AF752380

COMPUTER SCIENCE, TECHNOLOGY AND APPLICATIONS

ADVANCES IN EVOLUTIONARY ALGORITHMS RESEARCH

Computer Science, Technology and Applications

Additional books in this series can be found on Nova's website under the Series tab.

Additional e-books in this series can be found on Nova's website under the e-book tab.

COMPUTER SCIENCE, TECHNOLOGY AND APPLICATIONS

ADVANCES IN EVOLUTIONARY ALGORITHMS RESEARCH

GREGOR PAPA
EDITOR

nova publishers
New York

Copyright © 2015 by Nova Science Publishers, Inc.

All rights reserved. No part of this book may be reproduced, stored in a retrieval system or transmitted in any form or by any means: electronic, electrostatic, magnetic, tape, mechanical photocopying, recording or otherwise without the written permission of the Publisher.

We have partnered with Copyright Clearance Center to make it easy for you to obtain permissions to reuse content from this publication. Simply navigate to this publication's page on Nova's website and locate the "Get Permission" button below the title description. This button is linked directly to the title's permission page on copyright.com. Alternatively, you can visit copyright.com and search by title, ISBN, or ISSN.

For further questions about using the service on copyright.com, please contact:
Copyright Clearance Center
Phone: +1-(978) 750-8400 Fax: +1-(978) 750-4470 E-mail: info@copyright.com.

NOTICE TO THE READER

The Publisher has taken reasonable care in the preparation of this book, but makes no expressed or implied warranty of any kind and assumes no responsibility for any errors or omissions. No liability is assumed for incidental or consequential damages in connection with or arising out of information contained in this book. The Publisher shall not be liable for any special, consequential, or exemplary damages resulting, in whole or in part, from the readers' use of, or reliance upon, this material. Any parts of this book based on government reports are so indicated and copyright is claimed for those parts to the extent applicable to compilations of such works.

Independent verification should be sought for any data, advice or recommendations contained in this book. In addition, no responsibility is assumed by the publisher for any injury and/or damage to persons or property arising from any methods, products, instructions, ideas or otherwise contained in this publication.

This publication is designed to provide accurate and authoritative information with regard to the subject matter covered herein. It is sold with the clear understanding that the Publisher is not engaged in rendering legal or any other professional services. If legal or any other expert assistance is required, the services of a competent person should be sought. FROM A DECLARATION OF PARTICIPANTS JOINTLY ADOPTED BY A COMMITTEE OF THE AMERICAN BAR ASSOCIATION AND A COMMITTEE OF PUBLISHERS.

Additional color graphics may be available in the e-book version of this book.

Library of Congress Cataloging-in-Publication Data

Advances in evolutionary algorithms research / editors, Gregor Papa (Assistant Prof., Jožef Stefan Institute, Computer Systems Department, Jamova Cesta, Ljubljana, Slovenia).
pages cm. -- (Computer science, technology and applications)
Includes bibliographical references and index.
ISBN 978-1-63463-849-4 (hardcover)
1. Genetic algorithms. I. Papa, Gregor.
QA76.618.A2144 2015
006.3'823--dc23

2015013099

Published by Nova Science Publishers, Inc. † New York

CONTENTS

PREFACE

The field of Evolutionary algorithms produces various theoretical approaches that help searching for global optima within complex environments. These environments are often highly multidimensional, nonlinear, noisy, and with many constraints. Not only one, but frequently several, even conflicting, objectives need to be met while searching for the optimal solutions.

This book presents the advances in the research and applications of the evolutionary algorithms. There is a rich history of theoretical research and practical solutions in this field. Namely, evolutionary algorithms, with their intrinsic parallelism, have proved to be successful in a variety of problem domains in science, engineering and business. According to the no-free lunch theorem for optimization no super algorithm exists for all optimization problems. Therefore, the advances in this research field are also devoted to the identification of combination of problem classes and effective optimization methods, as well as the innovative and hybrid implementations of the algorithms.

The book consists of seven chapters covering the survey and theory on multimodal, multimemetic and multiobjective properties and algorithm performance. Further, the algorithms are applied to the real-world mechanical, biological, and chemical problems, as well as to the theoretical benchmarks.

Chapter 1 describes and reviews the state-of-the-art evolutionary approaches for multimodal optimization in terms of methodology, benchmarking, and application. Several evolutionary algorithms (DE, GA) and their various implementations (crowding, fitness sharing, species conserving) are tested for their performance in varied-line-spacing holographic grating problem that is issued in optical instruments for aberration corrections. Also, several current limitations of evolutionary multimodal optimization, as well as their possible solutions are noted.

Chapter 2 presents the island-based multimemetic algorithms used in the environments in which the availability of computational resources is unstable, which is relevant to many mechanical and biological systems. The instability is known to require the use of fault-aware strategies, in particular decentralized strategies suiting the lack of central command in this kind of complex networks. For this purpose, the use of self-balancing mechanisms provided an appealing way of coping with this volatility, endowing the search algorithm with enhanced resilience to churn, i.e., the network that is inherently dynamic and computing nodes independently enter and abandon it along time.

Chapter 3 introduces a new type of GA, named real structural genetic algorithm (RSGA) and applies it in constructing a class of genetic logic gates with compromised performance and cheaper structure. The RSGA integrating the advantages of the traditional real genetic algorithm (RGA) with a structured genetic algorithm (SGA) has been developed to simultaneously solve the parameter and structure optimization problems. A genetic transcriptional model with the cis-regulatory input function (CRIF) for genetic logic gate design is constructed by applying the RSGA to search for its cheaper structure.

Chapter 4 illustrates the application of multi-objective optimization to determine the optimal operating conditions of a continuous fermentation process. DPEA – Dual Population Evolutionary Algorithm was used to optimize the production of butanol in a continuous fermentation process coupled with a vacuum separation unit. Three different scenarios are used and compared to the optimization results with the standard continuous fermentation. After performing process simulation, obtaining the Pareto domain for both configurations, and ranking the Pareto-optimal solutions with the Net Flow Method, the optimal operating region was identified. As a result, higher butanol productivity and average butanol concentrations were observed in the vacuum fermentation compared to the standard continuous fermentation.

Chapter 5 presents the parallel implementation of scalarization approaches that are implemented on the GPU board. The performance of the algorithm is presented with different benchmark problems. The computation of the objective and the fitness functions for the individuals in the PSO are performed concurrently. The impact of such modification in the implementation might not be drastic for the benchmark problems (ZDT) since they usually consist of computationally cheap functions. But in case of computationally expensive functions (UF), the advantage of utilization of the streams is expected to be quite dramatic. It is also demonstrated that it is possible to achieve much faster GPU implementations for the multi-objective problems via careful and intelligent CUDA implementation.

Chapter 6 describes the development process of building a lighting system for a given target light distribution. The aim is to find an efficient algorithm to fit an analytic model to the measured data on LED and secondary lens combination with the symmetric spatial light distribution. Several versions of genetic algorithms and local search algorithms are used in an experimental study over a dataset of artificial instances that are generated so that the optimal solutions are known. The standard and the hybrid GA found appropriate solutions on all instances. While the GAs work well on a large set of their control parameters, the hybrid GA proved to be very robust against changing the population size and the local search procedure length.

Chapter 7 presents a success story of a practical application of variable implementations of methods from the evolutionary computation family (CMA-ES and DE) into the field of the computer aided design of mirrors, produced in the semiconductor technology and dedicated for use in ultrafast lasers. The design process consists of multiple stages, which involve the optimization problem definition, selection and an initial tuning of optimization methods and selection of starting points that incorporated the domain knowledge. In the course of the design process it was also necessary to follow the changes of the design criteria set by the user.

I would like to thank all the authors for their contributions to this book.

Gregor Papa

In: Advances in Evolutionary Algorithms Research
Editor: Gregor Papa
ISBN: 978-1-63463-849-4
© 2015 Nova Science Publishers, Inc.

Chapter 1

EVOLUTIONARY MULTIMODAL OPTIMIZATION: A SHORT SURVEY

Ka-Chun Wong*
Department of Computer Science, University of Toronto, Canada

Abstract

Real world problems always have different multiple solutions. For instance, optical engineers need to tune the recording parameters to get as many optimal solutions as possible for multiple trials in the varied-line-spacing holographic grating design problem. Unfortunately, most traditional optimization techniques focus on solving for a single optimal solution. They need to be applied several times; yet all solutions are not guaranteed to be found. Thus the multimodal optimization problem was proposed. In that problem, we are interested in not only a single optimal point, but also the others. With strong parallel search capability, evolutionary algorithms are shown to be particularly effective in solving this type of problem. In particular, the evolutionary algorithms for multimodal optimization usually not only locate multiple optima in a single run, but also preserve their population diversity throughout a run, resulting in their global optimization ability on multimodal functions. In addition, the techniques for multimodal optimization are borrowed as diversity maintenance techniques to other problems. In this chapter, we describe and review the state-of-the-arts evolutionary algorithms for multimodal optimization in terms of methodology, benchmarking, and application.

Keywords: multimodal optimization, methodology, benchmarking

1. Introduction and Background

Since the genetic algorithm was proposed by John H. Holland [1] in the early 1970s, researchers have been exploring the power of evolutionary algorithms [2]. For instance, biological pattern discovery [3] and computer vision [4]. In particular, its function optimization capability was highlighted [5] because of its high adaptability to different non-convex function landscapes, to which we cannot apply traditional optimization techniques.

*Corresponding Author address: Department of Computer Science, University of Toronto, Canada
E-mail address: wkc@cs.toronto.edu

Real world problems always have different multiple solutions [6, 7]. For instance, optical engineers need to tune the recording parameters to get as many optimal solutions as possible for multiple trials in the varied-line-spacing holographic grating design problem because the design constraints are too difficult to be expressed and solved in mathematical forms [8]. Unfortunately, most traditional optimization techniques focus on solving for a single optimal solution. They need to be applied several times; yet all solutions are not guaranteed to be found. Thus the multimodal optimization problem was proposed. In that problem, we are interested in not only a single optimal point, but also the others. Given an objective function, an algorithm is expected to find all optimal points in a single run. With strong parallel search capability, evolutionary algorithms are shown to be particularly effective in solving this type of problem [5]: Given function $f : \mathbb{X} \to \mathbb{R}$, we would like to find all global and local maxima (or minima) of f in a single run. Although the objective is clear, it is not easy to be satisfied in practice because some problems may have too many optima to be located. Nonetheless, it is still of great interest to researchers how these problems are going to be solved because the algorithms for multimodal optimization usually not only locate multiple optima in a single run, but also preserve their population diversity throughout a run, resulting in their global optimization ability on multimodal functions. Moreover, the techniques for multimodal optimization are usually borrowed as diversity maintenance techniques to other problems [9, 10].

2. Problem Definition

The multimodal optimization problem definition depends on the type of optimization (minimization or maximization). They are similar in principle and defined as follows:

2.1. Minimization

In this problem, given f:$\mathbb{X} \to \mathbb{R}$, we would like to find all global and local minimums of f in a single run.

Definition 1 Local Minimum [11]: A (local) minimum $\hat{x_l} \in \mathbb{X}$ of one (objective) function f:$\mathbb{X} \to \mathbb{R}$ is an input element with $f(\hat{x_l}) \leq f(x)$ for all x neighboring $\hat{x_l}$. If $\mathbb{X} \in \mathbb{R}^N$, we can write: $\forall \hat{x_l}\ \exists \varepsilon > 0 : f(\hat{x_l}) \leq f(x)\ \forall x \in \mathbb{X}, |x - \hat{x_l}| < \varepsilon$.

Definition 2 Global Minimum [11]: A global minimum $\hat{x_g} \in \mathbb{X}$ of one (objective) function f:$\mathbb{X} \to \mathbb{R}$ is an input element with $f(\hat{x_g}) \leq f(x)\ \forall x \in \mathbb{X}$.

2.2. Maximization

In this problem, given f:$\mathbb{X} \to \mathbb{R}$, we would like to find all global and local maximums of f in a single run.

Definition 3 Local Maximum [11]: A (local) maximum $\hat{x_l} \in \mathbb{X}$ of one (objective) function f:$\mathbb{X} \to \mathbb{R}$ is an input element with $f(\hat{x_l}) \geq f(x)$ for all x neighboring $\hat{x_l}$. If $\mathbb{X} \in \mathbb{R}^N$, we can write: $\forall \hat{x_l}\ \exists \varepsilon > 0 : f(\hat{x_l}) \geq f(x)\ \forall x \in \mathbb{X}, |x - \hat{x_l}| < \varepsilon$.

Definition 4 Global Maximum [11]: A global maximum $\hat{x_g} \in \mathbb{X}$ of one (objective) function f:$\mathbb{X} \rightarrow \mathbb{R}$ is an input element with $f(\hat{x_g}) \geq f(x)\ \forall x \in \mathbb{X}$.

3. Methodology

In the past literature, there were different evolutionary methods proposed for multimodal optimization. In this section, we discuss and categorize them into different methodologies.

3.1. Preselection

In 1970, the doctoral thesis by Cavicchio introduced different methods for genetic algorithms [12]. In particular, the preselection scheme was proposed to maintain the population diversity. In this scheme, the children compete with their parents for survival. If a child has a fitness (measured by an objective function) higher than its parent, the parent is replaced by the child in the next generation.

3.2. Crowding

In 1975, the work by De Jong [13] introduced the crowding technique to increase the chance of locating multiple optima. In the crowding technique, each child is compared to a random sub-population of cf members in the existing parent population (cf means crowding factor). The parent member which is most similar to the child itself is selected (measured by a distance metric). If the child has a higher fitness than the parent member selected, then it replaces the parent member in the population. Besides genetic algorithm, Thomsen has also incorporated crowding techniques [13] into differential evolution (CrowdingDE) for multimodal optimization [14]. In his study, the crowding factor is set to the population size and Euclidean distance is adopted as the dissimilarity metric. The smaller the distance, the more similar they are and vice versa. Although an intensive computation is accompanied, it can effectively transform differential evolution into an algorithm specialized for multimodal optimization. In 2012, CrowdingDE has been investigated and extended by Wong et al. [15], demonstrating competitive performance even when it is compared to the other state-of-the-arts methods.

3.3. Fitness Sharing

In 1989, Goldberg and Richardson proposed a fitness-sharing niching technique as a diversity preserving strategy to solve the multimodal optimization problem [16]. They proposed a shared fitness function, instead of an absolute fitness function, to evaluate the fitness of a individual in order to favor the growth of the individuals which are distinct from the others. The shared fitness function is defined as follows:

$$f'(x_i) = Shared\ Fitness = \frac{Actual\ Fitness}{Degree\ of\ Sharing} = \frac{f(x_i)}{\sum_{j=1}^{N} sh(d(x_i,x_j))}$$

where $f'(x_i)$ is the shared fitness of the ith individual x_i; $f(x_i)$ is the actual fitness of the ith individual x_i; $d(x_i,x_j)$ is the distance function between the two individuals x_i and x_j;

$sh(d)$ is the sharing function. With this technique, a population can be prevented from the domination of a particular type of individuals. Nonetheless, a careful adjustment to the sharing function $sh(d)$ definition is needed because it relates the fitness domain $f(x_i)$ to the distance domain $d(x_i, x_j)$ which are supposed to be independent of each other.

3.4. Species Conserving

Species conserving genetic algorithm (SCGA) [17] is a technique for evolving parallel subpopulations for multimodal optimization. Before each generation starts, the algorithm selects a set of species seeds which can bypass the subsequent procedures and be saved into the next generation. The algorithm then divides a population into several species based on a dissimilarity measure. The fittest individual is selected as the species seed for each species. After the identification of species seeds, the population undergoes the usual genetic algorithm operations: selection, crossover, and mutation. As the operations may remove the survival of less fit species, the saved species seeds are copied back to the population at the end of each generation.

To determine the species seeds in a population, the algorithm first sorts the population in a decreasing fitness order. Once sorted, it picks up the fittest individual as the first species seed and forms a species region around it. The next fittest individual is tested whether it is located in a species region. If not, it is selected as a species seed and another species region is created around it. Otherwise, it is not selected. Similar operations are applied to the remaining individuals, which are subsequently checked against all existing species seeds.

To copy the species seeds back to the population after the genetic operations have been executed, the algorithms need to scan all the individuals in the current population and identify to which species they belong. Once it is identified, the algorithm replaces the worst individual (lowest fitness) with the species seed in a species. If no individuals can be found in a species for replacement, the algorithm replaces the worst and un-replaced individual in the whole population. In short, the main idea is to preserve the population diversity by preserving the fittest individual for each species.

3.5. Covariance Matrix Adaptation

Evolution strategy is an effective method for numerical optimization. In recent years, its variant CMA-ES (Covariance Matrix Adaptation Evolution Strategy) showed a remarkable success [18]. To extend its capability, niching techniques have been introduced to cope with multimodal functions [19]. For instance, a concept called *adaptive individual niche radius* has been proposed to solve the *niche radius problem* commonly found in speciation algorithms [20].

3.6. Multiobjective Approach

At this point, we would like to note that the readers should not confuse evolutionary **multimodal** optimization (main theme of this chapter) with evolutionary **multiobjective** optimization. The former aims at solving a single function for multiple opima, while the latter aims at solving multiple functions for pareto front solutions. Nonetheless, the techniques involved are related. In particular, Deb and Saha demonstrated that, by decomposing a single multimodal objective function problem into a bi-objective problem, they can solve a multimodal function using a evolutionary multiobjective optimization algorithm [21]. Briefly, they keep the original multimodal objective function as the first objective. On the other hand, they use the gradient information to define peaks in the second objective.

3.7. Ensemble

As mentioned in the previous section, different niching algorithms have been proposed over the past years. Each algorithm has its own characteristics and design philosophy behind. Although it imposes difficult conditions to compare them thoroughly, it is a double-edged sword. Such a vast amount of algorithms can provide us a "swiss army knife" for optimizations on different problems. In particular, Yu and Suganthan proposed an ensemble method to combine those algorithms and form a powerful method called Ensemble of Niching Algorithms (ENA) [22]. An extensive work can also be found in [23].

3.8. Others

Researchers have been exploring many different ways to deal with the problem. Those methods include: clearing [24], repeated iterations [25], species-specific explosion [26], traps [27], stochastic automation [28], honey bee foraging behavior [29], dynamic niching [30], spatially-structured clearing [31], cooperative artificial immune network [32], particle swarm optimization [33–36] , and island model [37]. In particular, Stoean et al. have proposed a topological species conservation algorithm in which the proper topological separation into subpopulations has given it an advantage over the existing radius-based algorithms [38]. Comparison studies were conducted by Singh et al. [39], Kronfeld et al. [40], and Yu et al. [41]. Though different methods were proposed in the past, they are all based on the same fundamental idea: it is to strike an optimal balance between convergence and population diversity in order to locate multiple optima simultaneously in a single run [42,43].

4. Benchmarking

4.1. Benchmark Functions

There are many multimodal functions proposed for benchmarking in the past literature. In particular, the following five benchmark functions are widely adopted in literature: Deb's 1st function [26], Himmelblau function [25], Six-hump Camel Back function [44], Branin function [44], and Rosenbrock function [45]. In addition, five more benchmark functions (PP1 to PP5) can be found in [26,46]. For more vigorous comparisons, the IEEE Congress on Evolutionary Computation (CEC) usually releases a test suite for multimodal optimization every year. More than 15 test functions can be found there [47].

4.2. Performance Metrics

Several performance metrics have been proposed in the past literature [14, 17, 46, 48]. Among them, Peak Ratio (PR) and Average Minimum Distance to the Real Optima (D)

[26,46] are commonly adopted as the performance metrics.

- A peak is considered found when there exists a individual which is within 0.1 Euclidean distance to the peak in the last population. Thus the Peak Ratio is calculated using the equation (3):

$$Peak\ Ratio = \frac{Number\,of\,peaks\,found}{Total\,number\,of\,peaks} \tag{3}$$

- The average minimum distance to the optima (D) is calculated using the equation (4):

$$D = \frac{\sum_{i=1}^{n} \min_{indiv \in pop} d(peak_i, indiv)}{n} \tag{4}$$

  where n is the number of peaks, $indiv$ denotes a individual, $peak_i$ is the ith peak, pop denotes the last population, and $d(peak_i, indiv)$ denotes the distance between $peak_i$ and $indiv$.

As different algorithms perform different operations in one generation, it is unfair to set the termination condition as the number of generations. Alternatively, it is also unfair to adopt CPU time because it substantially depends on the implementation techniques for different algorithms. For instance, the sorting techniques to find elitists and the programming languages used. In contrast, fitness function evaluation is always the performance bottleneck [49] [1]. Thus the number of fitness function evaluations is suggested to be adopted as the running or the termination condition for convergence analysis.

4.3. Statistical Tests

Since evolutionary multimodal optimization is stochastic in nature, multiple runs are needed to evaluate each method on each test function. The means and standard deviations of performance metrics are usually reported for fair comparison. To justify the results, statistical tests are usually adopted to assess the statistical significances. For instance, t-tests, Mann-Whitney U-tests (MWU), and Kolmogorov-Smirnov test (KS).

5. Application

Holographic gratings have been widely used in optical instruments for aberration corrections. In particular, Varied-Line-Spacing (VLS) holographic grating is distinguished by the high order aberration eliminating capability in diffractive optical systems. It is commonly used in high resolution spectrometers and monochromaters. A recording optical system of VLS holographic grating is outlined in [8].

[1] For instance, over ten hours are needed to evaluate a calculation in computational fluid dynamics [50]

5.1. Problem Modelling

The core component descriptions of the optical systems are listed as follows [51]:

M_1, M_2 : Two spherical mirrors
C, D : Two coherent point sources
G : A grating blank

In this system, there are two light point sources C and D. They emit light rays which are then reflected by mirrors M_1 and M_2 respectively. After the reflection, the light rays are projected onto the grating blank G. More details are given in [8, 52]. The objective for the design is to find several sets of design variables (or recording parameters [8]) to form the expected groove shape of G (or the distribution of groove density [51]). The design variables are listed as follows:

γ : The incident angle of the ray O_1O
η_C: The incident angle of the ray CO_1
δ : The incident angle of the ray O_2O
η_D: The incident angle of the ray DO_2
p_C: The distance between C and M_1 (CO_1)
q_C: The distance between M_1 and G (O_1O)
p_D: The distance between D and M_2 (DO_2)
q_D: The distance between M_2 and G (O_2O)

Mathematically, the goal is to minimize the definite integral of the square error between the expected groove density and practical groove density [8]: $min\ J = \int_{-w_0}^{w_0} (n_p - n_e)^2 dw$ where w_0 is the half-width of the grating, n_p is the practical groove density, and n_e is the expected groove density. These two groove densities are complicated functions of the design variables. Ling et al. have further derived the above formula into a simpler one [51]:

$$min\ J = r_1^2 + \frac{w_0^2(2r_1r_3 + r_2^2)}{3} + \frac{w_0^4(r_3^2 + 2r_2r_4)}{5} + \frac{w_0^6 r_4^2}{7}$$

$$r_1 = \frac{j_{10}}{\lambda_0} - n_0\,, \qquad r_2 = \frac{j_{20}}{\lambda_0} - n_0 b_2$$

$$r_3 = \frac{3j_{30}}{2\lambda_0} - n_0 b_3\,, \quad r_4 = \frac{j_{40}}{2\lambda_0} - n_0 b_4$$

where j_{10}, j_{20}, j_{30} and j_{40} are the functions of the design variables, which are n_{10}, n_{20}, n_{30} and n_{40} respectively in [52]. Theoretically, the above objective is simple and clear. Unfortunately, there are many other auxiliary optical components in practice, which constraints are too difficult to be expressed and solved in mathematical forms. An optimal solution is not necessarily a feasible and favorable solution. Optical engineers often need to tune the design variables to find as many optimal solutions as possible for multiple trials. Multimodal optimization becomes necessary for this design problem.

Table 1. Results for all algorithms tested on the VLS holographic grating design problem (50 runs)

Measurement	CrowdingDE-STL [15]	CrowdingDE-TL [15]	CrowdingDE-SL [15]	CrowdingGA [13]	CrowdingDE [14]
Mean of Best Fitness	**8.29E-08**	7.17E-07	1.18E-07	9.02E-06	3.66E-06
StDev of Best Fitness	**2.91E-07**	5.01E-06	4.04E-07	3.40E-05	2.31E-05
Mean of Peaks Found	41.42	**45.54**	43.38	8.94	41.98
StDev of Peaks Found	13.07	**9.00**	10.69	5.04	14.26
Measurement	SharingGA [16]	SharingDE [14]	SDE [48]	SCGA [17]	UN [53]
Mean of Best Fitness	1.87E+04	1.74E+02	1.13E+00	1.24E+02	9.19E-04
StDev of Best Fitness	6.82E+04	2.65E+02	1.56E+00	4.59E+02	3.15E-03
Mean of Peaks Found	0.0	0.0	0.06	0.02	7.22
StDev of Peaks Found	0.0	0.0	0.31	0.14	3.92

5.2. Performance measurements

As the objective function is an unknown landscape, the exact optima information is not available. Thus the previous performance metrics cannot be adopted. We propose two new performance metrics in this section. The first one is the best fitness, which is the fitness value of the fittest individual in the last population. The second one is the number of distinct peaks, where a distinct peak is considered found when there exists a individual which fitness value is below a threshold 0.0001 and there isn't any other individual found as a peak before within 0.1 Euclidean distance in the last population. The threshold is chosen to 0.0001 because the fitness values of the solutions found in [8] are around this order of magnitude. On the other hand, the distance is chosen to 0.1 Euclidean distance because it has already been set for considering peaks found in peak ratio [26, 46]. Nonetheless, it is undeniable that such a threshold may not be suitable for this application because the landscape is unknown, although the value of 0.1 is the best choice we can adopt in this study.

5.3. Parameter setting

CrowdingDE-STL [15], CrowdingDE-TL [15], CrowdingDE-SL [15], Crowding Genetic Algorithm (CrowdingGA) [13], CrowdingDE [14], Fitness Sharing Genetic Algorithm (SharingGA) [16], SharingDE [14], Species Conserving Genetic Algorithm (SCGA) [17], SDE [48], and UN [53] are selected for illustrative purposes in this application. All the algorithms were run up to a maximum of 10000 fitness function evaluations. The above performance metrics were obtained by taking the average and standard deviation of 50 runs. The groove density parameters followed the setting in [8]: $n_0 = 1.400 \times 10^3(line/mm)$, $b_2 = 8.2453 \times 10^{-4}(1/mm)$, $b_3 = 3.0015 \times 10^{-7}(1/mm^2)$ and $b_4 = 0.0000 \times 10^{-10}(1/mm^3)$. The half-width w_0 was 90mm. The radii of spherical mirrors M_1 and M_2 were 1000mm. The recording wavelength (λ_0) was 413.1nm. The population size of all the algorithms was set to 50. The previous settings remained the same, except the algorithm-specific parameters: The species distance of SDE and SCGA was set to 1000. The scaling factor and niche radius of SharingDE and SharingGA were set to 1 and 1000 respectively. The discount factor of the temporal locality was set to 0.5. The survival selection method of the non-crowding algorithms was set to binary tournament [53].

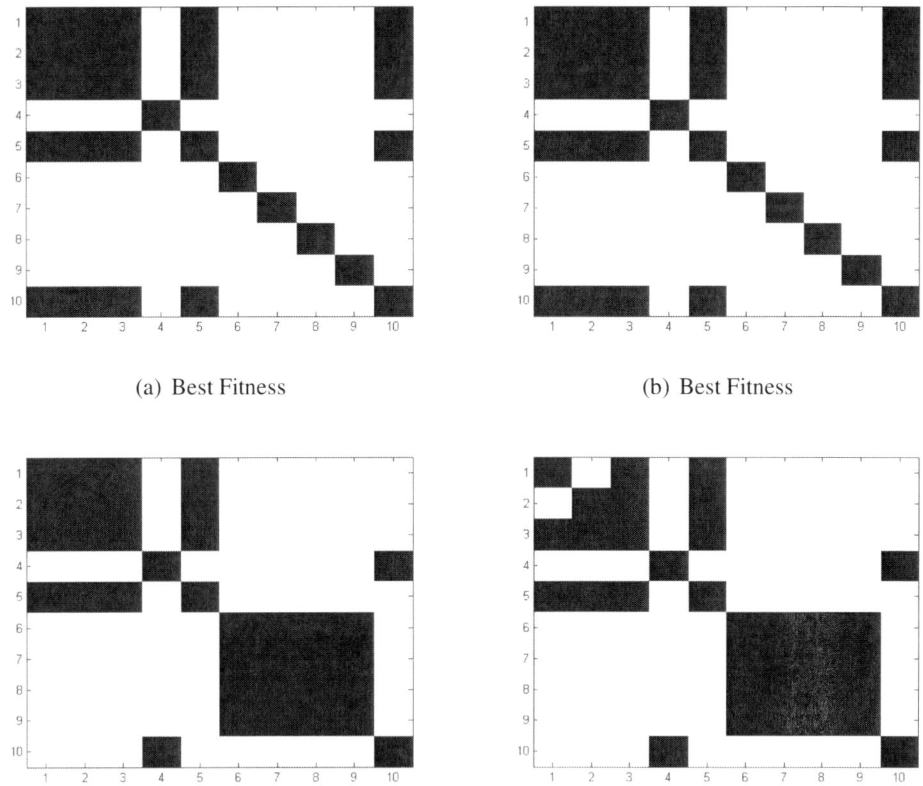

(a) Best Fitness (b) Best Fitness

(c) Peaks Found (d) Peaks Found

Figure 1. For Table 1, we depict the statistical significance test results for the pairwise performance differences between all algorithms tested on the VLS holgraphic grating design problem by Mann-Whitney U-test (MWU) and Two-sample Kolmogorov-Smirnov test (KS) with p=0.05. Each sub-figure correspond to the performance comparison using a metric by a statistical test. The vertical axis is the same as the horizontal axis. Each algorithm is represented by a number on each axis. The numbering of the algorithms follows the order in Table 1. For instance, 1 refers to CrowdingDE-STL, 2 refers to CrowdingDE-TL......10 refers to UN. The color of each block represents whether the algorithm indicated by the horizontal axis shows a performance different from the algorithm indicated by the vertical axis in a statistically significant way. The black color denotes the p-values higher than 0.05 whereas the white color denotes the p-values lower than 0.05. The even numbered sub-figures are the results obtained by MWU, whereas the odd numbered sub-figures are the results obtained by KS.

5.4. Results

The result is tabulated in Table 1. It can be observed that CrowdingDE-STL can achieve the best fitness, whereas CrowdingDE-TL can achieve the best number of peaks found. To compare the algorithms rigorously, statistical tests have also been used. The results are de-

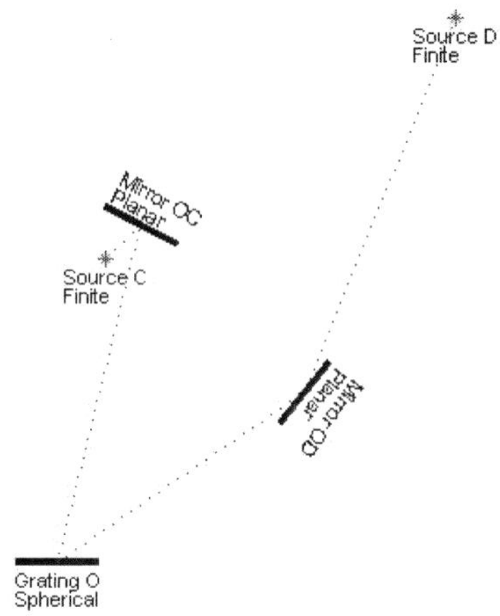

(a)

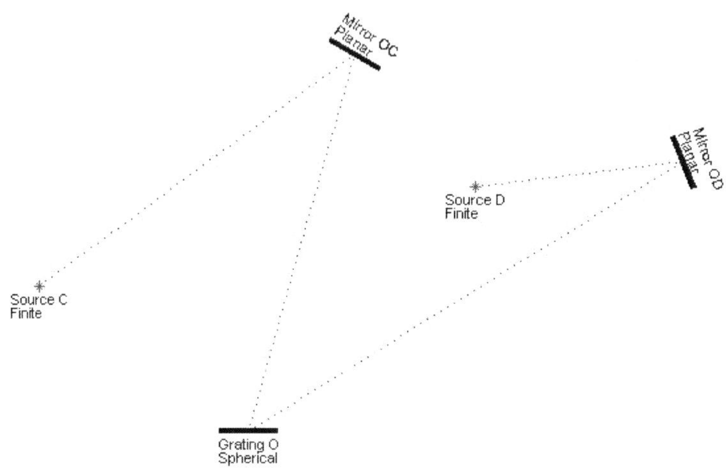

(b)

Figure 2. Configurations obtained by a single run of CrowdingDE-STL on the VLS holographic grating design problem. It can be seen that they are totally different and feasible configurations with which optical engineers can feel free to perform multiple trials after the single run.

picted in Figure 1. One can observe that there are some statistically significant performance differences among them. In particular, CrowdingDE-based methods are shown to have the results statistically different from CrowdingGA, SharingGA, SharingDE, SDE, and SCGA. Some configurations obtained after a run of CrowdingDE-STL on this problem are depicted in Figure 2. It can be seen that they are totally different and feasible configurations with which optical engineers can feel free to perform multiple trials after the single run.

6. Discussion

To conclude, we have briefly reviewed the state-of-the-arts methods of evolutionary multimodal optimization from different perspectives in this chapter. Different evolutionary multimodal optimization methodologies are described. To compare them fairly, we described different benchmarking techniques such as performance metrics, test functions, and statistical tests. An application to Varied-Line-Spacing (VLS) holographic grating is presented to demonstrate the real-world applicability of evolutionary multimodal optimization. Nonetheless, we would like to note several current limitations of evolutionary multimodal optimization as well as the possible solutions at the end of this chapter.

First, most of the past studies just focus on low dimensional test functions for benchmarking. More high dimensional test functions should be incorporated in the future. Second, we would like to point out that evolutionary multimodal optimization is actually far from just finding multiple optima because the algorithms for multimodal optimization usually not only locate multiple optima in a single run, but also preserve their population diversity throughout a run, resulting in their global optimization ability on multimodal functions. Moreover, the techniques for multimodal optimization are usually borrowed as diversity maintenance techniques to other problems. Third, the computational complexities of the methods are usually very high compared with the other methods since they involve population diversity maintenance, which implies that the related survival operators need to take into account the other individuals, resulting in additional time complexity.

References

[1] John H. Holland. *Adaptation in natural and artificial systems*. MIT Press, Cambridge, MA, USA, 1992.

[2] Ka-Chun Wong, Chengbin Peng, Yue Li, and Tak-Ming Chan. Herd clustering: A synergistic data clustering approach using collective intelligence. *Applied Soft Computing*, 23:61–75, 2014.

[3] Ka-Chun Wong, Chengbin Peng, Man-Hon Wong, and Kwong-Sak Leung. Generalizing and learning protein-dna binding sequence representations by an evolutionary algorithm. *Soft Computing - A Fusion of Foundations, Methodologies and Applications*, 15:1631–1642, 2011. 10.1007/s00500-011-0692-5.

[4] Chun-Ho Wu, Na Dong, Waihung Ip, Ching-Yuen Chan, Kei-Leung Yung, and Zengqiang Chen. Chaotic hybrid algorithm and its application in circle detection. In *EvoWorkshops*, pages 302–311, 2010.

[5] David E. Goldberg. *Genetic Algorithms in Search, Optimization and Machine Learning*. Addison-Wesley Longman Publishing Co., Inc., Boston, MA, USA, 1989.

[6] Ka-Chun Wong, Kwong-Sak Leung, and Man Hon Wong. Protein structure prediction on a lattice model via multimodal optimization techniques. In *GECCO '10: Proceedings of the 12th annual conference on Genetic and evolutionary computation*, pages 155–162, New York, NY, USA, 2010. ACM.

[7] Ka-Chun Wong, Yue Li, Chengbin. Peng, and Zhaolei Zhang. SignalSpider: probabilistic pattern discovery on multiple normalized ChIP-Seq signal profiles. *Bioinformatics*, Sep 2014.

[8] Ling Qing, Wu Gang, Yang Zaiyue, and Wang Qiuping. Crowding clustering genetic algorithm for multimodal function optimization. *Appl. Soft Comput.*, 8(1):88–95, 2008.

[9] Ka-Chun Wong, Tak-Ming Chan, Chengbin. Peng, Yue Li, and Zhaolei Zhang. DNA motif elucidation using belief propagation. *Nucleic Acids Res.*, 41(16):e153, Sep 2013.

[10] Ka-Chun Wong and Zhaolei Zhang. SNPdryad: predicting deleterious non-synonymous human SNPs using only orthologous protein sequences. *Bioinformatics*, Jan 2014.

[11] Thomas Weise. *Global Optimization Algorithms ? Theory and Application*. Thomas Weise, july 16, 2007 edition, July 2007. Online available at http://www.it-weise.de/projects/book.pdf.

[12] Daniel Joseph Cavicchio. Adaptive search using simulated evolution. 1970.

[13] Kenneth Alan De Jong. *An analysis of the behavior of a class of genetic adaptive systems*. PhD thesis, University of Michigan, Ann Arbor, MI, USA, 1975.

[14] R. Thomsen. Multimodal optimization using crowding-based differential evolution. In *CEC2004. IEEE Congress on Evolutionary Computation, 2004*, volume 2, pages 1382–1389, June 2004.

[15] Ka-Chun Wong, Chun-Ho Wu, Ricky KP Mok, Chengbin Peng, and Zhaolei Zhang. Evolutionary multimodal optimization using the principle of locality. *Information Sciences*, 194:138–170, 2012.

[16] David E. Goldberg and Jon Richardson. Genetic algorithms with sharing for multimodal function optimization. In *Proceedings of the Second International Conference on Genetic algorithms and their application*, pages 41–49, Hillsdale, NJ, USA, 1987. L. Erlbaum Associates Inc.

[17] Jian Ping Li, Marton E. Balazs, Geoffrey T. Parks, and P. John Clarkson. A species conserving genetic algorithm for multimodal function optimization. *Evol. Comput.*, 10(3):207–234, 2002.

[18] Nikolaus Hansen and Andreas Ostermeier. Completely derandomized self-adaptation in evolution strategies. *Evol. Comput.*, 9:159–195, June 2001.

[19] Ofer M. Shir, Michael Emmerich, and Thomas Bäck. Adaptive niche radii and niche shapes approaches for niching with the cma-es. *Evol. Comput.*, 18:97–126, March 2010.

[20] Ofer Shir and Thomas Back. Niche radius adaptation in the cma-es niching algorithm. In Thomas Runarsson, Hans-Georg Beyer, Edmund Burke, Juan Merelo-Guervos, L. Whitley, and Xin Yao, editors, *Parallel Problem Solving from Nature - PPSN IX*, volume 4193 of *Lecture Notes in Computer Science*, pages 142–151. Springer Berlin / Heidelberg, 2006.

[21] Kalyanmoy Deb and Amit Saha. Finding multiple solutions for multimodal optimization problems using a multi-objective evolutionary approach. In *Proceedings of the 12th Annual Conference on Genetic and Evolutionary Computation*, GECCO '10, pages 447–454, New York, NY, USA, 2010. ACM.

[22] E. L. Yu and P. N. Suganthan. Ensemble of niching algorithms. *Inf. Sci.*, 180:2815–2833, August 2010.

[23] Bo-Yang Qu and P.N. Suganthan. Novel multimodal problems and differential evolution with ensemble of restricted tournament selection. In *2010 IEEE Congress on Evolutionary Computation (CEC)*, pages 1 –7, july 2010.

[24] A. Petrowski. A clearing procedure as a niching method for genetic algorithms. In *Proceedings of IEEE International Conference on Evolutionary Computation, 1996*, pages 798–803, Nagoya, Japan, May 1996.

[25] David Beasley, David R. Bull, and Ralph R. Martin. A sequential niche technique for multimodal function optimization. *Evol. Comput.*, 1(2):101–125, 1993.

[26] Ka-Chun Wong, Kwong-Sak Leung, and Man-Hon Wong. An evolutionary algorithm with species-specific explosion for multimodal optimization. In *GECCO '09: Proceedings of the 11th Annual conference on Genetic and evolutionary computation*, pages 923–930, New York, NY, USA, 2009. ACM.

[27] Naoya Karatsu, Yuichi Nagata, Isao Ono, and Shigenobu Kobayashi. Globally multimodal function optimization by real-coded genetic algorithms using traps. In *2010 IEEE Congress on Evolutionary Computation (CEC)*, pages 1–8, 2010.

[28] K. Najim and A.S. Poznyak. Multimodal searching technique based on learning automata with continuous input and changing number of actions. *IEEE Transactions on Systems, Man, and Cybernetics, Part B: Cybernetics*, 26(4):666 –673, aug. 1996.

[29] K. Sundareswaran and V.T. Sreedevi. Development of novel optimization procedure based on honey bee foraging behavior. pages 1220 –1225, oct. 2008.

[30] A. Nickabadi, M.M. Ebadzadeh, and R. Safabakhsh. Evaluating the performance of dnpso in dynamic environments. pages 2640 –2645, oct. 2008.

[31] G. Dick. Automatic identification of the niche radius using spatially-structured clearing methods. In *2010 IEEE Congress on Evolutionary Computation (CEC)*, pages 1 –8, july 2010.

[32] Li Liu and Wenbo Xu. A cooperative artificial immune network with particle swarm behavior for multimodal function optimization. In *CEC 2008. (IEEE World Congress on Computational Intelligence). IEEE Congress on Evolutionary Computation, 2008*, pages 1550 –1555, june 2008.

[33] Zhen Ji, Huilian Liao, Yiwei Wang, and Q.H. Wu. A novel intelligent particle optimizer for global optimization of multimodal functions. In *CEC 2007. IEEE Congress on Evolutionary Computation, 2007*, pages 3272 –3275, sept. 2007.

[34] Xiaodong Li. Niching without niching parameters: Particle swarm optimization using a ring topology. *IEEE Transactions on Evolutionary Computation*, 14(1):150 –169, feb. 2010.

[35] Yau-Tarng Juang, Shen-Lung Tung, and Hung-Chih Chiu. Adaptive fuzzy particle swarm optimization for global optimization of multimodal functions. *Information Sciences*, 181(20):4539 – 4549, 2011. Special Issue on Interpretable Fuzzy Systems.

[36] Lili Liu, Shengxiang Yang, and Dingwei Wang. Force-imitated particle swarm optimization using the near-neighbor effect for locating multiple optima. *Information Sciences*, In Press, Uncorrected Proof:–, 2010.

[37] Mourad Bessaou, Alain Pétrowski, and Patrick Siarry. Island model cooperating with speciation for multimodal optimization. In *PPSN VI: Proceedings of the 6th International Conference on Parallel Problem Solving from Nature*, pages 437–446, London, UK, 2000. Springer-Verlag.

[38] C. Stoean, M. Preuss, R. Stoean, and D. Dumitrescu. Multimodal optimization by means of a topological species conservation algorithm. *IEEE Transactions on Evolutionary Computation*, 14(6):842 –864, dec. 2010.

[39] Gulshan Singh and Dr. Kalyanmoy Deb. Comparison of multi-modal optimization algorithms based on evolutionary algorithms. In *GECCO '06: Proceedings of the 8th annual conference on Genetic and evolutionary computation*, pages 1305–1312, New York, NY, USA, 2006. ACM.

[40] M. Kronfeld and A. Zell. Towards scalability in niching methods. In *2010 IEEE Congress on Evolutionary Computation (CEC)*, pages 1 –8, july 2010.

[41] E. L. Yu and P.N. Suganthan. Empirical comparison of niching methods on hybrid composition functions. In *CEC 2008. (IEEE World Congress on Computational Intelligence). IEEE Congress on Evolutionary Computation, 2008*, pages 2194 –2201, june 2008.

[42] M. Srinivas and L.M. Patnaik. Adaptive probabilities of crossover and mutation in genetic algorithms. *IEEE Transactions on Systems, Man and Cybernetics*, 24(4):656 –667, apr. 1994.

[43] Ka-Chun Wong, Kwong-Sak Leung, and Man-Hon Wong. Effect of spatial locality on an evolutionary algorithm for multimodal optimization. In *EvoApplications 2010, Part I, LNCS 6024*. Springer-Verlag, 2010.

[44] Zbigniew Michalewicz. *Genetic algorithms + data structures = evolution programs (3rd ed.).* Springer-Verlag, London, UK, 1996.

[45] Yun-Wei Shang and Yu-Huang Qiu. A note on the extended rosenbrock function. *Evol. Comput.*, 14(1):119–126, 2006.

[46] Rodica I. Lung, Camelia Chira, and D. Dumitrescu. An agent-based collaborative evolutionary model for multimodal optimization. In *GECCO '08: Proceedings of the 2008 GECCO conference companion on Genetic and evolutionary computation*, pages 1969–1976, New York, NY, USA, 2008. ACM.

[47] Xiaodong Li, Ke Tang, Mohammad N. Omidvar, Zhenyu Yang, and Kai Qin. Benchmark functions for the cec 2013 special session and competition on large-scale global optimization, 2013.

[48] Xiaodong Li. Efficient differential evolution using speciation for multimodal function optimization. In *GECCO '05: Proceedings of the 2005 conference on Genetic and evolutionary computation*, pages 873–880, New York, NY, USA, 2005. ACM.

[49] Yew S. Ong, Prasanth B. Nair, and Andrew J. Keane. Evolutionary optimization of computationally expensive problems via surrogate modeling. *AIAA Journal*, 41(4):687 –696, 2003.

[50] Yaochu Jin, M. Olhofer, and B. Sendhoff. A framework for evolutionary optimization with approximate fitness functions. *IEEE Transactions on Evolutionary Computation*, 6(5):481–494, 2002.

[51] Ling Qing, Wu Gang, and Wang Qiuping. Restricted evolution based multimodal function optimization in holographic grating design. In *The 2005 IEEE Congress on Evolutionary Computation, 2005*, volume 1, pages 789–794, Edinburgh, Scotland,, September 2005.

[52] Takeshi Namioka and Masato Koike. Aspheric wave-front recording optics for holographic gratings. *Appl. Opt.*, 34(13):2180–2186, 1995.

[53] Kenneth A. De Jong. *Evolutionary Computation. A Unified Approach.* MIT Press, Cambridge, MA, USA, 2006.

In: Advances in Evolutionary Algorithms Research
Editor: Gregor Papa
ISBN: 978-1-63463-849-4
© 2015 Nova Science Publishers, Inc.

Chapter 2

TOWARDS RESILIENT MULTIMEMETIC SYSTEMS ON UNSTABLE NETWORKS WITH COMPLEX TOPOLOGY

Rafael Nogueras and Carlos Cotta*
ETSI Informática, Universidad de Málaga, Málaga, Spain

Abstract

The use of parallel and distributed models of metaheuristics has steadily settled in the last decades into an accessible mechanism for improving both the efficiency and the effectiveness of the search process. While population-based techniques can be readily deployed on dedicated distributed systems, their use on unstable computational environments brings new challenges. These can include the algorithm being resilient to the volatility of the system and coping with the loss of sub-populations. In this sense, it must be noted that emergent computational environments such as P2P networks are prime examples of such systems. Given the enormous possibilities that these systems offer, it is of foremost interest to study the effective deployment of population-based optimization techniques on them. In this chapter we tackle this issue from the point of view of island-based multimemetic algorithms (MMAs), namely memetic systems that explicitly store memes (computational representations of problem solving procedures, e.g., local searchers) as a part of solutions and have them evolve alongside the latter. We model the environment as a faulty system in which the availability of computational resources is Weibull-distributed (this distribution is commonly used in survival analysis to model time-to-failure in mechanical and biological systems). We also consider that islands are interconnected using a non-regular complex topology as is typically the case in this kind of network. To be precise, we consider scale-free and small-world networks. We perform a broad experimentation on scenarios capturing different degrees of volatility and interconnection density, and analyze the resilience of the MMAs on several hard optimization problems.

Keywords: complex networks, island model, scale free network, small world network, multimemetic algorithms, resilience, churn

*E-mail address: ccottap@lcc.uma.es; Address: ETSI Informática, Universidad de Málaga, Campus de Teatinos, 29071 Málaga, Spain (Corresponding author)

1. Introduction

Population-based metaheuristics such as evolutionary algorithms are very amenable to deployment in distributed computational environments [1]. This constitutes a well-known approach for boosting the effectiveness of the search process [2] that has been studied and exploited over the last three decades [3, 4]. While initial developments in this field primarily focused on dedicated local area networks, the pervasiveness of computing resources permanently connected to the Internet has now led to the increasing relevance of peer-to-peer (P2P) networks [5] and volunteer computing networks [6]. Such emerging computational environments are becoming increasingly popular as a means of exploiting vast decentralized collections of computational resources. However, the deployment of optimization techniques in these environments is not exempt from difficulties. One of the most important is the so call *churn* phenomenon: the network is inherently dynamic and computing nodes independently enter and abandon it over time.

The presence of churn can have different effects on a distributed population-based metaheuristic. Considering the case of island-based models, namely the distribution of separate populations on the different computing nodes subject to sporadic interchange of solutions among them, it is clear that churn can lead to the loss of the current incumbent solution [7]. In general it impairs the progress of the search due to an implied loss of information when a computing node goes down and the disturbance caused by new nodes entering the system and being initialized from scratch. There are two possible ways of dealing with this: (i) utilize some fault-management policy (e.g., using redundant computation or restoration checkpoints) for corrective purposes upon node failure/reactivation [8–10] and (ii) endow the algorithm with fault-aware mechanisms to react to churn. Each approach has its own particular strengths and drawbacks. For example, fault-management strategies such as checkpoints are arguably simple and well-known in the context of distributed computation. They require some global monitorization and/or the availability of some means for safe external storage of computational states. On the other hand, if the algorithm can self adapt to churn (e.g., by dynamically resizing populations) it does not require central command or external storage. This in turn means they seem to fit better with the properties of decentralized networks.

In this chapter, we focus on island-based versions of multimemetic algorithms (MMAs) [11]. These are a subclass of memetic algorithms [12], namely optimization techniques based on the orchestrated interplay of elements from the population-based global search methods and trajectory-based local search techniques [13]. While classical MAs typically use some fixed mechanism for local-search, MMAs are based in the self-adaptation of local-search procedures which evolve alongside solutions. To study the deployment of island-based MMAs on dynamic networks we use a simulated computational environment that serves as a playground for experimenting with different degrees of resource volatility. The factor subject to scrutiny in this chapter is the interconnection topology of this computational environment. We consider here two complex network topologies, scale-free networks and ultra small-world networks. These are described in the next section.

2. Modeling a Dynamic Computational Environment

We consider a simulated distributed system composed of n nodes. This system is characterized by two elements: (i) the interconnection topology of the nodes and (ii) the dynamic pattern of availability/unavailability of each node. Let us describe each of these elements in more detail.

Regarding the interconnection topology we have considered two possibilities: scale-free (SF) networks and small-world (SW) networks. SF networks are commonly found in many natural, social and computational processes and are characterized by the existence of a power-law distribution in node degrees. In order to generate this kind of topology we use the Barabási-Albert (BA) model [14], whereby a network is grown by adding a new node at a time and in which the selection of new links is driven by preferential attachment [15]. More precisely, the construction of the network is controlled by a parameter m representing the number of connections each new node has. The BA algorithm begins by constructing a clique of m nodes and then adding the $n-m$ remaining nodes, picking m neighbors for each of the latter. These neighbors are selected with a probability proportional to their degrees. Figure 1 (top row) shows an example of this kind of network.

As for SW networks, these are characterized by very small average distances between nodes (typically growing logarithmically with the number of nodes) and a high clustering coefficient (the neighbors of a node are very likely to be neighbors themselves). There are several procedures for creating SW networks. The most classical approach is the Watts-Strogatz model [16] in which a regular ring lattice is built and edges are rewired with a certain probability. We have opted here for a different approach, namely the Barmpoutis-Murray (BM) model [17]. This model produces ultra-SW networks with very small average distance and very large average clustering. The construction of the network is controlled by a parameter M representing the total number of links. The algorithm tries to construct the largest clique that leaves enough links available to connect the rest of the network. This procedure is recursively repeated for the remaining nodes and links (if at a certain step it is found that no subnetwork can be built with the desired number of links and nodes, the algorithm backtracks and reduces by one, the size of the clique in the previous step). In the original BM model all these subnetworks are linked together through a fixed node in the first clique. This makes this node an articulation point, reducing the resilience of the network. For this reason, we have opted to modify the model so as to have each subnetwork link to the first clique at a randomly selected node. To compare with SF networks, note that running the BA model with parameter m produces a network with $M = nm - m(m+1)/2$ links, so we can use the latter value to build an analogous SW network. Figure 1 (bottom row) shows an example of this kind of networks.

Regarding the dynamics of the system, we follow the model in [10]. We assume all n nodes are initially available. Their permanence in the system is assumed to follow a Weibull distribution [18]. This distribution is often used in survival analysis to model time-to-failure in mechanical systems [19] and generalizes the exponential distribution in which the failure probability is time-independent. By means of a shape parameter η this failure probability can be made to increase with time ($\eta > 1$) or decrease with time ($\eta < 1$). We consider the former case and hence the longer a node has been active in the system the more likely it is

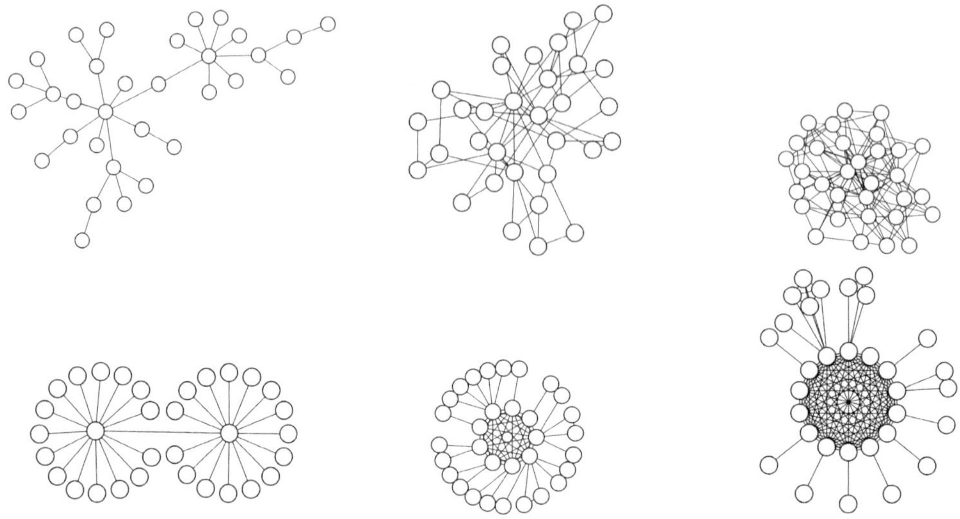

Figure 1. Example networks. The top row corresponds to SF networks and the bottom row to SW networks. For each kind of network and from left to right, the examples correspond to $m = 1$, $m = 2$, $m = 4$.

that it goes down. Mathematically, the probability of a node being available up to time t is

$$p(t, \eta, \beta) = e^{-(t/\beta)^{\eta}}. \tag{1}$$

where β is the so-called scale parameter. For simplicity, we consider the same distribution for node reactivations, i.e., the longer a node has been inactive the more likely it is that it will become available for computation again.

3. Fault-Aware Island-based Multimemetic Algorithms

We consider the deployment of an island-based MMA on the unstable computational environment described in the previous section. We have n panmictic islands, each of them running an MMA in which memes are attached to individuals and evolve alongside them. These memes are represented as pattern-based rewriting rules $A \rightarrow B$ following the model by Smith [20, 21]. Memes are subject to mutation and are transferred from parent to offspring via local selection (offspring inherit the meme of the best parent). The use of memes aside, the MMA resembles a steady-state evolutionary algorithm using tournament selection, one-point crossover, bit-flip mutation, and replacement of the worst parent. These islands are assumed to work in parallel and perform migration asynchronously. At the beginning of each cycle the island checks whether or not migrants have been received from any neighboring nodes. If this is the case, they are accepted into the population, replacing the worst existing individuals. Later, at the end of each cycle, migration is stochastically performed much like the remaining evolutionary operators. If done, migrants are randomly selected from the population – see [22]

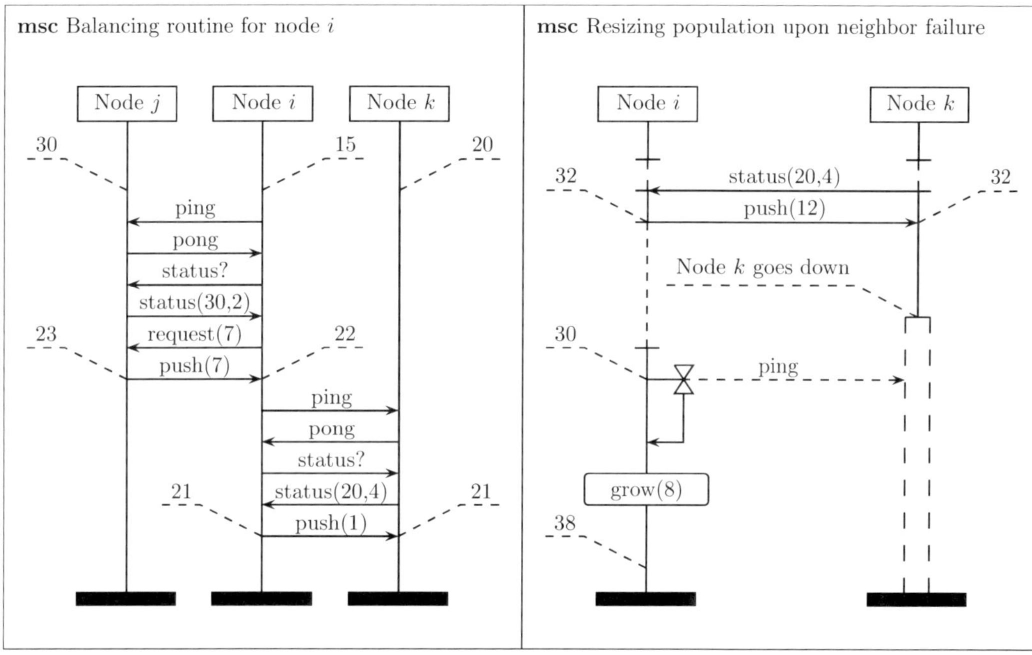

Figure 2. Message sequence charts of the balancing protocol. The basic routine for balancing among the active nodes is shown on the left. The right panel shows the protocol for enlarging a node population upon failure of a neighbor.

In order to cope with node failures and the subsequent loss of information, islands are embedded with self-balancing capabilities whereby each node resizes its population dynamically in response to churn. This resizing tries to (i) increase population sizes to compensate the loss of islands and (ii) balance the population sizes of neighboring islands. For this purpose, we use a variation of a direct-neighbor strategy [23] introduced elsewhere [24] and described below for the sake of completeness.

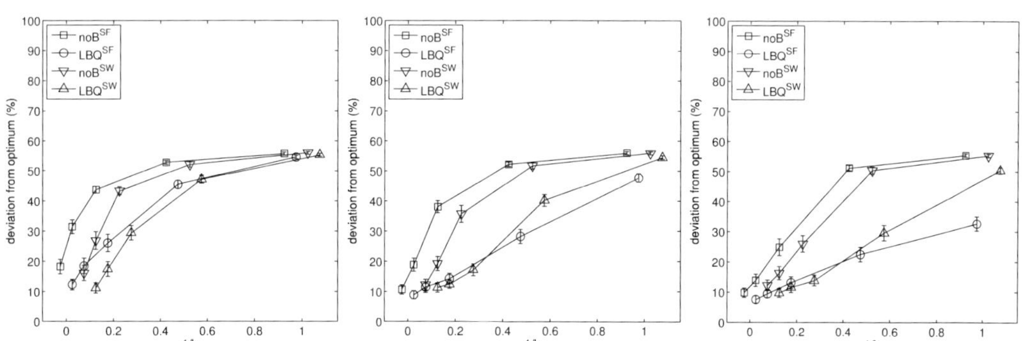

Figure 3. Deviation from the optimal solution as a function of the churn rate for $m = 1$ (left), $m = 2$ (middle) and $m = 4$ (right).

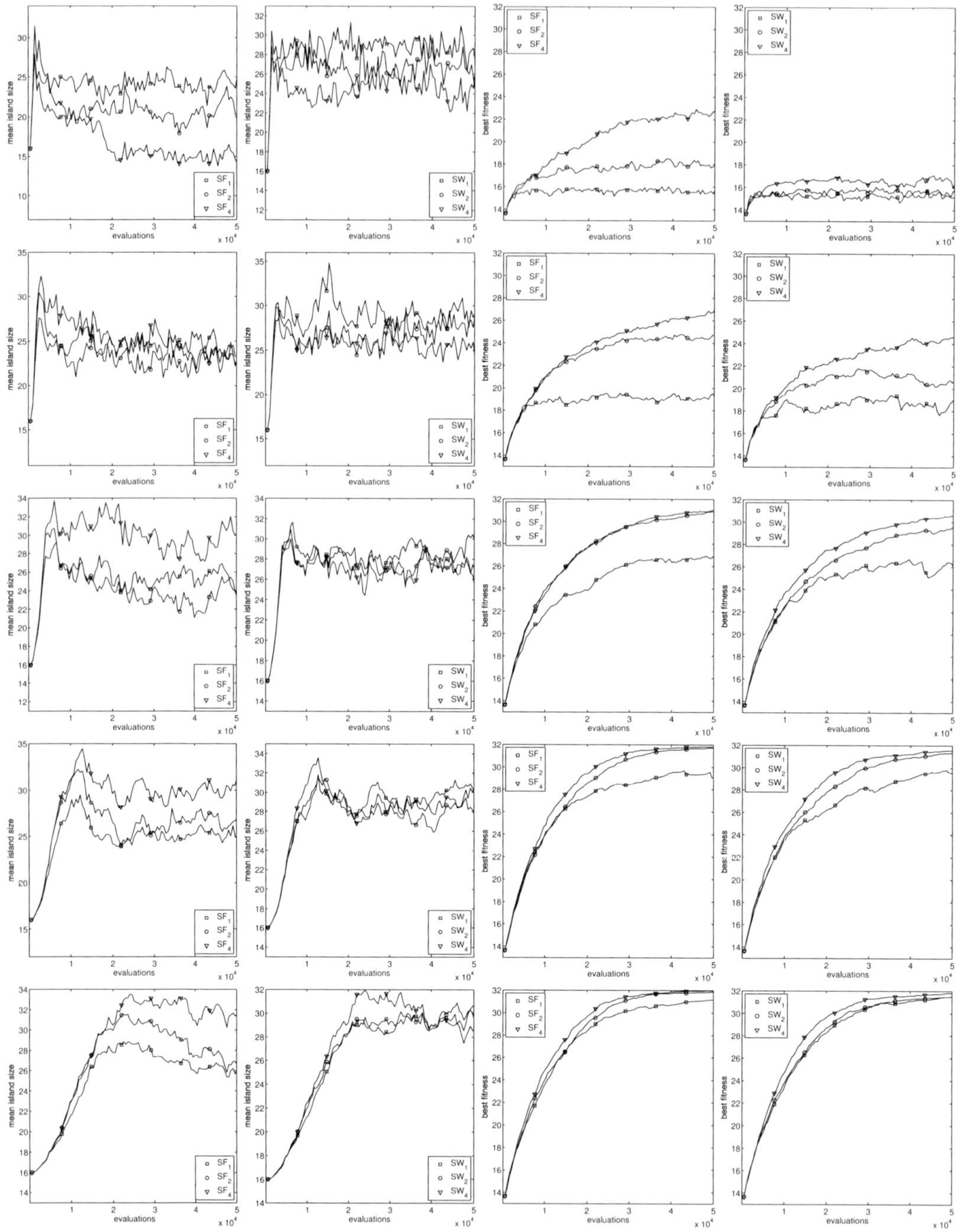

Figure 4. Evolution of mean island sizes for SF (leftmost column) and SW (middle-left column). Evolution of mean best fitness for SF (middle-right column) and SW (rightmost column). From top to bottom, $k = 1, 2, 5, 10$ and 20.

The balancing procedure is activated at the beginning of each evolutionary cycle in the corresponding island and is illustrated in Figure 2. The island communicates with its neighbors and gathers information on the size of their populations and the number of active neighbors they have. As it does this, it tries to balance the size of its population by sending or requesting individuals from neighbors. By doing so, the size of the islands will effectively converge to the same size (± 1 individual) in a few balancing attempts. When it is detected that a neighboring node has gone down (the ping message times out) the population is enlarged by a fraction of the size of the lost island, inversely proportional to the number of neighbors of this island. Thus, if in the last balancing attempt the lost island was found to have population μ and ν neighbors, the balancing node increases its population by μ/ν individuals (created from scratch). Note that when a node finally becomes available again, it starts the balancing procedure with a population of zero individuals. In the event that it had no active neighbor, it resorts to reinitialization from scratch using a fixed population size C_1.

4. Experiments

We considered $n = 32$ islands whose initial size is $\mu = 16$ individuals and a total number of evaluations $maxevals = 50000$. Meme lengths evolve within $l_{\min} = 3$ and $l_{\max} = 9$, mutating their length with probability $p_r = 1/9$. We used crossover probability $p_X = 1.0$, mutation probability $p_M = 1/\ell$, where ℓ is the genotype length, and migration probability $p_{mig} = 1/80$. Parameter m in the BA model of SF networks is $m \in \{1,2,4\}$ and we use the corresponding value of $M = nm - m(m+1)/2$ if the BM model of SW networks. Regarding node dynamics, we used the shape parameter $\eta = 1.5$ (and hence the probability of failure increases with time), and scale parameters $\beta = -1/\log(p(k))$ for $p(k) = 1 - (kn_\iota)^{-1}$, $k \in \{1,2,5,10,20\}$. To understand these scale parameters, it must be noted that $p(k)$ represents the probability of one island going down/up every k cycles (of course, the shape parameter is larger than 1 and hence the real failure probability is not constant). By doing this we obtained different scenarios ranging from a rather low ($k = 20$) churn up to an extremely high ($k = 1$) churn. Parameter C_1 used during eventual island reinitialization from scratch is set to $2\mu = 32$ (the asymptotic number of active islands under the parameterization chosen is $n/2$). We performed 25 simulations for each algorithm and churn scenario. We denoted by noB and LBQ, the algorithmic variants without balancing (i.e., no population resizing and reinitialization from scratch) and with balancing respectively, and used superscripts ^{SF} and ^{SW} to denote the use of SF or SW topology. We considered four test functions, namely Deb's trap (TRAP) function [25], Watson et al.'s Hierarchical-if-and-only-if (HIFF) and Hierarchical-Exclusive-OR (HXOR) functions [26] and Goldberg et al.'s Massively Multimodal Deceptive Problem (MMDP) [27] – see Appendix A for a description of these functions.

Figure 3 shows the results obtained in terms of deviation with respect to the optimal solution (averaged for the four problems) as a function of the churn rate, separately for each network density (detailed numerical data is provided in Tables 2–5 in Appendix B). First of all, it is clear that performance degrades for increasing churn rate. This fact notwithstanding, we can observe that variants using balancing perform notably better than their unbalanced counterparts. This can be shown to be statistically significant using a signrank

Table 1. Results of Holm Test ($\alpha = 0.05$) using SF_4 as control algorithm.

i	Strategy	z-statistic	p-value	α/i
1	SW_4	2.62950	0.00428	0.050
2	SF_2	3.40640	0.00033	0.025
3	SW_2	5.91638	< 0.00001	0.017
4	SW_1	8.78493	< 0.00001	0.013
5	SF_1	9.38254	< 0.00001	0.010

test [28] (p-value $= 0.0017$ in SW and $< 10^{-14}$ for SF). This confirms previous research on this kind of strategy and validates its usefulness on different network topologies. A more interesting perspective could be obtained by performing an analysis on the density of the network or on the network class. Starting with the latter, noB and LBQ offer qualitatively different results. On one hand, noB^{SW} seems to perform slightly better that noB^{SF}, although admittedly the difference is quite small. On the other hand, LBQ^{SF} provides a small improvement over LBQ^{SW} (statistically significant for $m = 2, 4$ according to signrank, p-value < 0.001). A potential interpretation of this can be stated in terms of the presence of larger cliques in SW networks. These can provide the means for a better distribution of solutions in scenarios without balancing, somewhat mitigating (if only minimally) the effect of churn. However, in the presence of balancing, such clusters induce less exchange of information than their SF counterparts (a balancing wave created when a node goes up or down can reach longer distances in SF networks due to the lower mean degree of nodes in this kind of networks). This is consistent with the evolution of island sizes shown in Figure 4 (left and middle-left). In the presence of high churn rates or low connectivity (i.e., low value of m) the SF network can become sporadically disconnected. If no additional corrections are introduced in the balancing procedure the result is the eventual decrease of population sizes. SW networks are much more robust in this sense, and manage to maintain a more stable population size. This reduction of population sizes may provide as an added effect a boost in convergence, as seen, for example, in Figure 4 (middle-right and right) for the case of the TRAP function. The difference between SW and SF becomes more marked for increasing churn and/or decreasing connectivity, in accordance with the previous hypothesis.

In more detail, we analyzed SF and SW separately for each value of m. The Quade test [29] indicated that at least one of the combinations $\langle$topology, $m\rangle$ is significantly different (p-value $\simeq 0$). We therefore performed a post hoc test, i.e., the Holm test [30] using SF_4 as control algorithm. The results of the test are shown in Table 1: the test is passed by all other topologies and values of m, indicating this topology is the most resilient.

5. Conclusion

This chapter has focused on the study of the performance of multimemetic algorithms in unstable computational environments with complex topologies such as those arising in P2P networks. This instability is known to require the use of fault-aware strategies, in particular decentralized strategies suiting the lack of central command in this kind of networks (or in overlay networks built on, for example, centralized volunteer computing infrastructures). For this purpose, the use of self-balancing mechanisms provide an appealing way of coping with this volatility, endowing the search algorithm with enhanced resilience to churn. Here we have been concerned with the effect that the underlying computational scenario, characterized by a certain churn rate, a kind of interconnection topology and a given network density, has on the performance of the algorithm. In addition to scale-free topologies typically considered when dealing with P2P networks, we have also considered the use of other models of complex networks, such as small-world networks with extremely short inter-node distance and high clustering coefficient. These networks can be shown to provide slightly better results for non-fault-aware MMAs, but are globally outperformed by scale-free networks, particularly in the most severe scenarios featuring high churn and/or low connectivity.

There are many avenues for future developments. On the one hand, it would be interesting to scale up network sizes and consider other scenarios of connectivity and churn rate. Another interesting line of research lies in the self-adaptation of the topology itself, so as to make network connectivity reactive to churn [31]. Last but not least, there exists the possibility of extending fault-aware capabilities in order to allow the algorithm to build a local model of its computational environment. Work is already in progress in these areas.

Acknowledgment

This chapter has been partially funded by the MINECO project EphemeCH (TIN2014-56494-C4-1-P), by the Junta de Andalucía project DNEMESIS (P10-TIC-6083) and by the Universidad de Málaga, Campus de Excelencia Internacional Andalucía Tech.

A. Test Suite

Deb's 4-bit fully deceptive function (TRAP) has an isolated single global optimum surrounded by low-fitness solutions as well as a local optimum towards which the gradient is oriented. Mathematically, TRAP is defined as:

$$f(b_1 \cdots b_4) = \begin{cases} 0.6 - 0.2 \cdot u(b_1 \cdots b_4) & \text{if } u(b_1 \cdots b_4) < 4 \\ 1 & \text{if } u(b_1 \cdots b_4) = 4 \end{cases} \tag{2}$$

where

$$u(b_1 \cdots b_i) = \sum_{j=1}^{i} b_j \tag{3}$$

is the unitation (number of 1s) of a binary block. By concatenating k such 4-bits blocks a higher-order problem is built. The fitness of the $4k$-bit string is in this case the sum of the function value for all blocks. We have considered $k = 32$ subproblems (and hence $opt = 32$).

Hierarchically consistent test problems are recursive epistatic functions defined for 2^k-bit strings. They use two auxiliary functions f and t with signatures:

$$f : \{0,1,\bullet\} \to \{0,1\} \quad \text{and} \quad t : \{0,1,\bullet\} \to \{0,1,\bullet\} \tag{4}$$

f is used to score the contribution of building blocks, and t is used to capture their interaction. In the case of the Hierarchical if-and-only-if (HIFF) f and t are defined as:

$$f(a,b) = \begin{cases} 1 & a = b \neq \bullet \\ 0 & \text{otherwise} \end{cases} \tag{5}$$

$$t(a,b) = \begin{cases} a & a = b \\ \bullet & \text{otherwise} \end{cases} \tag{6}$$

These two functions are then combined as follows:

$$\text{HIFF}_k(b_1 \cdots b_n) = \sum_{i=1}^{n/2} f(b_{2i-1}, b_{2i}) + 2 \cdot \text{HIFF}_{k-1}(b'_1, \cdots, b'_{n/2}) \tag{7}$$

where $b'_i = t(b_{2i-1}, b_{2i})$ and $\text{HIFF}_0(\cdot) = 1$. The Hierarchical-XOR (HXOR) is analogous but considers that f provides a fitness contribution of 1 when $a = 1$ and $b = 0$ or vice versa, and having in that case $t(a,b) = a$ (and $t(a,b) = \bullet$ otherwise). We have considered $k = 7$ (i.e., 128-bit strings, $opt = 576$).

Finally, the Massively Multimodal Deceptive Problem (MMDP) is a bipolar deceptive function with two global optima located at extreme unitation values (i.e., all zeros or all ones), and with a local deceptive attractor halfway between them. This location of the deceptive attractor results in massively more local optima than global optima (i.e., $\binom{L}{L/2}$ local vs 2 global, where L is the number of bits in each block). The basic MMDP is defined for 6-bit blocks as follows:

$$f(b_1 \cdots b_6) = \begin{cases} 1 & u(b_1 \cdots b_6) \in \{0,6\} \\ 0 & u(b_1 \cdots b_6) \in \{1,5\} \\ 0.360384 & u(b_1 \cdots b_6) \in \{2,4\} \\ 0.640576 & u(b_1 \cdots b_6) = 3 \end{cases} \tag{8}$$

As done for the TRAP function, we concatenate k copies of this basic block to create a harder problem. We have considered $k = 24$ (thus, $opt = 24$).

B. Numerical Data

Table 2. Deviation (in %) from the optimal solution (25 runs) of the different MMAs on TRAP and HIFF for SF networks. The median ($\tilde{x}$), mean ($\bar{x}$) and standard error of the mean ($\sigma_{\bar{x}}$) are indicated.

			TRAP		HIFF	
Topology	Strategy	k	$\tilde{x}$	$\bar{x} \pm \sigma_{\bar{x}}$	$\tilde{x}$	$\bar{x} \pm \sigma_{\bar{x}}$
SF_1	noB	20	6.25	7.03 ± 0.93	0.00	14.97 ± 3.44
		10	18.13	19.00 ± 1.33	39.41	36.40 ± 3.06
		5	33.13	33.36 ± 1.20	56.94	55.19 ± 1.03
		2	48.75	49.15 ± 0.70	61.46	61.01 ± 0.45
		1	53.47	52.93 ± 0.64	65.10	65.06 ± 0.19
	LBQ	20	1.88	2.63 ± 0.60	0.00	7.88 ± 2.45
		10	6.87	9.15 ± 1.41	0.00	13.83 ± 3.55
		5	15.00	15.78 ± 1.88	21.53	22.70 ± 3.78
		2	40.00	39.58 ± 0.90	52.43	51.64 ± 1.61
		1	51.82	50.90 ± 0.64	63.72	63.25 ± 0.42
SF_2	noB	20	0.00	1.30 ± 0.36	0.00	5.17 ± 2.22
		10	9.38	9.35 ± 1.09	0.00	11.84 ± 2.90
		5	26.25	27.02 ± 1.51	47.40	44.85 ± 2.55
		2	47.50	47.54 ± 0.75	62.67	61.56 ± 0.68
		1	53.75	54.08 ± 0.59	64.58	64.52 ± 0.23
	LBQ	20	0.00	0.40 ± 0.19	0.00	4.44 ± 1.86
		10	0.00	0.92 ± 0.29	0.00	8.53 ± 2.61
		5	2.50	3.48 ± 0.65	0.00	10.88 ± 2.46
		2	21.88	22.83 ± 1.25	21.88	21.71 ± 3.39
		1	44.38	44.15 ± 1.04	51.39	50.17 ± 1.79
SF_4	noB	20	0.00	0.40 ± 0.19	0.00	5.94 ± 2.27
		10	1.25	2.73 ± 0.67	0.00	12.30 ± 3.05
		5	16.25	15.98 ± 1.40	24.48	22.50 ± 4.09
		2	46.88	46.35 ± 1.13	61.28	60.32 ± 0.64
		1	52.50	52.55 ± 0.69	64.24	63.85 ± 0.33
	LBQ	20	0.00	0.10 ± 0.07	0.00	2.61 ± 1.49
		10	0.00	0.55 ± 0.36	0.00	4.72 ± 1.77
		5	2.50	3.05 ± 0.49	0.00	10.11 ± 2.90
		2	15.79	15.86 ± 1.38	19.44	15.71 ± 3.43
		1	30.00	29.10 ± 1.42	24.48	23.80 ± 3.20

Table 3. Deviation (in %) from the optimal solution (25 runs) of the different MMAs on TRAP and HIFF for SW networks. The median ($\tilde{x}$), mean ($\bar{x}$) and standard error of the mean ($\sigma_{\bar{x}}$) are indicated.

			TRAP		HIFF	
Topology	**Strategy**	k	$\tilde{x}$	$\bar{x} \pm \sigma_{\bar{x}}$	$\tilde{x}$	$\bar{x} \pm \sigma_{\bar{x}}$
SW_1	noB	20	6.87	5.85 ± 0.66	0.00	11.06 ± 3.58
		10	14.38	15.85 ± 1.67	27.43	25.01 ± 4.10
		5	32.50	32.82 ± 1.38	55.56	53.65 ± 1.25
		2	48.75	47.59 ± 0.94	61.92	61.13 ± 0.76
		1	53.75	53.59 ± 0.54	64.93	64.69 ± 0.21
	LBQ	20	0.00	1.50 ± 0.50	0.00	4.43 ± 1.65
		10	6.87	7.92 ± 1.25	0.00	12.25 ± 3.17
		5	18.75	18.48 ± 2.00	31.60	32.44 ± 2.79
		2	41.87	40.55 ± 1.36	55.38	54.41 ± 1.27
		1	53.13	52.55 ± 0.56	64.24	63.81 ± 0.36
SW_2	noB	20	2.50	3.79 ± 0.95	0.00	6.56 ± 2.29
		10	8.13	7.75 ± 1.25	19.44	17.09 ± 3.27
		5	28.75	29.52 ± 1.47	42.19	34.11 ± 4.09
		2	47.50	46.25 ± 1.30	62.36	61.80 ± 0.44
		1	53.75	53.20 ± 0.54	64.93	64.76 ± 0.23
	LBQ	20	0.00	1.52 ± 0.49	0.00	6.97 ± 2.26
		10	1.25	2.05 ± 0.51	0.00	5.11 ± 1.89
		5	7.50	7.55 ± 0.89	0.00	10.85 ± 2.86
		2	35.62	35.30 ± 1.03	47.40	40.28 ± 2.91
		1	51.25	50.79 ± 0.70	63.54	63.31 ± 0.30
SW_4	noB	20	0.00	1.60 ± 0.53	16.67	12.08 ± 2.50
		10	3.75	4.20 ± 0.97	19.44	15.22 ± 3.19
		5	16.25	16.27 ± 1.58	22.05	23.84 ± 3.78
		2	45.63	44.93 ± 1.07	60.48	59.63 ± 1.19
		1	52.86	52.18 ± 0.56	64.76	64.46 ± 0.22
	LBQ	20	0.00	0.55 ± 0.28	0.00	5.67 ± 2.14
		10	0.00	1.35 ± 0.44	0.00	7.19 ± 2.30
		5	3.13	4.35 ± 0.88	0.00	6.39 ± 2.43
		2	21.25	22.93 ± 1.15	22.57	22.94 ± 3.70
		1	49.38	48.92 ± 0.65	54.34	53.42 ± 1.31

Table 4. Deviation (in %) from the optimal solution (25 runs) of the different MMAs on HXOR and MMDP for SF networks. The median ($\tilde{x}$), mean ($\bar{x}$) and standard error of the mean ($\sigma_{\bar{x}}$) are indicated.

			HXOR		MMDP	
Topology	Strategy	k	$\tilde{x}$	$\bar{x} \pm \sigma_{\bar{x}}$	$\tilde{x}$	$\bar{x} \pm \sigma_{\bar{x}}$
SF_1	noB	20	41.32	40.87 ± 0.77	8.99	10.30 ± 1.01
		10	48.44	49.30 ± 0.88	19.98	21.22 ± 1.17
		5	57.47	57.11 ± 0.46	28.45	29.29 ± 0.76
		2	63.07	62.77 ± 0.25	38.12	38.61 ± 0.43
		1	64.76	64.90 ± 0.15	40.79	40.41 ± 0.52
	LBQ	20	34.38	33.93 ± 1.04	4.49	4.99 ± 0.56
		10	38.02	39.15 ± 0.97	11.65	11.96 ± 1.04
		5	44.97	46.07 ± 1.26	19.14	19.75 ± 1.38
		2	58.33	57.89 ± 0.56	33.30	33.02 ± 0.85
		1	64.41	64.21 ± 0.23	40.46	40.32 ± 0.48
SF_2	noB	20	30.90	31.56 ± 1.03	4.49	4.90 ± 0.49
		10	40.10	40.47 ± 1.04	14.32	13.96 ± 1.10
		5	53.30	53.11 ± 0.91	27.79	27.46 ± 0.88
		2	62.50	62.45 ± 0.33	37.29	37.46 ± 0.62
		1	64.76	64.43 ± 0.25	41.63	41.14 ± 0.36
	LBQ	20	29.17	28.44 ± 1.20	3.00	2.56 ± 0.32
		10	31.94	32.26 ± 0.82	4.49	4.36 ± 0.52
		5	35.42	34.97 ± 0.97	8.66	7.98 ± 0.55
		2	47.22	47.03 ± 0.53	21.80	21.48 ± 0.87
		1	60.42	60.48 ± 0.54	36.78	36.38 ± 0.57
SF_4	noB	20	33.33	31.78 ± 0.96	1.50	1.36 ± 0.28
		10	35.42	34.40 ± 0.74	5.99	6.49 ± 0.64
		5	44.44	44.15 ± 0.86	16.47	17.03 ± 0.80
		2	61.28	61.22 ± 0.43	36.63	37.17 ± 0.65
		1	64.93	64.76 ± 0.18	40.80	40.71 ± 0.49
	LBQ	20	27.78	26.58 ± 1.10	0.00	1.24 ± 0.33
		10	31.25	30.08 ± 0.94	1.50	2.76 ± 0.50
		5	34.38	33.13 ± 0.84	5.99	6.52 ± 0.56
		2	43.40	43.79 ± 0.94	14.65	14.78 ± 0.78
		1	51.56	52.06 ± 0.67	26.48	25.79 ± 1.07

Table 5. Deviation (in %) from the optimal solution (25 runs) of the different MMAs on HXOR and MMDP for SW networks. The median ($\tilde{x}$), mean ($\bar{x}$) and standard error of the mean ($\sigma_{\bar{x}}$) are indicated.

			HXOR		MMDP	
Topology	Strategy	k	$\tilde{x}$	$\bar{x} \pm \sigma_{\bar{x}}$	$\tilde{x}$	$\bar{x} \pm \sigma_{\bar{x}}$
SW_1	noB	20	38.37	37.46 ± 1.05	10.15	10.16 ± 1.11
		10	47.92	48.01 ± 0.96	17.97	18.72 ± 1.44
		5	57.29	57.36 ± 0.56	29.62	29.57 ± 0.85
		2	63.02	62.96 ± 0.25	36.96	37.07 ± 0.62
		1	65.10	64.59 ± 0.28	40.79	41.45 ± 0.48
	LBQ	20	32.64	31.00 ± 1.77	5.99	7.85 ± 1.12
		10	35.59	36.40 ± 1.33	13.48	13.43 ± 1.32
		5	43.92	45.87 ± 1.18	19.98	21.02 ± 1.12
		2	59.38	59.10 ± 0.68	33.96	34.65 ± 0.76
		1	64.41	63.99 ± 0.29	41.24	41.31 ± 0.37
SW_2	noB	20	34.03	34.17 ± 1.26	4.49	4.65 ± 0.69
		10	39.76	40.22 ± 0.82	11.65	11.98 ± 1.11
		5	53.30	53.16 ± 1.06	26.30	26.28 ± 0.80
		2	63.02	62.48 ± 0.39	36.63	36.42 ± 0.71
		1	64.90	64.79 ± 0.17	41.12	41.08 ± 0.43
	LBQ	20	33.33	32.26 ± 0.84	4.49	4.75 ± 0.55
		10	35.76	35.44 ± 0.75	5.99	7.30 ± 0.74
		5	40.10	39.13 ± 0.79	11.65	11.34 ± 0.72
		2	54.69	54.48 ± 0.66	30.64	30.78 ± 0.61
		1	63.54	63.44 ± 0.30	40.79	40.66 ± 0.35
SW_4	noB	20	33.33	33.19 ± 1.05	1.50	2.38 ± 0.50
		10	38.89	38.84 ± 0.63	7.16	7.20 ± 0.81
		5	44.97	46.28 ± 0.90	17.64	17.72 ± 1.21
		2	61.63	61.28 ± 0.51	36.12	36.00 ± 0.75
		1	64.93	64.65 ± 0.21	40.79	40.21 ± 0.48
	LBQ	20	31.25	30.54 ± 0.98	1.50	2.43 ± 0.47
		10	34.72	33.51 ± 1.09	4.49	4.45 ± 0.52
		5	37.50	36.28 ± 0.82	8.66	8.57 ± 0.55
		2	48.61	48.68 ± 0.80	23.63	23.88 ± 0.87
		1	61.81	61.36 ± 0.55	38.46	38.15 ± 0.43

References

[1] Enrique Alba. *Parallel Metaheuristics: A New Class of Algorithms*. Wiley-Interscience, 2005.

[2] Enrique Alba and Marco Tomassini. Parallelism and evolutionary algorithms. *IEEE Transactions on Evolutionary Computation*, 6(5):443–462, Oct 2002.

[3] Martina Gorges-Schleuter. ASPARAGOS: an asynchronous parallel genetic optimization strategy. In J. David Schaffer, editor, *Third International Conference on Genetic Algorithms*, pages 422–427, San Francisco, CA, 1989. Morgan Kaufmann.

[4] Reiko Tanese. Distributed genetic algorithms. In *3rd International Conference on Genetic Algorithms*, pages 434–439, San Francisco, CA, USA, 1989. Morgan Kaufmann Publishers Inc.

[5] Dejan S. Milojičić, Vana Kalogeraki, Rajan Lukose, Kiran Nagaraja, Jim Pruyne, Bruno Richard, Sami Rollins, and Zhichen Xu. Peer-to-peer computing. *Technical Report* HPL-2002-57, Hewlett-Packard Labs, 2002.

[6] Luis F.G. Sarmenta. Bayanihan: Web-based volunteer computing using java. In Yoshifumi Masunaga, Takuya Katayama, and Michiharu Tsukamoto, editors, *Worldwide Computing and Its Applications – WWCA'98*, volume 1368 of *Lecture Notes in Computer Science*, pages 444–461. Springer Berlin Heidelberg, 1998.

[7] J. Ignacio Hidalgo, Juan Lanchares, Francisco Fernández de Vega, and Daniel Lombraña. Is the island model fault tolerant? In *Proceedings of the 9th Annual Conference Companion on Genetic and Evolutionary Computation*, GECCO '07, pages 2737–2744, New York, NY, USA, 2007. ACM.

[8] Daniel Lombraña González, Juan Luís Jiménez Laredo, Francisco Fernández de Vega, and Juan Julián Merelo Guervós. Characterizing fault-tolerance of genetic algorithms in desktop grid systems. In Peter Cowling and Peter Merz, editors, *Evolutionary Computation in Combinatorial Optimization*, volume 6022 of *Lecture Notes in Computer Science*, pages 131–142. Springer Berlin Heidelberg, 2010.

[9] Juan Luis Jiménez Laredo, Pascal Bouvry, Diego Lombraña González, Francisco Fernández de Vega, Maribel García Arenas, Juan Julián Merelo Guervós, and Carlos M. Fernandes. Designing robust volunteer-based evolutionary algorithms. *Genetic Programming and Evolvable Machines*, 15(3):221–244, 2014.

[10] Rafael Nogueras and Carlos Cotta. Studying fault-tolerance in island-based evolutionary and multimemetic algorithms. *Journal of Grid Computing*, [Online first] DOI:10.1007/s10723-014-9315-6, 2015.

[11] N. Krasnogor, B.P. Blackburne, E.K. Burke, and J.D. Hirst. Multimeme algorithms for protein structure prediction. In J.J. Merelo et al., editors, *Parallel Problem Solving From Nature VII*, volume 2439 of *Lecture Notes in Computer Science*, pages 769–778. Springer, Berlin, 2002.

[12] Ferrante Neri, Carlos Cotta, and Pablo Moscato. *Handbook of Memetic Algorithms*, volume 379 of *Studies in Computational Intelligence*. Springer, Berlin Heidelberg, 2012.

[13] P. Moscato. On Evolution, Search, Optimization, Genetic Algorithms and Martial Arts: Towards Memetic Algorithms. *Technical Report Caltech Concurrent Computation Program*, Report. 826, California Institute of Technology, Pasadena, California, USA, 1989.

[14] Réka Albert and Albert-László Barabási. Statistical mechanics of complex networks. *Review of Modern Physics*, 74(1):47–97, Jan 2002.

[15] Albert-László Barabási and Réka Albert. Emergence of Scaling in Random Networks. *Science*, 286(5439):509–512, 1999.

[16] Duncan J. Watts and Steven H. Strogatz. Collective dynamics of 'small-world' networks. *Nature*, 393:440–442, 1998.

[17] Dionysios Barmpoutis and Richard M. Murray. *Networks with the smallest average distance and the largest average clustering.* arXiv, 1007.4031 [q-bio], 2010.

[18] Waloddi Weibull. A statistical distribution function of wide applicability. *Journal of Applied Mechanics*, 18(3):293–297, 1951.

[19] Elisa T. Lee and John W. Wang. *Statistical Methods for Survival Data Analysis*. John Wiley & Sons, Inc., Hoboken, NJ, 2003.

[20] James E. Smith. Self-adaptation in evolutionary algorithms for combinatorial optimisation. In Carlos Cotta, Marc Sevaux, and Kenneth Sörensen, editors, *Adaptive and Multilevel Metaheuristics*, volume 136 of *Studies in Computational Intelligence*, pages 31–57. Springer Berlin Heidelberg, 2008.

[21] James E. Smith. Self-adaptative and coevolving memetic algorithms. In Ferrante Neri, Carlos Cotta, and Pablo Moscato, editors, *Handbook of Memetic Algorithms*, volume 379 of *Studies in Computational Intelligence*, pages 167–188. Springer-Verlag, Berlin Heidelberg, 2012.

[22] Rafael Nogueras and Carlos Cotta. An analysis of migration strategies in island-based multimemetic algorithms. In T. Bartz-Beielstein, J. Branke, B. Filipič, and J. Smith, editors, *Parallel Problem Solving From Nature – PPSN XIII*, volume 8672 of *Lecture Notes in Computer Science*, pages 731–740, Berlin Heidelberg, 2014. Springer.

[23] Franco Zambonelli. Exploiting biased load information in direct-neighbour load balancing policies. *Parallel Computing*, 25(6):745 – 766, 1999.

[24] R. Nogueras and C. Cotta. Studying self-balancing strategies in island-based multimemetic algorithms. *Journal of Computational and Applied Mathematics*, 2015. doi:10.1016/j.cam.2015.03.047.

[25] Kalyanmoy Deb and David E. Goldberg. Analyzing deception in trap functions. In L. Darrell Whitley, editor, *Second Workshop on Foundations of Genetic Algorithms*, pages 93–108, Vail, Colorado, USA, 1993. Morgan Kaufmann.

[26] Richard A. Watson, Gregory S. Hornby, and Jordan B. Pollack. Modeling building-block interdependency. In Agoston E. Eiben, Thomas Bäck, Marc Schoenauer, and Hans-Paul Schwefel, editors, *Parallel Problem Solving from Nature – PPSN V*, volume 1498 of *Lecture Notes in Computer Science*, pages 97–106. Springer, Berlin Heidelberg, 1998.

[27] David E. Goldberg, Kalyanmoy Deb, and Jeffrey Horn. Massive multimodality, deception, and genetic algorithms. In *Parallel Problem Solving from Nature – PPSN II*, pages 37–48, Brussels, Belgium, 1992. Elsevier.

[28] F. Wilcoxon. Individual comparisons by ranking methods. *Biometrics*, 1:80–83, 1945.

[29] Dana Quade. Using weighted rankings in the analysis of complete blocks with additive block effects. *Journal of the American Statistical Association*, 74:680–683, 1979.

[30] S. Holm. A simple sequentially rejective multiple test procedure. *Scandinavian Journal of Statistics*, 6:65–70, 1979.

[31] R. Nogueras and C. Cotta. Self-balancing multimemetic algorithms in dynamic scale-free networks. In A.M. Mora and G. Squillero, editors, *Applications of Evolutionary Computation*, volume 9028 of *Lecture Notes in Computer Science*, pages 177–188, Berlin Heidelberg, 2015. Springer.

In: Advances in Evolutionary Algorithms Research
Editor: Gregor Papa
ISBN: 978-1-63463-849-4
© 2015 Nova Science Publishers, Inc.

Chapter 3

RSGA-BASED GENETIC LOGIC CIRCUIT DESIGN

Chia-Hua Chuang and Chun-Liang Lin*
Department of Electrical Engineering,
National Chung Hsing University, Taiwan, ROC

ABSTRACT

This chapter intends to introduce a new type of genetic algorithms (GAs), named real structural genetic algorithm (RSGA) and applies itin constructing a class of genetic logic gates with compromised performance and cheaper structure. The RSGA integrating the advantages of the traditional real genetic algorithm (RGA) with a structured genetic algorithm (SGA) has been developed to simultaneously solve the parameter and structure optimization problems. A genetic transcriptional model with the cis-regulatory input function (CRIF) for genetic logic gate design is constructed byapplying the RSGA to search for its cheaper structure. To assemble the logic gates, a genetic counter with a clock pulse generator based on an existing genetic oscillator is designed. The clock's frequency is an inverse integral multiple to that of the genetic oscillator. A genetic waveform-shaping circuit with several cascaded buffers is constructed to shape logic high/low levels of an oscillation input and generate a pulse-width-modulated (PWM) output with various duty cycles. Based on the topology of the digital sequential logic circuits, the synchronous genetic counter circuit is synthesized and triggered by the clock pulse to realize a frequency synthesizer.

Keywords: real structural genetic algorithm, parameter and structure optimization,genetic logic gates, cis-regulatory input function

INTRODUCTION

Genetic algorithms (GAs) which is inspired by the mechanisms of natural selection and evolution genetics have been widely applied for solving optimization problems in various

*Corresponding Author address: National Chung Hsing University, Taichung 402, Taiwan, ROC; Email: chunlin@dragon.nchu.edu.tw.

fields [1-7]. For conventional binary genetic algorithm (BGA), it emphasizes binary coding in chromosomes, but requires an excessive amount of computational time when dealing with high-dimensional problems. Alternate forms of GAs have been developed to overcome the weaknesses of premature convergence and in efficient computational performance. Real genetic algorithm (RGA) using a floating point representation for parameter optimization has been proven to have significant improvements on computational speed and high precision [2]. In addition, structured genetic algorithm (SGA) and hierarchical genetic algorithm (HGA) have been proposed to handle structure optimization problem, which enable simultaneous optimizations of parameters in different chromosome structures [3, 4]. A novel real structured genetic algorithm (RSGA) which combines the advantages of RGA and SGA has been proposed for digital filter and optimal control designs yielding a compact structure with appropriate performance simultaneously [5-7].

Recently, synthetic biology is developed to understand the behavior of biological systems from system-level as well as construct a class of artificial genetic circuits using the approaches of mathematics and engineering. By using mathematical models to capture the quantitative and qualitative characteristics of biological systems, synthetic genetic circuits with specific functions can be designed from the engineering perspective. As Boolean logic gate is the essential unit of computers, the genetic logic gate is a fundamental element for constructing the more complicated bio-computer in synthetic biology. In biological systems, genetic expression is controlled by transcription factor (TF)-a protein. To describe the biochemical phenomena, many mathematical models for genetic logic gate design have recently been developed in [8-16]. A genetic transcriptional model with cis-regulatory input function (CRIF) describes the combined effect of the promoters and logic phenotype. By selecting strengths and related DNA binding sites in the gene's cis-regulatory region, the various kinds of genetic logic gates can be constructed accordingly. By assembling the fundamental genetic logic gates, more complicated genetic logic circuits can be synthesized.

There are many evolutionary algorithms proposed to construct synthetic genetic logic circuits. The major purpose of these approaches is to convert the problem into a tracking control problem. In the known circuit topology, GAs are used to search for the optimal parameters to achieve the desired performance. By regulating the transcription rate of mRNA and synthesis rate of protein, a class of robust genetic logic circuits are constructed under stochastic perturbational environments [17, 18]. In addition to the parameter optimization, structure optimization problem is also considered for reducing the size of genetic circuits. In [19, 20], the RSGA is applied to synthesize robust genetic oscillators with the minimal number of genes while ensuring satisfactory performance. It is also applicable to the genetic logic gate design, which generates a regular structure of the model and a function of model simplification. A class of genetic combinational and sequential circuits is synthesized by assembling the RSGA-based logic gates.

This chapter introduces the RSGA and applies it to construct the CRIF models with a compact structure and optimal performance for a class of genetic logic gates. With the RSGA, a structured genetic mapping is utilized to regulate the model structure so that the CRIF models reveal the desired functional values of logical expressions on each of their functional arguments. Through synchronous cascades of the RSGA-based genetic logic gates based on analogous topology of the digital logic circuits in electronics, a genetic sequential logic circuit with a function of frequency synthesizer based on an existing genetic oscillator has been realized [21, 22].Analogous to electronic waveform-shaping circuits, a genetic waveform-shaping circuit constructed by several cascaded genetic "Buffers" is proposed, which shapes logic high/low levels of an oscillation input and generate a pulse-width-modulated (PWM) output with various duty cycles. By regulating the threshold level of the buffer, a clock pulse with its frequency consistent to the genetic oscillator is synthesized, which is served as the rising or falling triggered edges of a clock signal. Based on the topology of the digital sequential logic circuits, a synchronous genetic counter circuit is triggered by the clock pulse to generate a clock signal whose frequency is an inverse integer multiple to the genetic oscillator. In silico numerical examples are provided to demonstrate the design procedure.

REAL STRUCTURAL GENETIC ALGORITHM

The RSGA [5-7] is an optimization algorithm, which combines the advantages of RGA and SGA for obtaining the global optimal solutions with structure and parameter optimizations.

Initialization

In RSGA, the chromosome structure consists of control genes and parameter genes which are both real numbers within the interval $(R_{\min}, R_{\max})$ where $0.5R_{\max} - R_{\min} > 0$, as illustrated in Figure 1. The model of the generalized chromosome structure is defined as follows

$$Y = \langle C, P \rangle = \langle [c_i], [p_i] \rangle \tag{1}$$

where $Y = [y_i]_{1\times\left(n+\sum_{i=1}^{n} n_{p_i}\right)}$ denotes an ordered set with the control genes $C = [c_i]_{1\times n}$ and the parameter genes $P = [p_i]_{1\times\left(\sum_{i=1}^{n} n_{p_i}\right)}$ with n_{p_i} denoting the appropriate size of the parameter vector p_i.

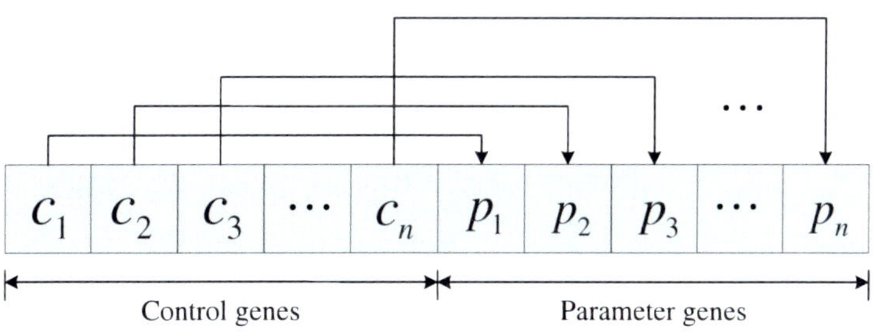

Figure 1. Chromosome structure of the RSGA.

Structured Genetic Mapping

The structured genetic mapping in RSGA has three operations to control the activity of the parameter genes: activate, inhibit, and linear ratio scaling. Representation of the chromosome structure via the structured genetic mapping from C to P is defined as

$$\tilde{Y} = \langle C, \tilde{P} \rangle = \langle [c_i], [\tilde{p}_i] \rangle = \langle [c_i], [c_i] \otimes [p_i] \rangle \tag{2}$$

with

$$\tilde{p}_i \equiv \begin{cases} p_i, & \text{if } B_{\max} \le c_i \\ p_i t, & \text{if } B_{\min} \le c_i \le B_{\max},\ t = \dfrac{c_i - B_{\min}}{B_{\max} - B_{\min}} \\ \phi, & \text{if } c_i \le B_{\min} \end{cases} \tag{3}$$

where $\tilde{Y}$ is the new chromosome structure consisting of $C = [c_i]$ and new parameter genes $\tilde{P} = [\tilde{p}_i]$ after structured genetic mapping, $\otimes$ acts as the genetic switch to determine the status of parameter genes, ϕ denotes an empty string, and t denotes the effective gain. The activation function of the control genes c_i is determined by $B_{\min}$ and $B_{\max}$, which corresponds to the boundaries for OFF (inactive) and ON (active) respectively. The control genes c_i regulate the corresponding parameter genes p_i with linear ratio scaling when c_i is within the boundary of $B_{\min}$ and $B_{\max}$. If the value of the control genes exceeds $B_{\max}$ the corresponding parameter genes are maintained; the parameter genes are deactivated, if otherwise. The values of $B_{\min}$ and $B_{\max}$ in each generation are regulated by a boundary sizing formula characterized by

$$\begin{cases} B_{\max} = B_{\min} = R_{\text{mid}}, & \text{if } g_i = g_{\text{init}} \\ B_{\max} = R_{\text{mid}} + 0.5\Delta B,\ B_{\min} = R_{\text{mid}} - 0.5\Delta B, & \text{if } 0 < g_i < g_f \\ B_{\max} = R_{\max},\ B_{\min} = R_{\min}, & \text{if } g_i = g_f \end{cases} \tag{4}$$

where $R_{\text{mid}} = \frac{1}{2}(R_{\max} + R_{\min})$, g_i denotes the current generation, g_{init} and g_f are the initial and final generations respectively, and the generation-related constant $\Delta B = k g_i$ with k being a positive constant.

Fitness Function

The objective function J_{tot} consisting of the corresponding costs of two parts relatedtothe parameter and structure is defined by

$$J_{tot} = \rho J_s + (1-\rho) J_p \tag{5}$$

where J_s and J_p reveal, respectively, the normalized indices of structure complexity and performance, and the constant $\rho \in [0,1]$ is the weighting factor. The "windowing" technique converts the objective function J_{tot} into the fitness function F defined by

$$F = \mu (J_{tot} - J_l) + F_u \tag{6}$$

where $\mu = \frac{F_u - F_l}{J_l - J_u}$ with J_u and J_l denoting the largest and smallest values of J_{tot} in the current generation respectively, and F_l and F_u being the minimum and maximum fitness values respectively.

Genetic Operators

Reproduction

Reproduction follows the principle of survival of the fittest in the process of natural selection. A new population in the next generation is created from the current populations according to the reproduction probability defined by

$$P_r = \frac{F_i}{\sum_{j=1}^{m} F_j} \tag{7}$$

where P_r is the reproduction probability, F_i is the fitness value of the i th member, and m is the population size. A higher probability tends to be assigned to chromosomes associated with higher fitness value among the population.

Crossover

Crossover operator provides a mechanism to mix the information of two chosen chromosomes. As the popular GAs, the number of individuals joining the operation is determined by the crossover probability P_c. The crossover process of randomly selected pairs of individuals is determined by an extrapolation/interpolation method defined as

$$\begin{cases} \tilde{x}_{di} = x_{di} - \lambda(x_{di} - x_{mi}) \\ \tilde{x}_{mi} = x_{mi} + \lambda(x_{di} - x_{mi}) \end{cases} \tag{8}$$

when $x_{di} > R_{\max}$ or $x_{mi} < R_{\min}$ and

$$\begin{cases} \tilde{x}_{di} = x_{di} + \lambda(x_{di} - x_{mi}) \\ \tilde{x}_{mi} = x_{mi} - \lambda(x_{di} - x_{mi}) \end{cases} \tag{9}$$

when $R_{\min} \le x_{mi} \le x_{di} \le R_{\max}$; where x_{di} and x_{mi} refer to parent generation, and $\tilde{x}_{di}$ and $\tilde{x}_{mi}$ are offspring of x_{di} and x_{mi}, respectively, and $\lambda = \lambda_0 \left(1 - \frac{g_i}{g_f}\right)$ with a uniform random number $\lambda_0 \in [0,1]$. The operation starts by extrapolation and switches to interpolation when the parameters of the offspring exceed the permissible range. Interpolation avoids parameters from crossing over the admissible range in the boundary value search.

Mutation

The mutation operator applies randomly chosen individuals to generate fine tuning in chromosomes. The number of individuals to be varied is determined by the mutation probability P_m. In mutation operator, it adopts the non-uniform mutation method which changes genes in a chromosome. The mutation operation is specified by

$$\tilde{x}_{ij} = \begin{cases} x_{ij} + \Delta\left(g_i, x_{ij\max} - x_{ij}\right), & \text{if } h = 0 \\ x_{ij} - \Delta\left(g_i, x_{ij} - x_{ij\min}\right), & \text{if } h = 1 \end{cases} \tag{10}$$

where $x_{ij} \notin \{\phi\}$ and $\Delta(g_i, y) = y\lambda_0 \left(1 - \frac{g_i}{g_{fin}}\right)$, x_{ij} is the j th element of the i th individuals in the current generation, $x_{ij,\max}$ and $x_{ij,\min}$ are the maximal and minimal of x_{ij}, the value of h is 0 or 1 dependent on the random production, $\lambda_0 \in [0,1]$ is a uniform random number, and y is a scaling factor.

Dynamic Crossover/Mutation Probability

To regulate the mutation and crossover probabilities for both of the control and parameter genes, the dynamic mutation and crossover probability adjustments are described by

$$P_{new} = P_{cur}\Delta P \tag{11}$$

with $\Delta P = \dfrac{1}{1+\left(\dfrac{g_i}{g_c}\right)^{2q}}$, where P_{new} is the new probability, P_{cur} is the current probability, ΔP is the dynamic probability factor, g_c is the cutoff generation, and q is the order of the dynamic probability.

For the control genes, the dynamic crossover/mutation probability is defined as

$$P_{c,new} = P_{c,cur}\Delta P \tag{12}$$

and

$$P_{m,new} = P_{m,cur}\Delta P \tag{13}$$

where $P_{c,new}$ and $P_{m,new}$ are, respectively, new crossover and mutation probabilities, and $P_{c,cur}$ and $P_{m,cur}$ are the current crossover and mutation probabilities, respectively.

The crossover/mutation probability for the parameter genes is defined as follows

$$\begin{cases} P_{c,new} = P_{c,cur}\Delta P, & g_i < g_c, \\ P_{c,new} = P_{c,cur}\Delta P, & g_i \geq g_c \end{cases} \tag{14}$$

and

$$\begin{cases} P_{m,new} = P_{m,cur}\Delta P, & g_i < g_c, \\ P_{m,new} = P_{m,cur}\Delta P, & g_i \geq g_c \end{cases} \tag{15}$$

This would ensure that the emphasis of the optimization will be switched toward parameter optimization after reaching g_c. The above arrangement ensuring the effect of the crossover and mutation for parameter genes will not vanish.

One is referred to [5-7] for more details regarding the operations of RSGA above.

DESIGN OF GENETIC LOGIC GATES

Transcription Model

In genetic systems, DNA is transcribed to messenger RNA (mRNA) when an enzyme RNA polymerase (RNAp) binds to the corresponding promoter. Protein is produced from mRNA when ribosome binds to mRNA in the translation process. For a gene with multiple binding sites, the genetic transcription model with *cis*-regulatory input function (CRIF)can be described by the dynamic Hill differential equation:

$$\dot{x} = \alpha f(u) - \beta x + \alpha_0 \tag{16}$$

with its steady-state solution

$$x_{ss} = \frac{\alpha}{\beta} f(u) + \frac{\alpha_0}{\beta} \tag{17}$$

where x is the concentration of protein, x_{ss} is its steady-state, α, β and α_0 are synthesis, degradation and basal production rates, respectively, and $f(\cdot)$ is the CRIF model with u denoting a vector of concentrations of TFs.

The model of a gene with a single TF can be used to synthesize a class of Boolean logic functions, such as NOT and Buffer. For those cases, the general CRIF model is as follows

$$f(u_1) = \frac{m_1 + m_2 \left(\frac{u_1}{K_1}\right)^{h_1}}{1 + \left(\frac{u_1}{K_1}\right)^{h_1}} \tag{18}$$

where u_1 denotes the concentration of TF, K_1 denotes the binding strength of the TF to the promoter, h_1 is the Hill coefficients related to the cooperativity between TF and the corresponding biding sites, and m_1 and m_2 are the weighting coefficients operating at structured genetic mapping in RSGA. In the numerator part of (18), the first term represents RNAp bound to the promoter and the second term represents the corresponding TF bound to the corresponding operation site. By the appropriate CRIF, the desired protein response can be obtained after performing the genetic transcription and translation processes.

Similarly, the model with two TFs can be used to synthesize fundamental logic functions including AND, OR, NAND, NOR, and XOR. For these cases, a general CRIF model is constructed as

$$f(u_1, u_2) = \frac{m_1 + m_2 \left(\frac{u_1}{K_1}\right)^{h_1} + m_3 \left(\frac{u_2}{K_2}\right)^{h_2} + m_4 \left(\frac{u_1}{K_1}\right)^{h_1} \left(\frac{u_2}{K_2}\right)^{h_2}}{1 + \left(\frac{u_1}{K_1}\right)^{h_1} + \left(\frac{u_2}{K_2}\right)^{h_2} + \left(\frac{u_1}{K_1}\right)^{h_1} \left(\frac{u_2}{K_2}\right)^{h_2}} \tag{19}$$

where K_1 and K_2 denote, respectively, the independent binding strength of the TF proteins $u = (u_1, u_2)$ with u_1 and u_2 denoting, respectively, concentrations of two TFs. In the numerator part of (19), the first term represents RNAp bond to the promoter, the second and third terms represent the TFs u_1 and u_2 bound to the respective operation sites, the final term represents the regulators $u=(u_1,u_2)$ bound to the operation sites, and $m_i \in R_+$, $i=1,2,3$ are the weighting coefficients.

For a gene with three TFs, the model can be used to synthesize fundamental logic functions including AND, OR, NAND, NOR, and XOR. For these cases, a general CRIF model is constructed as

$$f(u_1,u_2,u_3)=\frac{N(u_1,u_2,u_3)}{D(u_1,u_2,u_3)} \tag{20}$$

with

$$\begin{aligned} N(u_1,u_2,u_3) &= m_1 + m_2\left(\frac{u_1}{K_1}\right)^{h_1} + m_3\left(\frac{u_2}{K_2}\right)^{h_2} + m_4\left(\frac{u_3}{K_3}\right)^{h_3} \\ &+ m_5\left(\frac{u_1}{K_1}\right)^{h_1}\left(\frac{u_2}{K_2}\right)^{h_2} + m_6\left(\frac{u_2}{K_2}\right)^{h_2}\left(\frac{u_3}{K_3}\right)^{h_3} + m_7\left(\frac{u_3}{K_3}\right)^{h_3}\left(\frac{u_1}{K_1}\right)^{h_1} \\ &+ m_8\left(\frac{u_1}{K_1}\right)^{h_1}\left(\frac{u_2}{K_2}\right)^{h_2}\left(\frac{u_3}{K_3}\right)^{h_3} \end{aligned} \tag{21}$$

$$\begin{aligned} D(u_1,u_2,u_3) &= 1 + \left(\frac{u_1}{K_1}\right)^{h_1} + \left(\frac{u_2}{K_2}\right)^{h_2} + \left(\frac{u_3}{K_3}\right)^{h_3} + \left(\frac{u_1}{K_1}\right)^{h_1}\left(\frac{u_2}{K_2}\right)^{h_2} \\ &+ \left(\frac{u_2}{K_2}\right)^{h_2}\left(\frac{u_3}{K_3}\right)^{h_3} + \left(\frac{u_3}{K_3}\right)^{h_3}\left(\frac{u_1}{K_1}\right)^{h_1} + \left(\frac{u_1}{K_1}\right)^{h_1}\left(\frac{u_2}{K_2}\right)^{h_2}\left(\frac{u_3}{K_3}\right)^{h_3} \end{aligned} \tag{22}$$

where K_1, K_2, and K_3 denote, respectively, the independent binding strength of the regulated proteins $u=(u_1,u_2,u_3)$ with u_1, u_2 and u_3 denoting, respectively, concentrations of three TFs. In (21), the first term represents RNAp bond to the promoter, the second to fourth terms represent the TFs u_1, u_2 and u_3 bound to the respective operation sites, the fifth to the seventh terms represent any two TFs bound to the respective operation sites, the final term represents the TF $u=(u_1,u_2,u_3)$ bound to the operation sites, and $m_i \in R_+$, $i=1,2,\ldots,8$ are the weighting coefficients.

RSGA-Based Genetic Logic Gate

Structured Genetic Mapping

For the genetic logic gate with single TF in (18), the weighting coefficients are regarded as parameter genes and set the control genes, whose number is equal to the number of weighting coefficients, to control the corresponding weighting coefficients. If the cored coefficients $m_1, m_2 \in R_+$ are to be determined, the structured genetic mapping can be designed as

$$Y = [c_1 \; c_2 \; m_1 \; m_2 \; h_1] \tag{23}$$

where c_1 and c_2 are control genes that govern the changes of parameters m_1 and m_2 for structured genetic mapping respectively. The control genes determine the parameter genes in ON/OFF status or linear scaling multiplication.

Similarly, the structured genetic mapping with the weighting coefficients $m_1, m_2, m_3, m_4 \in R_+$ for the genetic logic gate with two TFs in (19)can be designed as

$$Y = [c_1 \; c_2 \; c_3 \; c_4 \; m_1 \; m_2 \; m_3 \; m_4 \; h_1 \; h_2] \tag{24}$$

where c_1, c_2, c_3 and c_4 are control genes that govern the changes of parameters m_1, m_2, m_3 and m_4 for structured mapping respectively.

For the genetic logic gate with three TFs in(21), the structured genetic mapping with the weighting coefficients $m_i,\; i = 1,2,\ldots,8$ can be designed as

$$Y = [c_1 \; c_2 \; c_3 \; c_4 \; c_5 \; c_6 \; c_7 \; c_8 \; m_1 \; m_2 \; m_3 \; m_4 \; m_5 \; m_6 \; m_7 \; m_8 \; h_1 \; h_2 \; h_3] \tag{25}$$

where $c_i,\; i = 1,2,\ldots,8$ are control genes that govern the changes of parameters $m_i,\; i = 1,2,\ldots,8$ for structured mapping respectively.

Fitness Function

A logic gate in electronics is an idealized device performing a logical operation on one or more logical inputs, and generating a single logical output, i.e. a Boolean function. An ideal logic gate implies for instance zero rise time and unlimited fan-out. As for genetic logic gates, they are synthesized via a variety of proteins. Responses of protein concentration take time, which are usually far longer than those in electronic devices.

To fulfill the requirement of an ideal logic gate, the objective function J_{tot} for multi-objective assessment is defined as

$$J_{total} = \rho J_1 + (1-\rho) J_2 \tag{26}$$

with

$$J_1 = \begin{cases} |1 - f(\cdot)|, & \text{for logic "1"} \\ |f(\cdot)|, & \text{for logic "0"} \end{cases} \tag{27}$$

$$J_2 = \begin{cases} \left| r(\cdot) - f(\cdot) \right|, & \text{for logic "0" changing to logic "1"} \\ \left| 1 - r(\cdot) - f(\cdot) \right|, & \text{for logic "1" changing to logic "0"} \end{cases} \quad (28)$$

and

$$r(u) = \frac{1}{1 + e^{-\kappa(u-0.5)}} \quad (29)$$

where J_1 and J_2 denote, respectively, the costs of the accuracy of logic values and sharpness of the contrast between high and low-logic levels, $r(\cdot)$ is a reference sigmoidal function with κ being a constant specifying the slope of transition from logic “0” to logic “1”.

Case Study

Suppose that the total generation number is set to be 1000, the population size is 200 and the weighting factor ρ is 0.4, and $R_{\max}$ and $R_{\min}$ are 4 and 0, respectively. The designs of the genetic logic gate by the RSGA approach are obtained in the follows. For the case of the promoter binding one TF, the optimal parameters are shown in Table 1 and the bio-CRIF models of NOT and Buffer gates are, respectively, obtained as

$$f_{\text{NOT}}(u_1) = \frac{m_1}{1 + \left(\frac{u_1}{K_1} \right)^{h_1}} \quad (30)$$

and

$$f_{\text{Buffer}}(u_1) = \frac{m_2 \left(\frac{u_1}{K_1} \right)^{h_1}}{1 + \left(\frac{u_1}{K_1} \right)^{h_1}} \quad (31)$$

Table 1.Model parameters of the RSGA-based genetic logic gates with single TF

	m_1	m_2	h_1
NOT	1	0	3.9999
Buffer	0	1.0625	3.9999

It is seen from the above two RSGA-based CRIF models that the input of logic NOT gate is a repressor and it produces protein only in absence of the repressor; otherwise, the presence of the repressor obstructs the bound of RNAp and promoter. For the genetic Buffer, the input is an activator which advances the bound of RNAp and promoter to produce protein. Concentration responses of the RSGA-based NOT and Buffer gates are shown in Figure 2. Figures 3(a) and 3(b) reveal the constructions for the two logic gates.

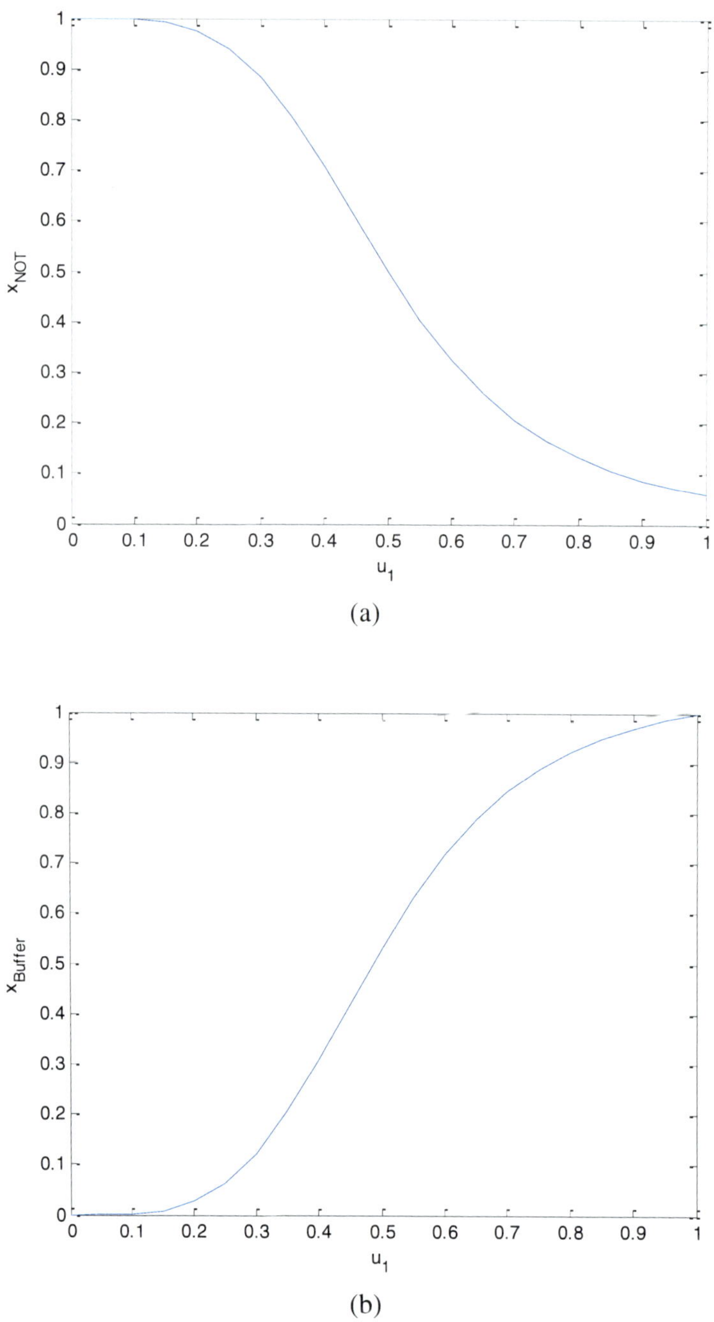

Figure 2. I/O responses of the RSGA-based genetic logic gates with single TF. (a) NOT gate; and (b) Buffer.

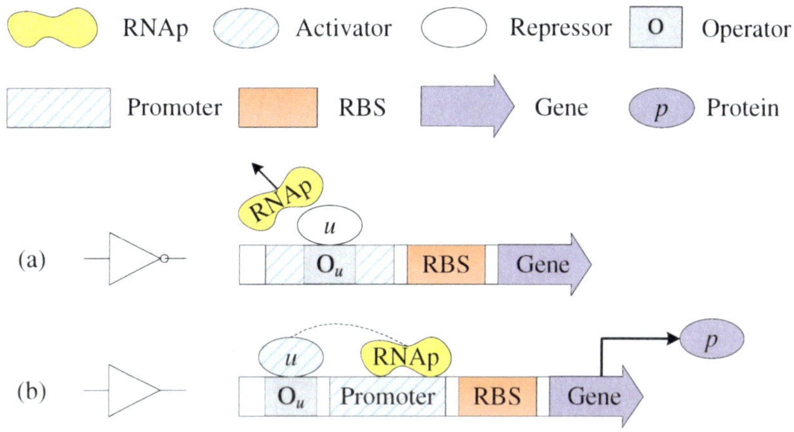

Figure 3. Constructions of the RSGA-based genetic logic gates with single TF. (a) NOT; and (b) Buffer.

Similarly, the optimal parameters for the genetic logic gates with double and triple inputs are shown in Tables 2 and 3, respectively. For the RSGA-based logic gate design with two TFs, the concentration responses are shown in Figure 4. The constructions are illustrated in Figure 5. For the logic AND, OR and XOR gates, the genetic expressions are regulated by two activator TFs. For the AND gate, the protein is produced only in the presence of both TFs. The gene of the OR gate is activated when any one of two TFs (or both) presents. For the XOR gate, the gene is activated in the presence of any one of two TFs; it is inhibited when both TFs are present or absent. For the logic NAND and NOR gates, their expressions are controlled by two repressor TFs. For the three-input RSGA-based logic gates, the concentration responses are shown in Figure 6. The constructions are illustrated, respectively, in Figs. 7(a)-7(e).

Table 2.Model parameters of the RSGA-based genetic logic gates with double TFs

	m_1	m_2	m_3	m_4	h_1	h_2
AND	0	0	0	1.1291	3.9998	3.9999
OR	0	1.0628	1.0625	0.9958	3.9934	3.9998
NAND	1	1	1.0002	0	3.9626	3.9971
NOR	1	0	0	0	3.9998	4
XOR	0	1.0626	1.0624	0	3.9991	3.9999

Table 3.Model parameters of the RSGA-based genetic logic gates with triple TFs

	AND	OR	NAND	NOR	XOR
m_1	0	0	0.9990	1.0022	0
m_2	0	1.0770	0.9999	0	1.0617
m_3	0	1.0854	1.0010	0	1.0651
m_4	0	1.0804	1.0038	0	1.0610
m_5	0	0.9934	0.9999	0	0

Table 3. (Continued)

	AND	OR	NAND	NOR	XOR
m_6	0	0.9932	0.9987	0	0
m_7	0	0.9938	0.9997	0	0
m_8	1.2496	1.0003	0	0	1.2047
h_1	3.9999	3.8417	3.5118	3.9999	3.9984
h_2	3.9994	3.6859	3.9972	3.9988	3.9425
h_3	3.9997	3.9279	3.6298	4	3.9950

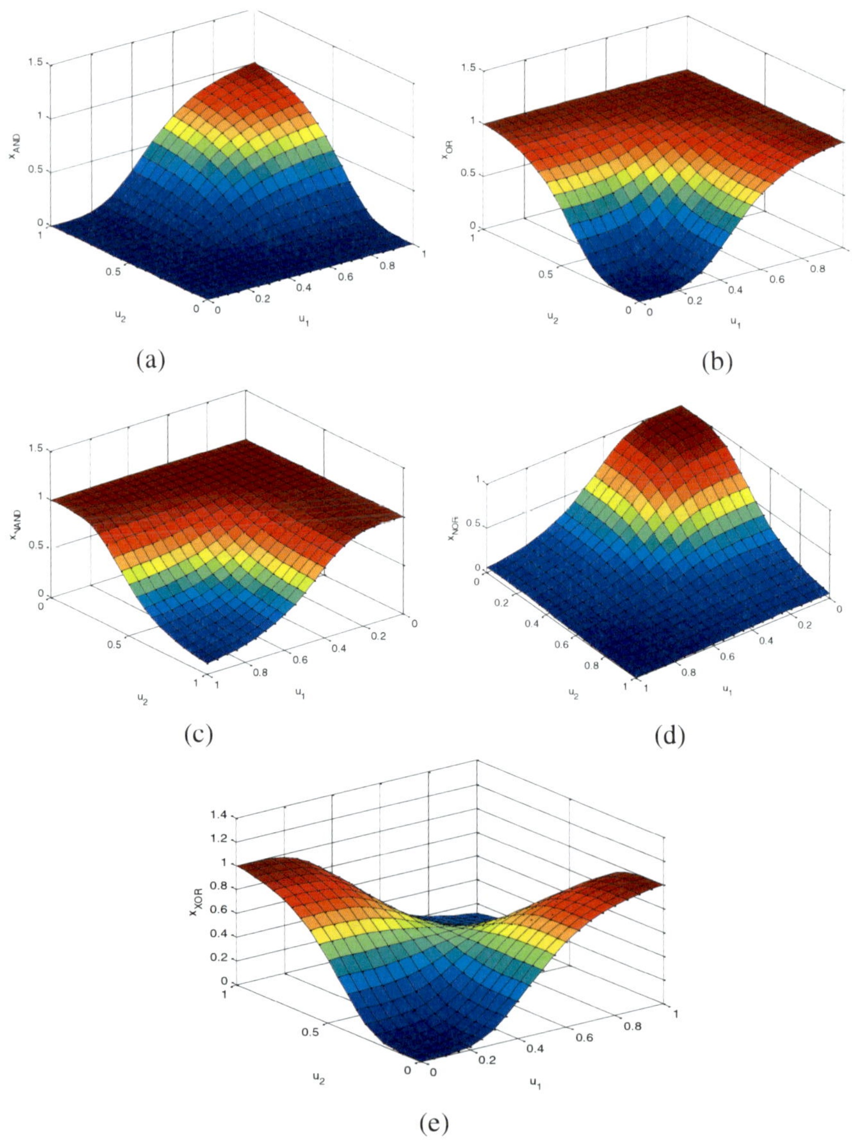

Figure 4. I/O responses of the RSGA-based genetic logic gates with double TFs. (a) AND; (b) OR; (c) NAND; (d) NOR; and (e) XOR.

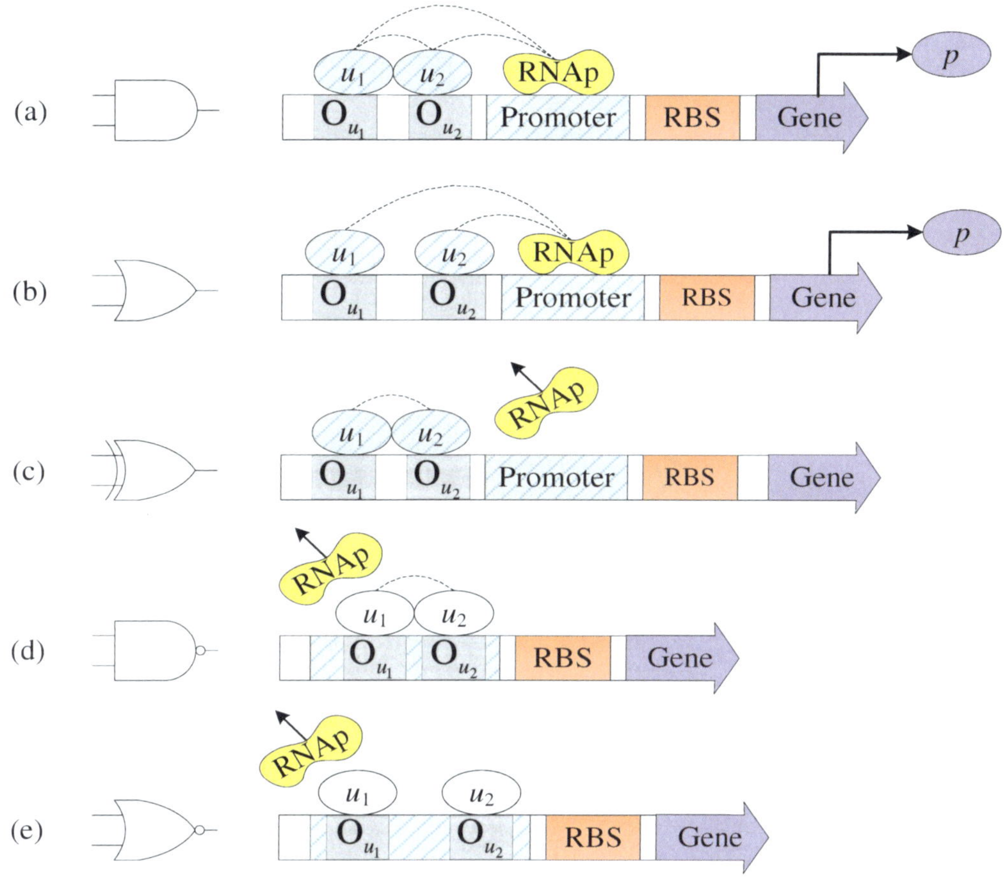

Figure 5. Constructions of the RSGA-based genetic logic gates with double TFs. (a) AND; (b) OR; (c) XOR; (d) NAND; and (e) NOR.

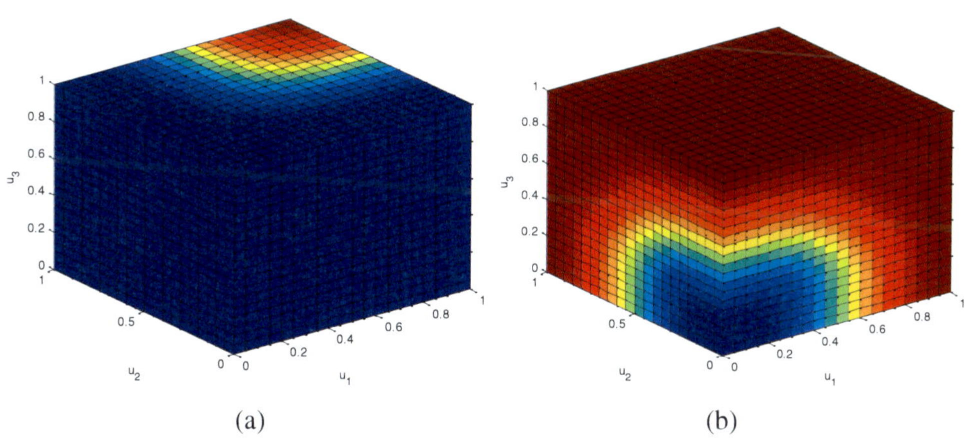

Figure 6. (Continued).

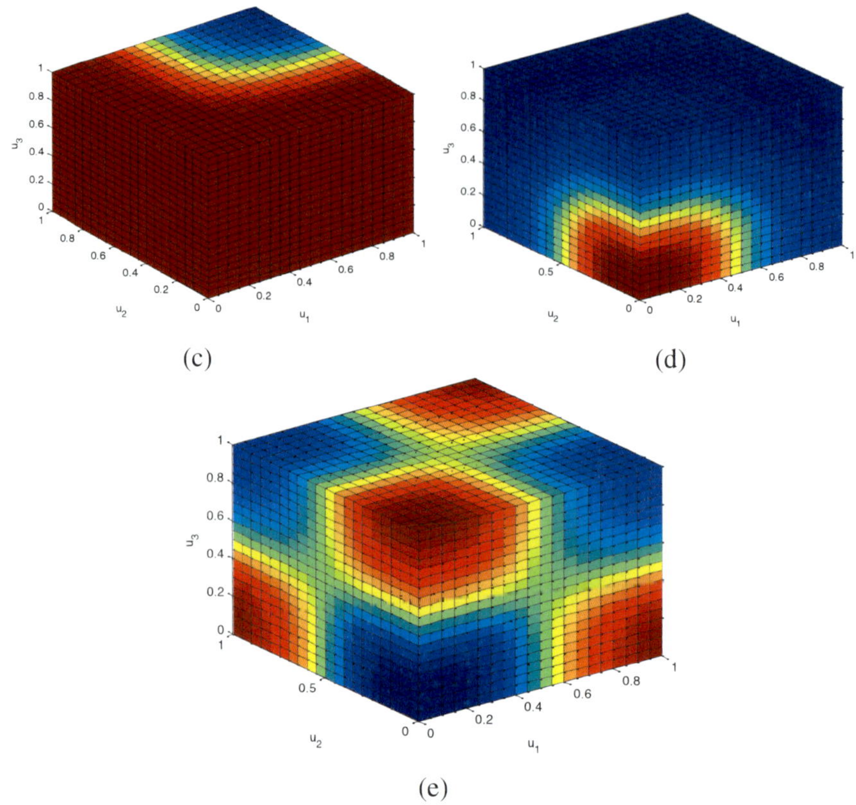

Figure 6. I/O responses of the RSGA-based genetic logic gates with triple TFs. (a) AND; (b) OR; (c) NAND; (d) NOR; and (e) XOR.

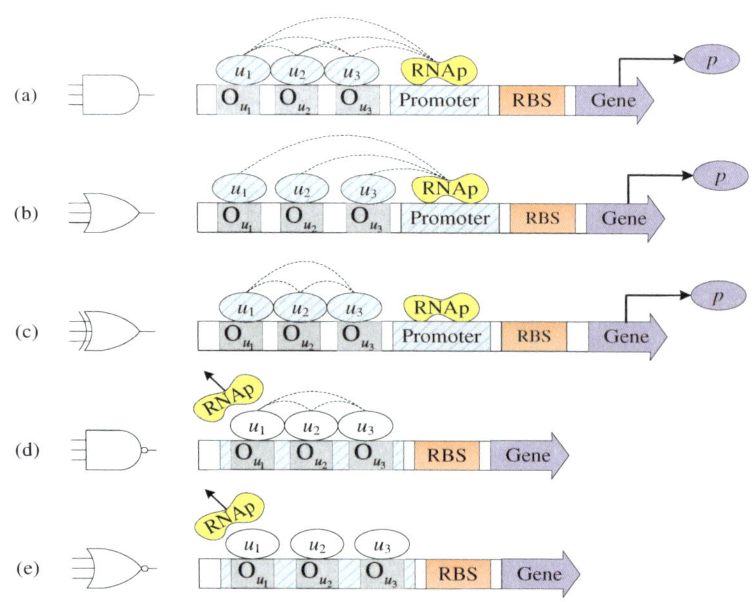

Figure 7. Constructions of the RSGA-based genetic logic gates with triple TFs. (a) AND; (b) OR; (c) XOR; (d) NAND; and (e) NOR.

DESIGN OF GENETIC FREQUENCY SYNTHESIZER

Genetic Waveform-Shaping Circuit

In electronics, a waveform-shaping circuit is designed to shape the input signal to the desired form according to the input and output (I/O) characteristic curve. For the oscillation input and clock output, the I/O characteristic curve of the desired waveform-shaping circuit is displayed in Figure8. A step function (dashed line) with the threshold level y_T is used in electronics. For the input signal with its value larger than the threshold level, it is treated as "logic high". Otherwise, it is referred to "logic low". However, in the real biological world, an ideal step function doesn't exist. A sigmoid function (solid line in Figure8) might be used instead. From the I/O characteristic curve of a sigmoid function, there are two operational regions: saturation and transition. The input signal in the saturation region can be cut-off and hold on the high level or the low level for approximation. In the transition region, the gain in the operation point y_T must be more than (normalized) 1 because it ensures that the input is larger or less than the threshold level will be amplified or shrunk. By cascading the next sigmoid function, the oscillation input will gradually reach the saturation region and remain at the high or low level.

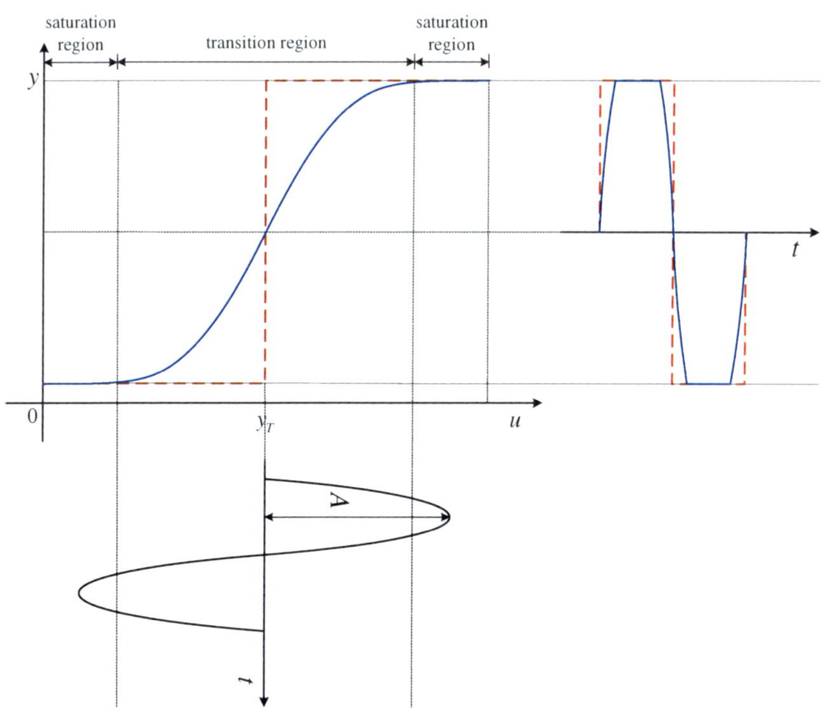

Figure 8. I/O characteristics of the waveform-shaping circuit design.

According to this idea, a waveform-shaping circuit can be used to regulate the time duration of the logic high/low levels of an oscillation signal in a sinusoidal cycle and generate a PWM signal with different duty cycle defined by

$$D = \frac{T_{\text{on}}}{T_0} \cdot 100\% \tag{32}$$

where D is the duty cycle, T_0 is the basal period of oscillation signal and T_{on} being the period of "logic high" in a basal period. For the PWM signal with different duty cycle, the threshold is obtained by considering

$$y_T = A\sin\left(\omega_0 t + \varphi\right) + y_{d,0},\ t = t_h \pm \frac{T_{\text{on}}}{2} \tag{33}$$

with

$$t_h = \frac{1}{\omega_0}\sin^{-1}\left(1\right) - \frac{\varphi}{\omega_0},\ t_h \in \left[0\quad T_0\right] \tag{34}$$

where A is the amplitude, ω_0 is the basal frequency, φ is the phase, and $y_{d,0}$ is the base level to ensure nonnegative protein concentration. To select the threshold level approaching to $y_{d,0} + A$, the clock pulse from low to high is generated. For the clock pulse from high to low, one can choose the threshold level which is close to $y_{d,0} - A$. In other words, the PWM signals with different duty cycles can be synthesized from an oscillation signal via a waveform-shaping circuit in different threshold levels. The ideal PWM signals are shown in Figure9.

In genetic logic circuits, a genetic Buffer [20] is proposed to serve as a buffer between two cascade genetic circuits to enhance logic signal transfer. It's used here to aid the genetic waveform-shaping circuit design:

$$\dot{\boldsymbol{x}}_{\boldsymbol{k}} = \boldsymbol{\alpha}_{\boldsymbol{k}}\boldsymbol{m}_{\boldsymbol{2}} \frac{\left(\dfrac{u_k}{K_k}\right)^{h_k}}{1+\left(\dfrac{u_k}{K_k}\right)^{h_k}} - \beta_k x_k + \alpha_{0,k},\ k = 1,\ldots,\boldsymbol{M} \tag{35}$$

with its steady-state solution is easily obtained as

$$x_{k,ss} = \frac{\alpha_k m_2}{\beta_k} \cdot \frac{\left(\dfrac{u_k}{K_k}\right)^{h_k}}{1+\left(\dfrac{u_k}{K_k}\right)^{h_k}} + \frac{\alpha_{0,k}}{\beta_k} \tag{36}$$

where x_k is the output concentration of the kth Buffer, $x_{k,ss}$ denotes its steady-state concentration, u_k, K_k and h_k are respectively the input concentration, Hill constant, and Hill coefficient of the kth Buffer and α_k, β_k and $\alpha_{0,k}$ are, respectively, synthesis, decay and basal rates of the kth Buffer.

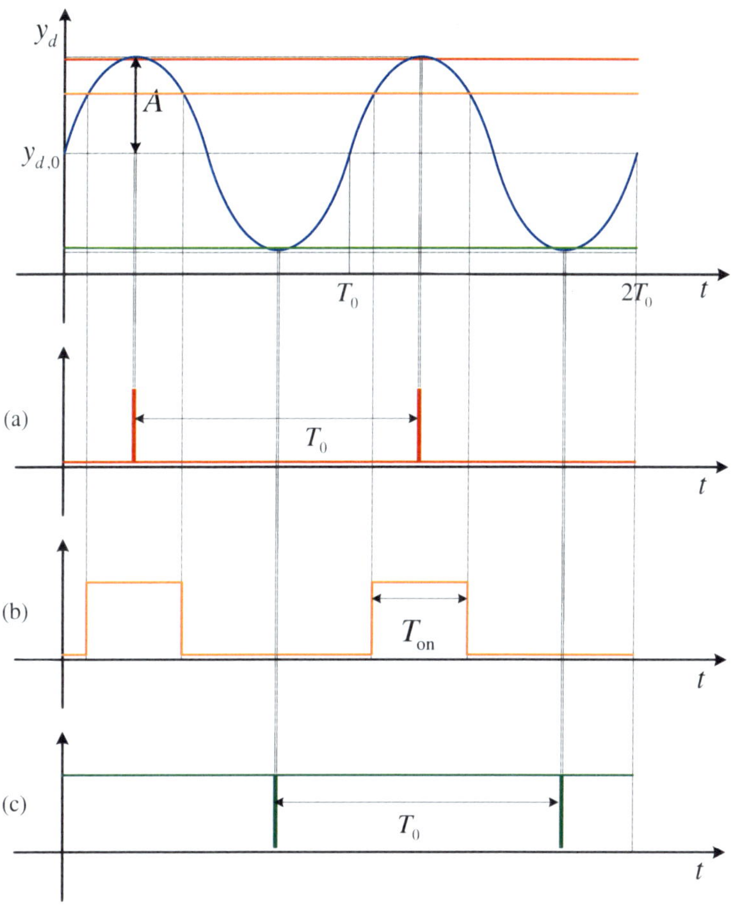

Figure 9. Ideal PWM signals. (a) clock pulse from low to high; (b) $(T_{on}/T_0)\cdot 100\%$ dutycycle; and (c) clock pulse from high to low.

The second term in the right side of (36) is minimal level and α_k/β_k is the difference between minimal level and maximal level. For a Buffer gate, the relationship between input concentration and CRIF model without m_2 for the different Hill constants is shown in Figure 10(a). Figure 10(b) shows the relationship between input concentration and promoter activity function for the different Hill coefficients. Output concentration of the genetic Buffer is the half maximal output concentration when the input concentration equals K_k and thus K_k refers to the threshold level y_T.

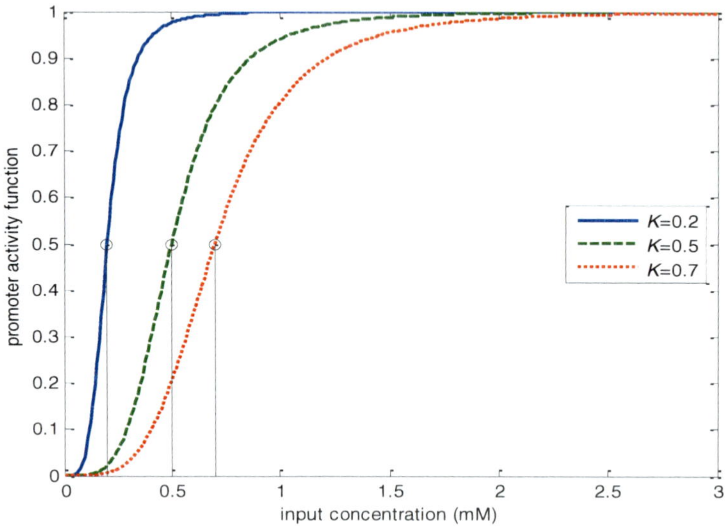

(a)

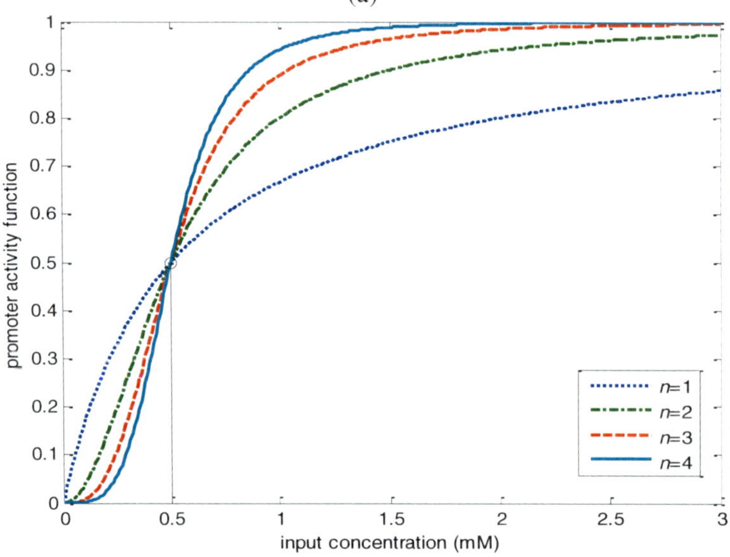

(b)

Figure10. Promoter activity functions of genetic Buffer with (a) different Hill constants; and (b) different Hill coefficients.

In each stage, the corresponding inputs and the threshold levels are given by

$$u_k = \begin{cases} A\sin\left(\omega_0 t + \varphi\right) + y_{d,0}, & k = 1 \\ x_{k-1}, & 1 < k \le M \end{cases} \tag{37}$$

and

$$K_k = \begin{cases} y_T, & k = 1 \\ \dfrac{\alpha_{k-1} m_{k-1} + \alpha_{0,k-1}}{2\beta_{k-1}}, & 1 < k \le M \end{cases} \quad (38)$$

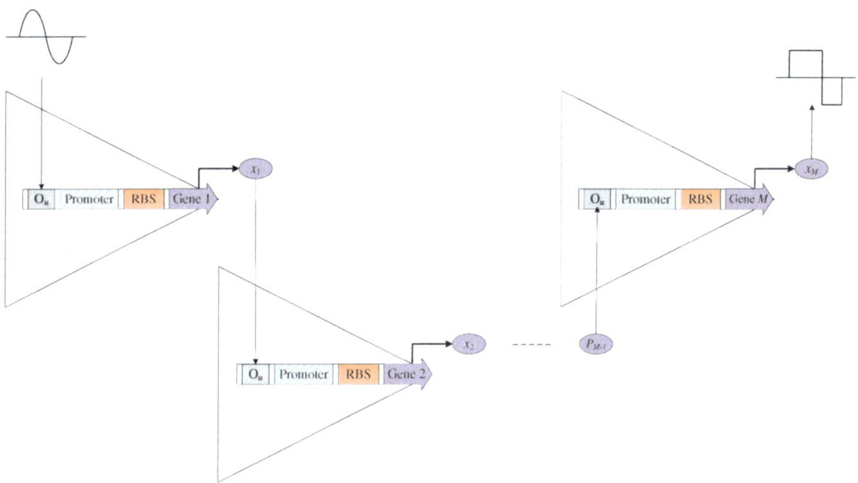

Figure 11. Topology of the designed genetic waveform-shaping circuit.

In the first stage, the input signal is the oscillation signal and the threshold level is chosen according to the desired duty cycle in (33). In the next stage, the input signal is the output concentration of the previous Buffer and the threshold level is the half maximal output level in the previous one. Topology of the genetic waveform-shaping circuit is shown in Figure 11. The oscillation signal activates the transcription expression of the first gene in the genetic waveform-shaping circuit, whose product activates the next gene. Stage by stage, the oscillation can be reshaped to the crisp clock signal or PWM signal. However, one can observe that the problem of slow convergence to the maximal level is occurred for the larger threshold level K_k in Figure 10 (a). To resolve this problem, one can again cascade a Buffer with the design parameters of (36) in the last stage of the genetic waveform-shaping circuit to compensate the output level. The gain at the operating point K_k is obtained as

$$A_k = \left.\frac{\partial x_{k,ss}}{\partial u_k}\right|_{u_k = K_k} = \frac{\alpha_k m_k h_k}{4\beta_k K_k} \quad (39)$$

where A_k is the gain of the kth Buffer. The gain is proportional to the Hill coefficient h_k and the synthesis rate α_k and is inversely proportional to the Hill constant K_k and the decay rate β_k at the operating point $u_k = K_k$. To ensure that the necessary condition of the gain at the operating point K_k, A_k should be large than 1. At first, one chooses the appropriate Hill constant for the desired synthesized PWM signal according to (38) and then selects synthesis rate α_k and decay rate β_k satisfying (39) to guarantee that the input concentration will be amplified or decayed when its concentration is larger or less than the threshold level K_k. From the system parameters in the previous stage, one chooses the suitable system parameters in the next stage satisfying (38)and (39).

Genetic Frequency Synthesizer Circuit

Genetic Flip-Flop

Table 4. True table of the clocked JK flip-flop

Present State	Inputs of JK Flip-Flop		Next State
x_Q	x_J	x_K	x_Q
0	0	0	0
0	0	1	0
0	1	0	1
0	1	1	1
1	0	0	1
1	0	1	0
1	1	0	1
1	1	1	0

Table 5. Excitations of the clocked JK flip-flop

Present State	Next State	Inputs of JK Flip-Flop	
x_Q	x_Q	x_J	x_K
0	0	0	X
0	1	1	X
1	0	X	1
1	1	X	0

In electronics, there are four kinds of flip-flops: RS flip-flop, D flip-flop, T flip-flop and JK flip-flop. In which, the JK flip-flop has two inputs and four possible logic outputs. The true table and excitation table are illustrated in Tables 4 and 5, respectively. Based on the topology of the digital logic circuits, the genetic JK flip-flops are also divided into the rising edge-triggered one and the falling edge-triggered one shown as in Figure12. For the rising edge-triggered genetic JK flip-flop, its model is described by

$$\begin{aligned}
\dot{x}_R &= \alpha_R f_{\text{AND}}\left(x_K, x_{CLK}, x_Q\right) - \beta_R x_R, \\
\dot{x}_S &= \alpha_S f_{\text{AND}}\left(x_J, x_{CLK}, x_{\bar{Q}}\right) - \beta_S x_S, \\
\dot{x}_Q &= \alpha_Q f_{\text{NOR}}\left(x_R, x_{\bar{Q}}\right) - \beta_Q x_Q, \\
\dot{x}_{\bar{Q}} &= \alpha_{\bar{Q}} f_{\text{NOR}}\left(x_S, x_Q\right) - \beta_{\bar{Q}} x_{\bar{Q}}
\end{aligned} \tag{40}$$

where x_{CLK} is the concentration of clock pulse from low to high, x_R, x_S, x_Q, and $x_{\bar{Q}}$ denote, respectively, the protein concentrations of the genes R, S, Q, and $\bar{Q}$, α_R, α_S, α_Q, and $\alpha_{\bar{Q}}$ are the corresponding synthesis rates, and β_R, β_S, β_Q, and $\beta_{\bar{Q}}$ are the corresponding decay rates. There are two three-input AND gates and two two-input NOR gates, see Figure13. The rising edge-triggered genetic JK flip-flop becomes active only when the clock pulse goes from low to high. The proteins x_K, x_{CLK} and x_Q activate the transcription of the gene R. The proteins x_J, x_{CLK} and $x_{\bar{Q}}$ activate the transcription of the gene S. The products of the genes R and $\bar{Q}$ inhibit the transcription of the gene Q and the products of the genes S and Q inhibit the transcription of the gene $\bar{Q}$.

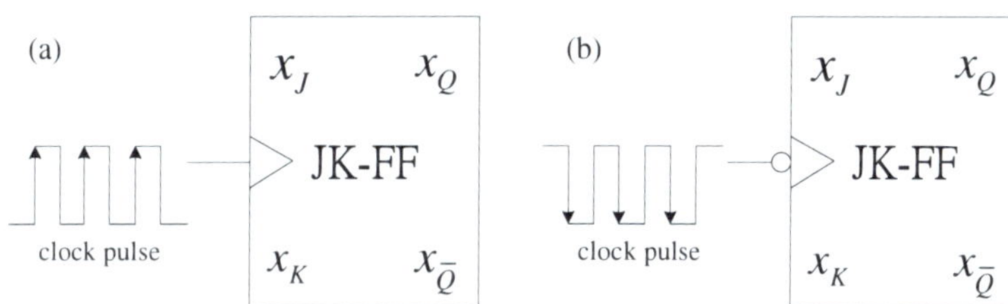

Figure 12.A class of the genetic clocked JK flip-flops. (a) a rising edge-triggered one; and (b) a falling edge-triggered one.

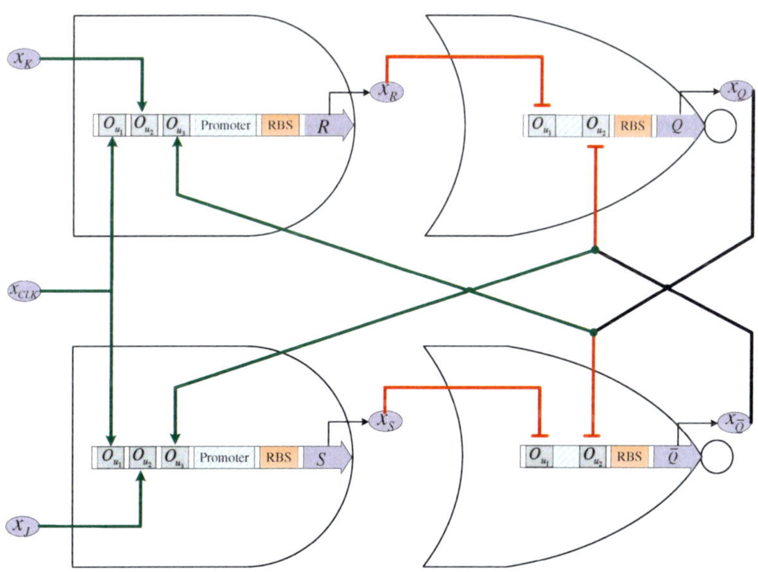

Figure 13. Topology of the rising edge-triggered JK flip-flop.

For the falling edge-triggered genetic JK flip-flop, the model is described by

$$\begin{aligned}
\dot{x}_R &= \alpha_R f_{\text{NAND}}\left(x_K, x_{CLK}, x_Q\right) - \beta_R x_R, \\
\dot{x}_S &= \alpha_S f_{\text{NAND}}\left(x_J, x_{CLK}, x_{\bar{Q}}\right) - \beta_S x_S, \\
\dot{x}_Q &= \alpha_Q f_{\text{NAND}}\left(x_S, x_{\bar{Q}}\right) - \beta_Q x_Q, \\
\dot{x}_{\bar{Q}} &= \alpha_{\bar{Q}} f_{\text{NAND}}\left(x_R, x_Q\right) - \beta_{\bar{Q}} x_{\bar{Q}}
\end{aligned} \tag{41}$$

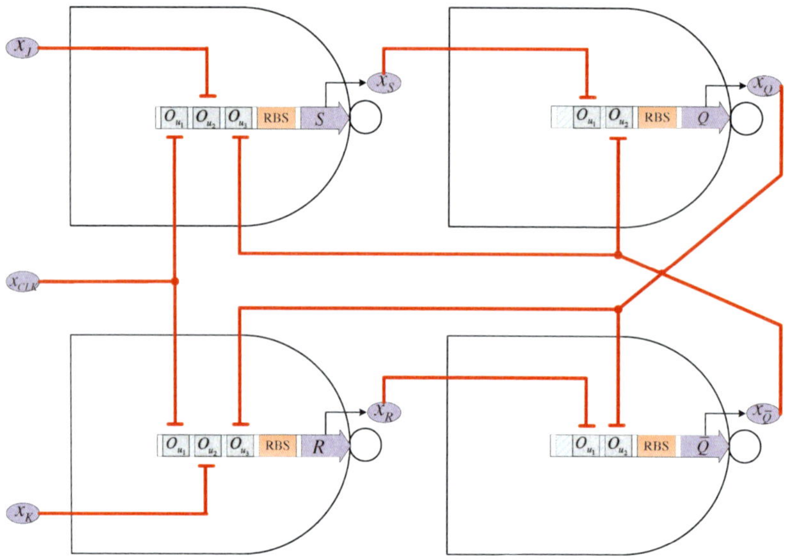

Figure 14. Topology of the falling edge-triggered JK flip-flop.

The falling edge-triggered genetic JK flip-flop becomes active only when the clock pulse goes from high to low. This circuit is composed of two three-input NAND gates and two two-input NAND gates with its topology structure shown in Figure14. The proteins x_K, x_{CLK} and x_Q inhibit the transcription of the gene R. The proteins x_J, x_{CLK} and x_Q inhibit the transcription of the gene S. The products of the genes S and $\bar{Q}$ inhibit the transcription of the gene Q and the products of the genes R and Q inhibit the transcription of the gene $\bar{Q}$.

Genetic Counter

Table 6. State table for designing the clock signal with double basal period

Present State	Next State	Inputs of JK Flip-Flop	
x_{Q_1}	x_{Q_1}	x_{J_1}	x_{K_1}
0	1	1	X
1	0	X	1

To synthesize the clock signal with double basal period, one can use a rising or falling edge-triggered genetic JK flip-flop. The digitized state responses are summarized in Table 6 according to the stimulations given in Table 5.

The synchronous genetic counter circuits with the rising or falling edge-triggered JK flip-flop are constructed respectively as follows

$$\begin{aligned}
\dot{x}_{R_1} &= \alpha_{R_1} f_{\text{AND}}\left(x_{K_1}, x_{CLK}, x_{Q_1}\right) - \beta_{R_1} x_{R_1}, \\
\dot{x}_{S_1} &= \alpha_{S_1} f_{\text{AND}}\left(x_{J_1}, x_{CLK}, x_{\bar{Q}_1}\right) - \beta_{S_1} x_{S_1}, \\
\dot{x}_{Q_1} &= \alpha_{Q_1} f_{\text{NOR}}\left(x_{R_1}, x_{\bar{Q}_1}\right) - \beta_{Q_1} x_{Q_1}, \\
\dot{x}_{\bar{Q}_1} &= \alpha_{\bar{Q}_1} f_{\text{NOR}}\left(x_{S_1}, x_{Q_1}\right) - \beta_{\bar{Q}_1} x_{\bar{Q}_1}
\end{aligned} \tag{42}$$

or

$$\begin{aligned}
\dot{x}_{R_1} &= \alpha_{R_1} f_{\text{NAND}}\left(x_{K_1}, x_{CLK}, x_{Q_1}\right) - \beta_{R_1} x_{R_1}, \\
\dot{x}_{S_1} &= \alpha_{S_1} f_{\text{NAND}}\left(x_{J_1}, x_{CLK}, x_{\bar{Q}_1}\right) - \beta_{S_1} x_{S_1}, \\
\dot{x}_{Q_1} &= \alpha_{Q_1} f_{\text{NAND}}\left(x_{S_1}, x_{\bar{Q}_1}\right) - \beta_{Q_1} x_{Q_1}, \\
\dot{x}_{\bar{Q}_1} &= \alpha_{\bar{Q}_1} f_{\text{NAND}}\left(x_{R_1}, x_{Q_1}\right) - \beta_{\bar{Q}_1} x_{\bar{Q}_1}
\end{aligned} \tag{43}$$

with inputs of genetic JK flip-flop given by

$$x_{K_1} = x_{J_1} = 1 \tag{44}$$

where x_{CLK} is the clock pulse signal from low to high for (42) and from high to low for (43). Figure 15 shows the topology of the synchronous genetic counter circuit for the clock signal with a double basal period.

Similarly, the clock signal with quadruple basal period is synthesized by using two rising or falling edge-triggered JK flip-flops. The digitized state responses are illustrated in Table 7 according to the stimulations given in Table 5.

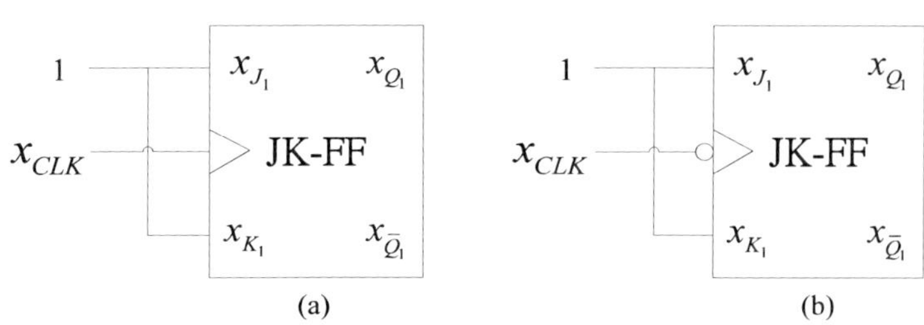

Figure 15. Topology of the synchronous genetic counter for the clock signal with double basal period. (a) a rising edge-triggered JK flip-flop; and (b) a falling edge-triggered JK flip-flop.

Table 7. State table for designing the clock signal with a quadruple basal period

Present State		Next State		Inputs of 2nd JK Flip-Flop		Inputs of 1st JK Flip-Flop	
x_{Q_2}	x_{Q_1}	x_{Q_2}	x_{Q_1}	x_{J_2}	x_{K_2}	x_{J_1}	x_{K_1}
0	0	0	1	0	X	1	X
0	1	1	0	1	X	X	1
1	0	1	1	X	0	1	X
1	1	0	0	X	1	X	1

According to the Karnaugh map (K-map) in the digital logic theory shown in Figure 16, the synchronous genetic counter circuit for the rising edge-triggered JK flip-flops is constructed as

$$
\begin{aligned}
\dot{x}_{R_1} &= \alpha_{R_1} f_{\text{AND}}\left(x_{K_1}, x_{CLK}, x_{Q_1}\right) - \beta_{R_1} x_{R_1}, \\
\dot{x}_{S_1} &= \alpha_{S_1} f_{\text{AND}}\left(x_{J_1}, x_{CLK}, x_{\bar{Q}_1}\right) - \beta_{S_1} x_{S_1}, \\
\dot{x}_{Q_1} &= \alpha_{Q_1} f_{\text{NOR}}\left(x_{R_1}, x_{\bar{Q}_1}\right) - \beta_{Q_1} x_{Q_1}, \\
\dot{x}_{\bar{Q}_1} &= \alpha_{\bar{Q}_1} f_{\text{NOR}}\left(x_{S_1}, x_{Q_1}\right) - \beta_{\bar{Q}_1} x_{\bar{Q}_1}, \\
\dot{x}_{R_2} &= \alpha_{R_2} f_{\text{AND}}\left(x_{K_2}, x_{CLK}, x_{Q_2}\right) - \beta_{R_2} x_{R_2}, \\
\dot{x}_{S_2} &= \alpha_{S_2} f_{\text{AND}}\left(x_{J_2}, x_{CLK}, x_{\bar{Q}_2}\right) - \beta_{S_2} x_{S_2}, \\
\dot{x}_{Q_2} &= \alpha_{Q_2} f_{\text{NOR}}\left(x_{R_2}, x_{\bar{Q}_2}\right) - \beta_{Q_2} x_{Q_2}, \\
\dot{x}_{\bar{Q}_2} &= \alpha_{\bar{Q}_2} f_{\text{NOR}}\left(x_{S_2}, x_{Q_2}\right) - \beta_{\bar{Q}_2} x_{\bar{Q}_2}, \\
\dot{x}_{G_1} &= \alpha_{G_1} f_{\text{AND}}\left(x_{K_2}, x_{Q_2}\right) - \beta_{G_1} x_{G_1}
\end{aligned}
\tag{45}
$$

with inputs of each genetic JK flip-flop given by

$$
\begin{aligned}
x_{K_1} &= x_{J_1} = 1, \\
x_{K_2} &= x_{J_2} = x_{Q_1}
\end{aligned}
\tag{46}
$$

where x_{G_1} is the clock signal with a quadruple basal period.

One also can use two falling edge-triggered JK flip-flop to assemble the genetic counter with the clock pulse signal from high to low to replace (45). The topology of the synchronous genetic counter circuit for the clock signal with quadruple basal period is displayed in Figure17.

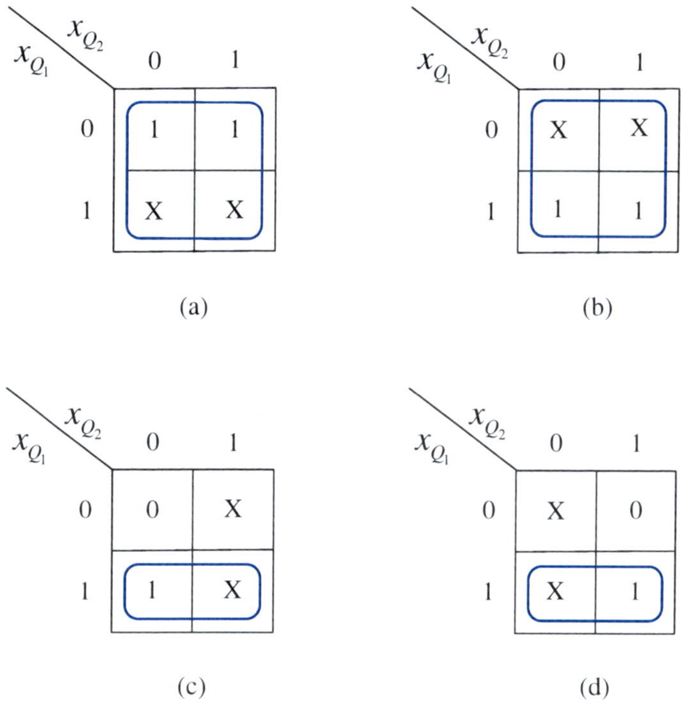

Figure 16. Karaugh map of the synchronous genetic counter for the clock signal with a quadruple basal period. (a) x_{J_1} ; (b) x_{K_1} ; (c) x_{J_2} ; and (d) x_{K_2} .

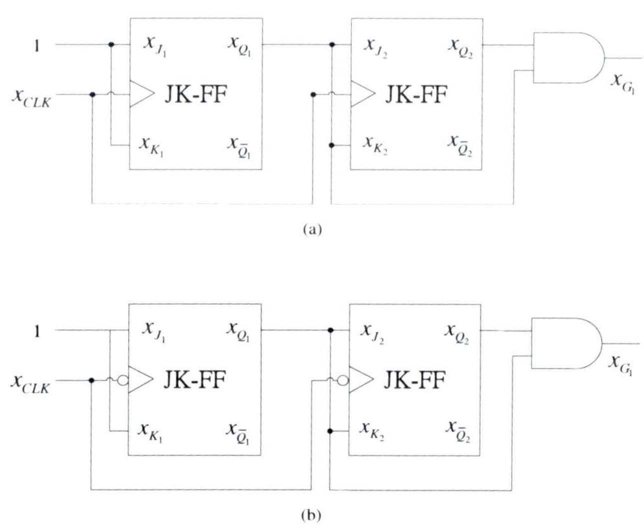

Figure 17. Topology of the synchronous genetic counter for the clock signal with a quadruple basal period. (a) two rising edge-triggered JK flip-flops; and (b) two falling edge-triggered JK flip-flops.

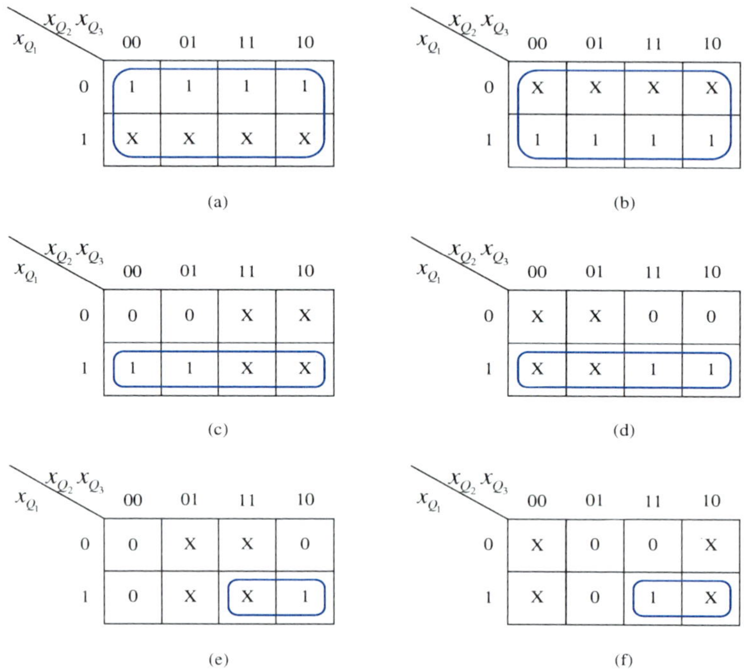

Figure 18. Karaugh map of the synchronous genetic counter for the clock signal with eight-fold basal period. (a) x_{J_1} ; (b) x_{K_1} ; (c) x_{J_2} ; (d) x_{K_2} ; (e) x_{J_3} ; and (f) x_{K_3} .

Table 8.State table for designing the clock signal with an eight-fold basal period

Present State			Next State			Inputs of 3rd JK Flip-Flop		Inputs of 2nd JK Flip-Flop		Inputs of 1st JK Flip-Flop	
x_{Q_3}	x_{Q_2}	x_{Q_1}	x_{Q_3}	x_{Q_2}	x_{Q_1}	x_{J_3}	x_{K_3}	x_{J_2}	x_{K_2}	x_{J_1}	x_{K_1}
0	0	0	0	0	1	0	X	0	X	1	X
0	0	1	0	1	0	0	X	1	X	X	1
0	1	0	0	1	1	0	X	X	0	1	X
0	1	1	1	0	0	1	X	X	1	X	1
1	0	0	1	0	1	X	0	0	X	1	X
1	0	1	1	1	0	X	0	1	X	X	1
1	1	0	1	1	1	X	0	X	0	1	X
1	1	1	0	0	0	X	1	X	1	X	1

To synthesize the clock signal with an eight-fold basal period, three rising or falling edge-triggered JK flip-flops are used. According to the stimulations given in Table 5, the digitized state responses are summarized in Table 8. The K-map is displayed in Figure18 and the synchronous genetic counter circuit with three rising edge-triggered JK flip-flops is constructed as

$$\begin{aligned}
\dot{x}_{R_1} &= \alpha_{R_1} f_{\text{AND}}\left(x_{K_1}, x_{CLK}, x_{Q_1}\right) - \beta_{R_1} x_{R_1}, \\
\dot{x}_{S_1} &= \alpha_{S_1} f_{\text{AND}}\left(x_{J_1}, x_{CLK}, x_{\bar{Q}_1}\right) - \beta_{S_1} x_{S_1}, \\
\dot{x}_{Q_1} &= \alpha_{Q_1} f_{\text{NOR}}\left(x_{R_1}, x_{\bar{Q}_1}\right) - \beta_{Q_1} x_{Q_1}, \\
\dot{x}_{\bar{Q}_1} &= \alpha_{\bar{Q}_1} f_{\text{NOR}}\left(x_{S_1}, x_{Q_1}\right) - \beta_{\bar{Q}_1} x_{\bar{Q}_1}, \\
\dot{x}_{R_2} &= \alpha_{R_2} f_{\text{AND}}\left(x_{K_2}, x_{CLK}, x_{Q_2}\right) - \beta_{R_2} x_{R_2}, \\
\dot{x}_{S_2} &= \alpha_{S_2} f_{\text{AND}}\left(x_{J_2}, x_{CLK}, x_{\bar{Q}_2}\right) - \beta_{S_2} x_{S_2}, \\
\dot{x}_{Q_2} &= \alpha_{Q_2} f_{\text{NOR}}\left(x_{R_2}, x_{\bar{Q}_2}\right) - \beta_{Q_2} x_{Q_2}, \\
\dot{x}_{\bar{Q}_2} &= \alpha_{\bar{Q}_2} f_{\text{NOR}}\left(x_{S_2}, x_{Q_2}\right) - \beta_{\bar{Q}_2} x_{\bar{Q}_2}, \\
\dot{x}_{R_3} &= \alpha_{R_3} f_{\text{AND}}\left(x_{K_3}, x_{CLK}, x_{Q_3}\right) - \beta_{R_3} x_{R_3}, \\
\dot{x}_{S_3} &= \alpha_{S_3} f_{\text{AND}}\left(x_{J_3}, x_{CLK}, x_{\bar{Q}_3}\right) - \beta_{S_3} x_{S_3}, \\
\dot{x}_{Q_3} &= \alpha_{Q_3} f_{\text{NOR}}\left(x_{R_3}, x_{\bar{Q}_3}\right) - \beta_{Q_3} x_{Q_3}, \\
\dot{x}_{\bar{Q}_3} &= \alpha_{\bar{Q}_3} f_{\text{NOR}}\left(x_{S_3}, x_{Q_3}\right) - \beta_{\bar{Q}_3} x_{\bar{Q}_3}, \\
\dot{x}_{G_1} &= \alpha_{G_1} f_{\text{AND}}\left(x_{K_2}, x_{Q_2}\right) - \beta_{G_1} x_{G_1}, \\
\dot{x}_{G_2} &= \alpha_{G_2} f_{\text{AND}}\left(x_{K_3}, x_{Q_3}\right) - \beta_{G_2} x_{G_2}
\end{aligned} \tag{47}$$

with inputs of genetic JK flip-flop given by

$$\begin{aligned}
x_{K_1} &= x_{J_1} = 1, \\
x_{K_2} &= x_{J_2} = x_{Q_1}, \\
x_{K_3} &= x_{J_3} = x_{G_1}
\end{aligned} \tag{48}$$

where x_{G_2} is the clock signal with an eight-fold basal period. Similarly, one can use three falling edge-triggered JK flip-flops to assemble the genetic counter with the clock pulse signal from high to low to replace to (47). The topology of the synchronous genetic counter circuit for the clock signal with eight-fold basal period is shown in Figure19.

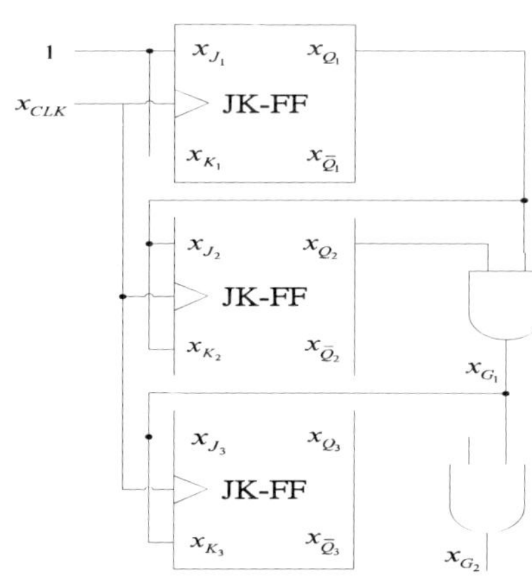

Figure 19. Topology of the synchronous genetic counter for the clock signal with an eight-fold basal period.

From the above results, to synthesize the clock signal with 2^{δ}-fold basal period in which δ is a positive integer, a synchronous genetic counter circuit with δ number of rising edge-triggered genetic JK flip-flops is constructed as

$$\begin{aligned}
\dot{x}_{R_1} &= \alpha_{R_1} f_{\text{AND}}\left(x_{K_1}, x_{CLK}, x_{Q_1}\right) - \beta_{R_1} x_{R_1}, \\
\dot{x}_{S_1} &= \alpha_{S_1} f_{\text{AND}}\left(x_{J_1}, x_{CLK}, x_{\bar{Q}_1}\right) - \beta_{S_1} x_{S_1}, \\
\dot{x}_{Q_1} &= \alpha_{Q_1} f_{\text{NOR}}\left(x_{R_1}, x_{\bar{Q}_1}\right) - \beta_{Q_1} x_{Q_1}, \\
\dot{x}_{\bar{Q}_1} &= \alpha_{\bar{Q}_1} f_{\text{NOR}}\left(x_{S_1}, x_{Q_1}\right) - \beta_{\bar{Q}_1} x_{\bar{Q}_1}, \\
&\vdots \\
\dot{x}_{R_\delta} &= \alpha_{R_\delta} f_{\text{AND}}\left(x_{K_\delta}, x_{CLK}, x_{Q_\delta}\right) - \beta_{R_\delta} x_{R_\delta}, \\
\dot{x}_{S_\delta} &= \alpha_{S_\delta} f_{\text{AND}}\left(x_{J_\delta}, x_{CLK}, x_{\bar{Q}_\delta}\right) - \beta_{S_\delta} x_{S_\delta}, \\
\dot{x}_{Q_\delta} &= \alpha_{Q_\delta} f_{\text{NOR}}\left(x_{R_\delta}, x_{\bar{Q}_\delta}\right) - \beta_{Q_\delta} x_{Q_\delta}, \\
\dot{x}_{\bar{Q}_\delta} &= \alpha_{\bar{Q}_\delta} f_{\text{NOR}}\left(x_{S_\delta}, x_{Q_\delta}\right) - \beta_{\bar{Q}_\delta} x_{\bar{Q}_\delta}, \\
\dot{x}_{G_1} &= \alpha_{G_1} f_{\text{AND}}\left(x_{K_2}, x_{Q_2}\right) - \beta_{G_1} x_{G_1}, \\
&\vdots \\
\dot{x}_{G_{\delta-1}} &= \alpha_{G_{\delta-1}} f_{\text{AND}}\left(x_{K_\delta}, x_{Q_\delta}\right) - \beta_{G_{\delta-1}} x_{G_{\delta-1}}
\end{aligned} \tag{49}$$

with the inputs of each genetic JK flip-flop given by

$$\begin{aligned}
x_{J_1} &= x_{K_1} = 1, \\
x_{J_2} &= x_{K_2} = x_{Q_1}, \\
x_{J_3} &= x_{K_3} = x_{G_1}, \\
&\vdots \\
x_{J_\delta} &= x_{K_\delta} = x_{G_{\delta-2}}
\end{aligned} \tag{50}$$

where x_{Q_1}, x_{Q_2}, and x_{Q_δ} are, respectively, the clock signals with double, quadruple and 2^{δ}-fold basal period. Figure 20 shows the topology of the synchronous genetic counter circuit for the clock signals with 2^{δ}-fold basal period.

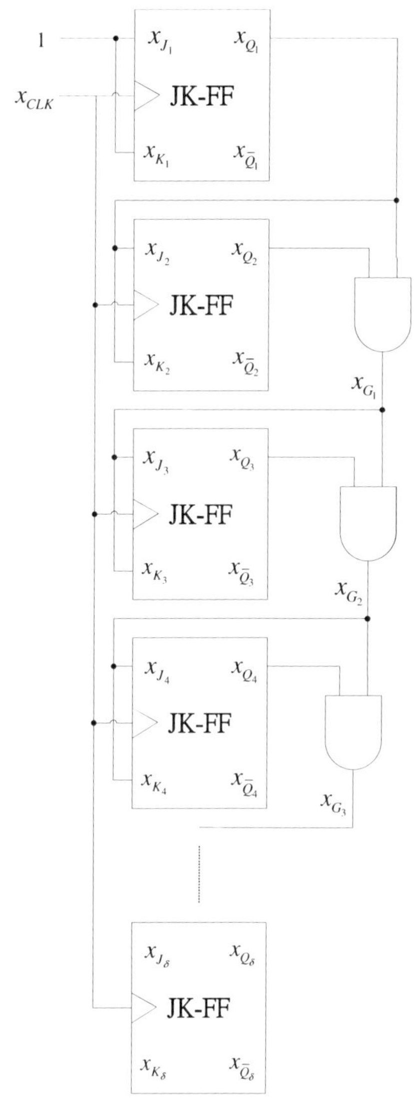

Figure 20. Topology of the synchronous genetic counter for the clock signal with a 2^{δ} fold basal period.

Table 9.State table for designing the clock signal with a five-fold basal period

Present State			Next State			Inputs of 3rd JK Flip-Flop		Inputs of 2nd JK Flip-Flop		Inputs of 1st JK Flip-Flop	
x_{Q_3}	x_{Q_2}	x_{Q_1}	x_{Q_3}	x_{Q_2}	x_{Q_1}	x_{J_3}	x_{K_3}	x_{J_2}	x_{K_2}	x_{J_1}	x_{K_1}
0	0	0	0	0	1	0	X	0	X	1	X
0	0	1	0	1	0	0	X	1	X	X	1
0	1	0	0	1	1	0	X	X	0	1	X
0	1	1	1	0	0	1	X	X	1	X	1
1	0	0	0	0	0	X	1	0	X	0	X

To synthesize the clock signal with a five-fold basal period, the state responses are summarized in Table 9 according to the stimulations given in Table 5. The K-map is displayed in Figure21 and the synchronous genetic counter circuit with three rising edge-triggered genetic JK flip-flops and a falling edge-triggered genetic JK flip-flop is constructed as

$$
\begin{aligned}
\dot{x}_{R_1} &= \alpha_{R_1} f_{\text{AND}}\left(x_{K_1}, x_{CLK_1}, x_{Q_1}\right) - \beta_{R_1} x_{R_1}, \\
\dot{x}_{S_1} &= \alpha_{S_1} f_{\text{AND}}\left(x_{J_1}, x_{CLK_1}, x_{\bar{Q}_1}\right) - \beta_{S_1} x_{S_1}, \\
\dot{x}_{Q_1} &= \alpha_{Q_1} f_{\text{NOR}}\left(x_{R_1}, x_{\bar{Q}_1}\right) - \beta_{Q_1} x_{Q_1}, \\
\dot{x}_{\bar{Q}_1} &= \alpha_{\bar{Q}_1} f_{\text{NOR}}\left(x_{S_1}, x_{Q_1}\right) - \beta_{\bar{Q}_1} x_{\bar{Q}_1}, \\
\dot{x}_{R_2} &= \alpha_{R_2} f_{\text{AND}}\left(x_{K_2}, x_{CLK_1}, x_{Q_2}\right) - \beta_{R_2} x_{R_2}, \\
\dot{x}_{S_2} &= \alpha_{S_2} f_{\text{AND}}\left(x_{J_2}, x_{CLK_1}, x_{\bar{Q}_2}\right) - \beta_{S_2} x_{S_2}, \\
\dot{x}_{Q_2} &= \alpha_{Q_2} f_{\text{NOR}}\left(x_{R_2}, x_{\bar{Q}_2}\right) - \beta_{Q_2} x_{Q_2}, \\
\dot{x}_{\bar{Q}_2} &= \alpha_{\bar{Q}_2} f_{\text{NOR}}\left(x_{S_2}, x_{Q_2}\right) - \beta_{\bar{Q}_2} x_{\bar{Q}_2}, \\
\dot{x}_{R_3} &= \alpha_{R_3} f_{\text{AND}}\left(x_{K_3}, x_{CLK_1}, x_{Q_3}\right) - \beta_{R_3} x_{R_3}, \\
\dot{x}_{S_3} &= \alpha_{S_3} f_{\text{AND}}\left(x_{J_3}, x_{CLK_1}, x_{\bar{Q}_3}\right) - \beta_{S_3} x_{S_3}, \\
\dot{x}_{Q_3} &= \alpha_{Q_3} f_{\text{NOR}}\left(x_{R_3}, x_{\bar{Q}_3}\right) - \beta_{Q_3} x_{Q_3}, \\
\dot{x}_{\bar{Q}_3} &= \alpha_{\bar{Q}_3} f_{\text{NOR}}\left(x_{S_3}, x_{Q_3}\right) - \beta_{\bar{Q}_3} x_{\bar{Q}_3}, \\
\dot{x}_{R_4} &= \alpha_{R_4} f_{\text{NAND}}\left(x_{K_4}, x_{CLK_2}, x_{Q_4}\right) - \beta_{R_4} x_{R_4}, \\
\dot{x}_{S_4} &= \alpha_{S_4} f_{\text{NAND}}\left(x_{J_4}, x_{CLK_2}, x_{\bar{Q}_4}\right) - \beta_{S_4} x_{S_4}, \\
\dot{x}_{Q_4} &= \alpha_{Q_4} f_{\text{NAND}}\left(x_{S_4}, x_{\bar{Q}_4}\right) - \beta_{Q_4} x_{Q_4}, \\
\dot{x}_{\bar{Q}_4} &= \alpha_{\bar{Q}_4} f_{\text{NAND}}\left(x_{R_4}, x_{Q_4}\right) - \beta_{\bar{Q}_4} x_{\bar{Q}_4} \\
\dot{x}_{G_1} &= \alpha_{G_1} f_{\text{AND}}\left(x_{Q_1}, x_{Q_2}\right) - \beta_{G_1} x_{G_1}, \\
\dot{x}_{G_2} &= \alpha_{G_2} f_{\text{OR}}\left(x_{Q_3}, x_{Q_4}\right) - \beta_{G_2} x_{G_2},
\end{aligned}
$$

with the inputs of each genetic JK flip-flop given by

$$
\begin{aligned}
x_{J_1} &= x_{\bar{Q}_3},\ x_{K_1} = 1, \\
x_{J_2} &= x_{K_2} = x_{Q_1}, \\
x_{J_3} &= x_{G_1},\ x_{K_3} = 1, \\
x_{J_4} &= x_{Q_3},\ x_{K_4} = x_{\bar{Q}_3}
\end{aligned} \tag{51}
$$

where x_{G_2} is the clock signal with a five-fold basal period. The topology of the synchronous genetic counter circuit for the clock signal with a five-fold basal period is displayed in Figure22 and the corresponding ideal signals are shown in Figure23.

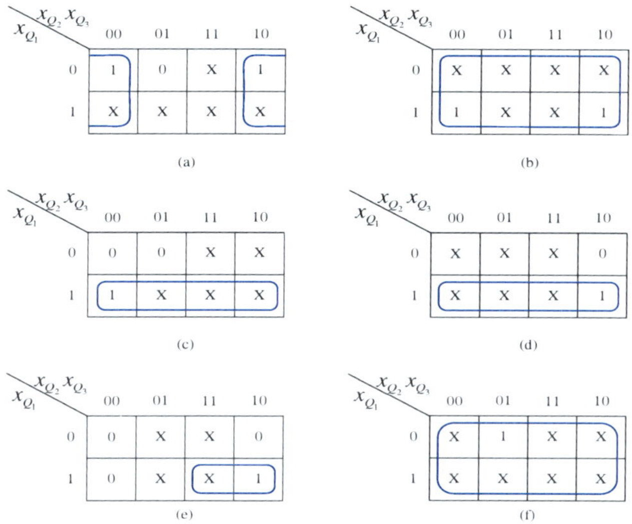

Figure 21. Karaugh map of the synchronous genetic counter for the clock signal with a five-fold basal period. (a) x_{J_1} ; (b) x_{K_1} ; (c) x_{J_2} ; (d) x_{K_2} ; (e) x_{J_3} ; and (f) x_{K_3} .

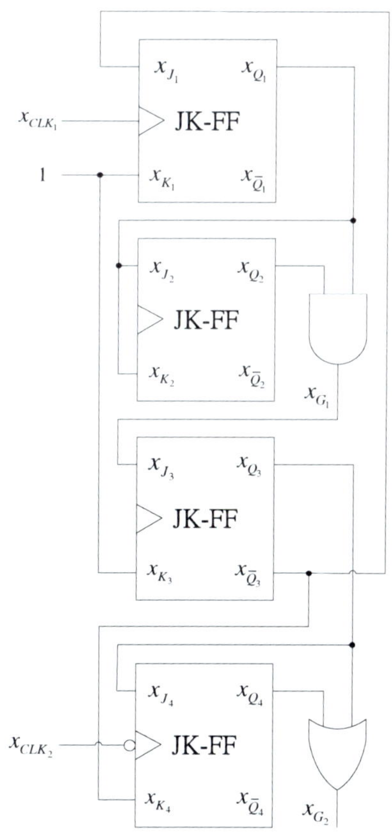

Figure 22. Topology of the synchronous genetic counter with two rising and one falling edge-triggered JK flip-flops for the clock signal with a five-fold basal period.

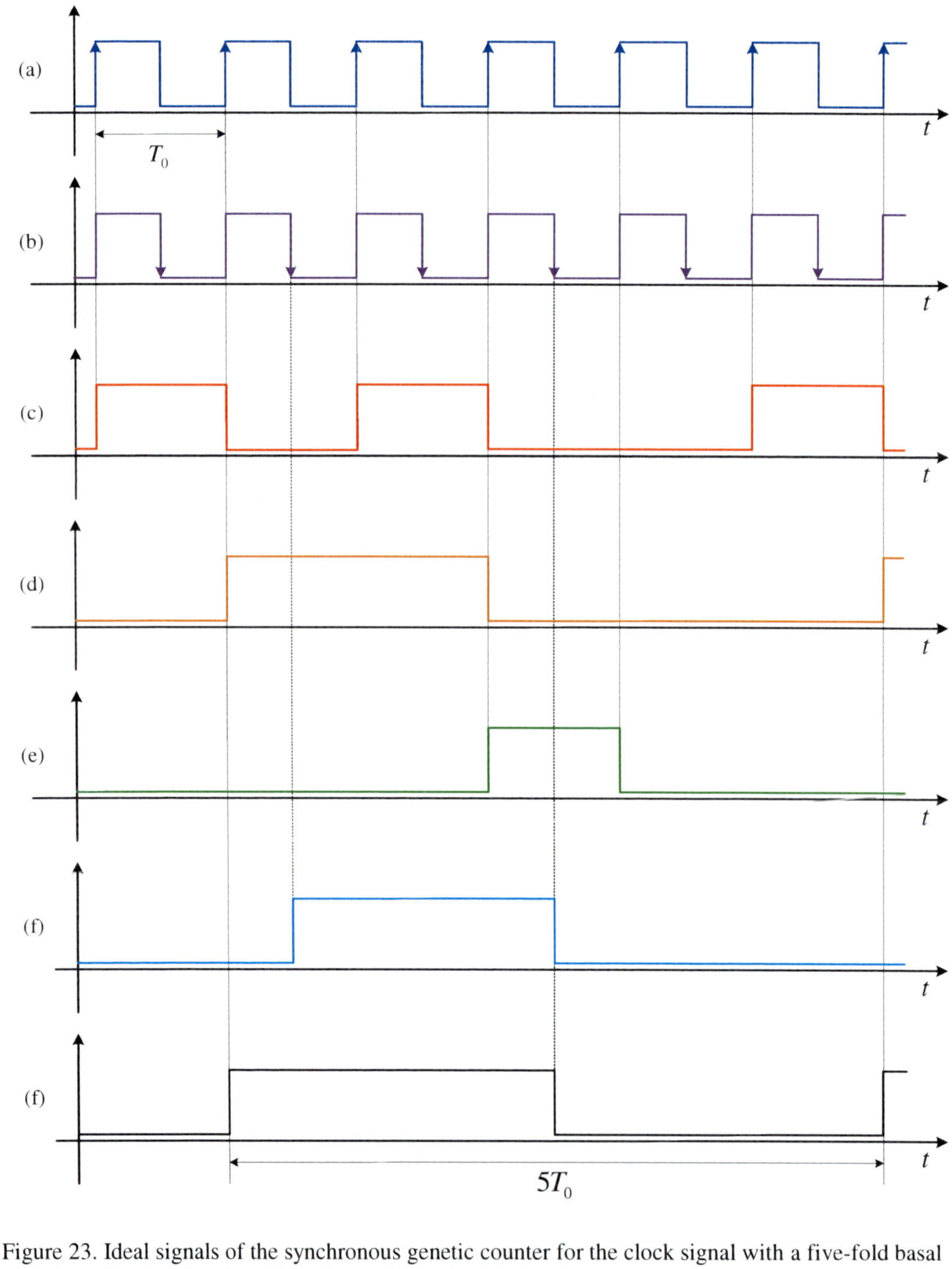

Figure 23. Ideal signals of the synchronous genetic counter for the clock signal with a five-fold basal period.(a) Clock pulse signal from low to high; (b) Clock pulse signal from high to low; (c) Output signal x_{Q_1} of the 1st genetic JK flip-flop; (d) Output signal x_{Q_2} of the 2nd genetic JK flip-flop; (e) Output signal x_{Q_3} of the 3rd genetic JK flip-flop; (f) Output signal x_{Q_4} of the 4th genetic JK flip-flop; and (g) Output signal of logic OR of (e) and (f).

SIMULATION RESULTS

Consider the dynamic model of the synthesized genetic oscillator given in [22]

$$\begin{aligned} \dot{x}_{lacI} &= 0.3425\frac{1}{1+x_{cI}^4} - 0.1165x_{lacI}, & x_{lacI}(0) &= 0.7, \\ \dot{x}_{tetR} &= 0.3425\frac{1}{1+x_{lacI}^4} - 0.1165x_{tetR}, & x_{tetR}(0) &= 1.2, \\ \dot{x}_{cI} &= 0.3425\frac{1}{1+x_{tetR}^4} - 0.1165x_{cI}, & x_{cI}(0) &= 1.7 \end{aligned} \quad (52)$$

The oscillation with the basal period $T_0 = 32\sec$, the amplitude $A = 0.63$, and the base level $y_{d,0} = 1.1731$ is displayed in Figure24. Suppose that the protein concentration x_{cI} is the desired oscillation input. To design the clock pulse signal with $D = 10\%$, the designed genetic waveform-shaping circuit is described by

$$\begin{aligned} \dot{x}_1 &= \frac{x_{cI}^4}{1.76^4 + x_{cI}^4} - x_1, \\ \dot{x}_2 &= \frac{x_1^4}{0.5^4 + x_1^4} - x_2, \\ \dot{x}_3 &= \frac{x_{cI}^4}{0.5^4 + x_2^4} - x_3, \\ \dot{x}_4 &= \frac{x_3^4}{0.5^4 + x_3^4} - x_4, \\ \dot{x}_5 &= \frac{x_4^4}{0.5^4 + x_4^4} - x_5, \\ \dot{x}_6 &= 1.0872\frac{x_5^4}{0.5^4 + x_5^4} - x_6 \end{aligned} \quad (53)$$

where x_6 is the PWM signal with $D = 10\%$. The circuit has six genetic Buffers.

In the first Buffer, the threshold level 1.76 is set and the corresponding parameters including rate constants, Hill constants, and Hill coefficients and satisfying (37)-(39)are chosen for the second to the fifth Buffers. The last Buffer is to compensate the output of the maximal level by choosing the appropriate rate constants in. In each stage, the I/O characteristic curves are shown in Figure25(a).

The concentration response of the generated clock pulse signal is shown in Figure25(b).

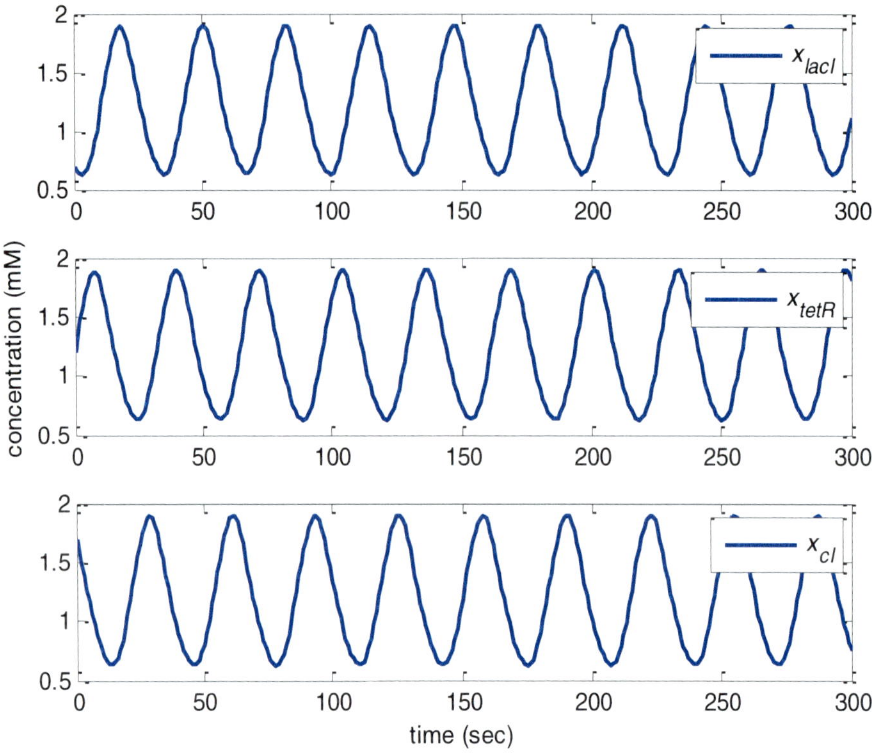

Figure 24. Responses of the genetic oscillator.

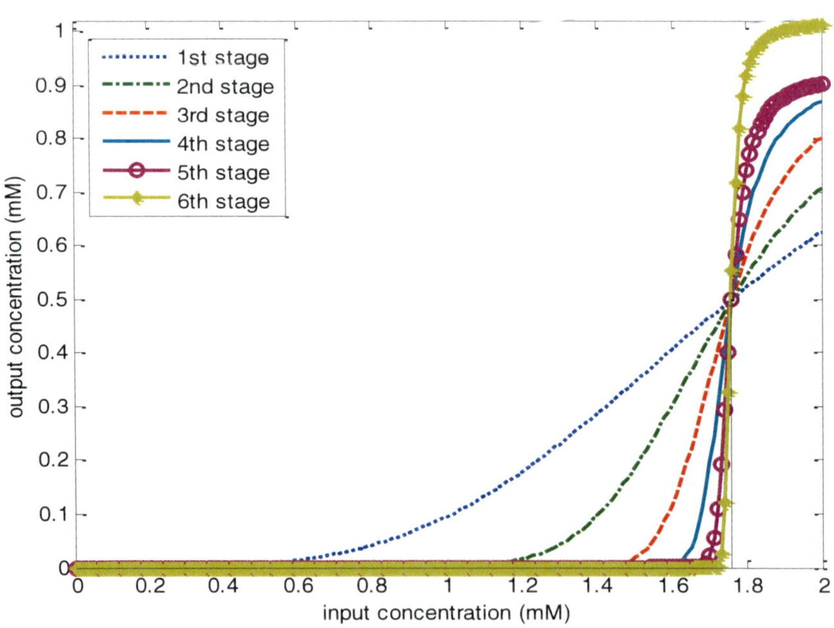

(a)

Figure 25. (Continued).

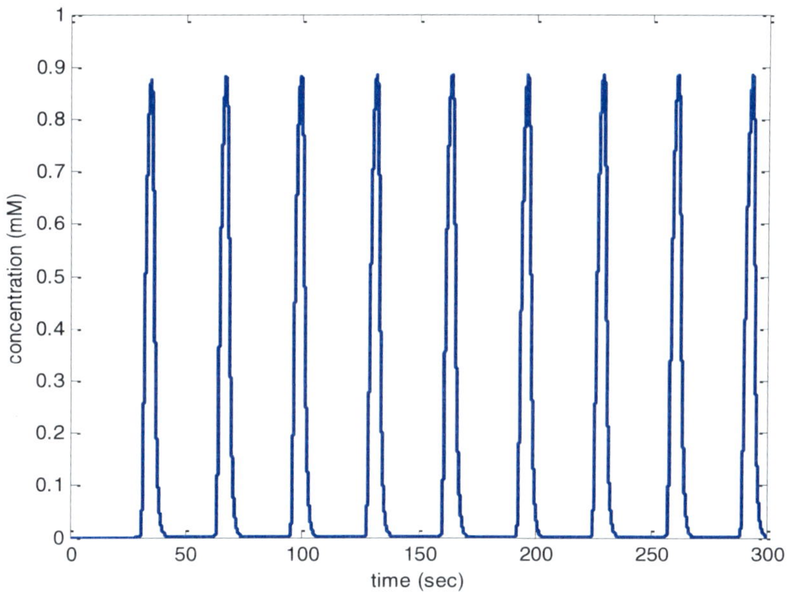

(b)

Figure 25. A clock pulse signal with $D = 10\%$. (a) I/O characteristic curve of designed genetic waveform-shaping circuit in each stage; (b) Response of the designed clock pulse signal.

Similarly, the clock pulse signal with $D = 90\%$ is generated by the following genetic waveform-shaping circuit

$$\begin{aligned}
\dot{x}_1 &= \frac{x_{cI}^4}{0.6761^4 + x_{cI}^4} - x_1, \\
\dot{x}_2 &= \frac{x_1^4}{0.5^4 + x_1^4} - x_2, \\
\dot{x}_3 &= \frac{x_2^4}{0.5^4 + x_2^4} - x_3, \\
\dot{x}_4 &= \frac{x_3^4}{0.5^4 + x_3^4} - x_4, \\
\dot{x}_5 &= \frac{x_4^4}{0.5^4 + x_4^4} - x_5, \\
\dot{x}_6 &= 1.1083\frac{x_5^4}{0.5^4 + x_5^4} - x_6
\end{aligned} \tag{54}$$

where x_6 is the PWM signal with $D = 90\%$. The first Buffer gate is designed with the threshold level 0.6761 and the second to the fifth Buffers choose the corresponding threshold level 0.5 satisfying (38).

The Buffer in the last stage functions to compensate the output of maximal level.

In each stage, the I/O characteristic curves are shown in Figure26(a). The concentration response of the designed clock pulse is shown in Figure26(b).

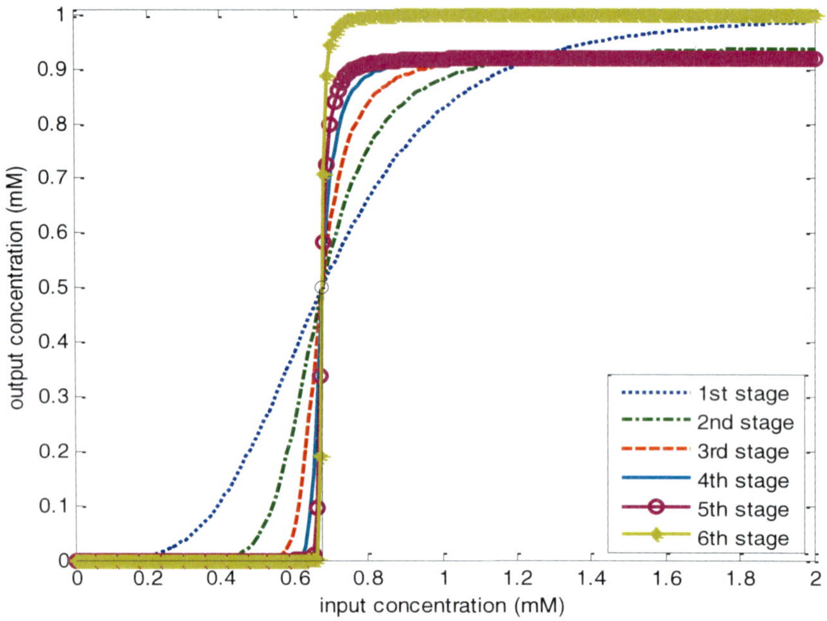

(a)

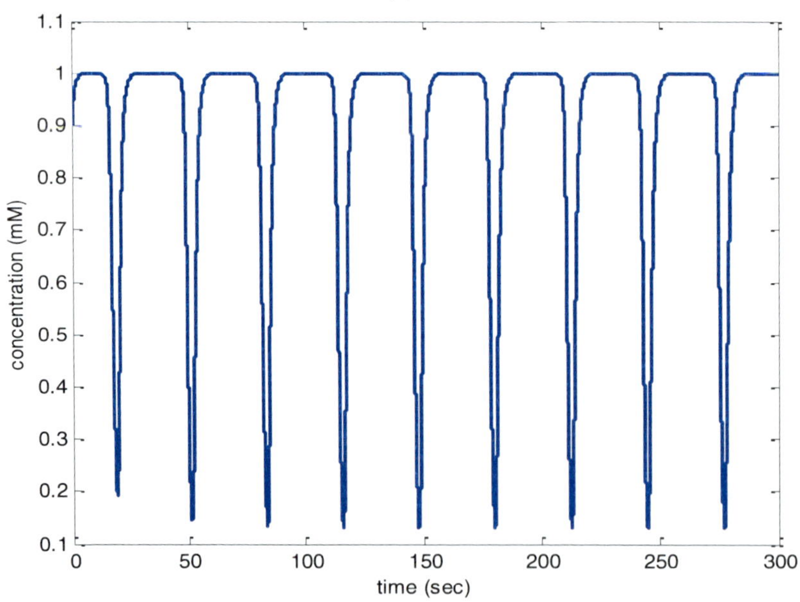

(b)

Figure 26. A clock pulse signal with $D = 90\%$. (a) I/O characteristic curve of designed genetic waveform-shaping circuit in each stage; (b) Response of the designed clock pulse signal.

According to the proposed approach, the oscillation signal can be rectified and filtered as a direct current (DC) output. The genetic waveform-shaping circuit with $D = 100\%$ is described by

$$\begin{aligned}
\dot{x}_1 &= \frac{x_{cI}^4}{0.5^4 + x_{cI}^4} - x_1, \\
\dot{x}_2 &= \frac{x_1^4}{0.5^4 + x_1^4} - x_2, \\
\dot{x}_3 &= \frac{x_2^4}{0.5^4 + x_2^4} - x_3, \\
\dot{x}_4 &= 1.0851\frac{x_3^4}{0.5^4 + x_3^4} - x_4,
\end{aligned} \tag{55}$$

where x_4 is the DC signal with full duty cycle. There are four genetic Buffers. In the first Buffer, the threshold level 0.5 is chosen and the second to the fifth Buffers choose the threshold level 0.5. In each stage, the I/O characteristic curves are shown in Figure27(a). The concentration response of the designed direct current (DC) signal is shown in Figure27(b).

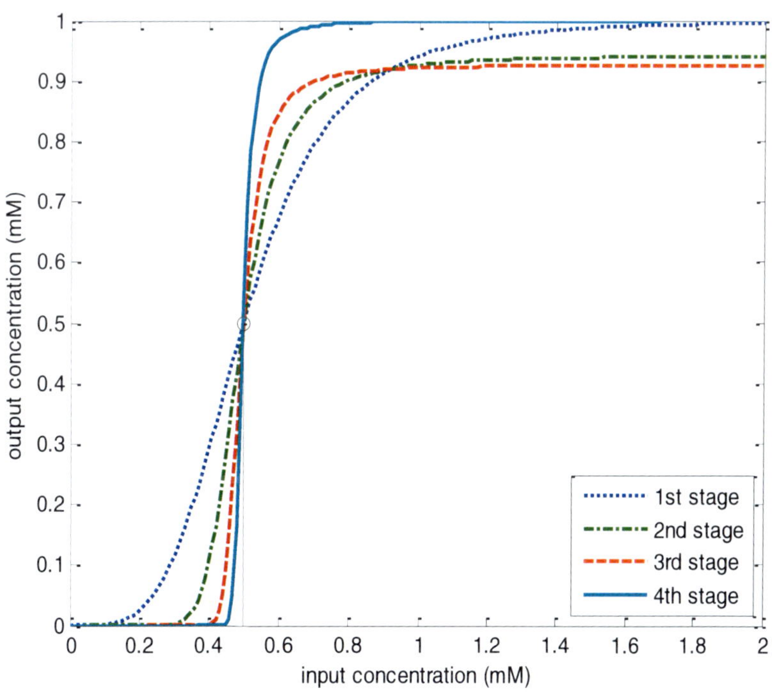

(a)

Figure 27. (Continued).

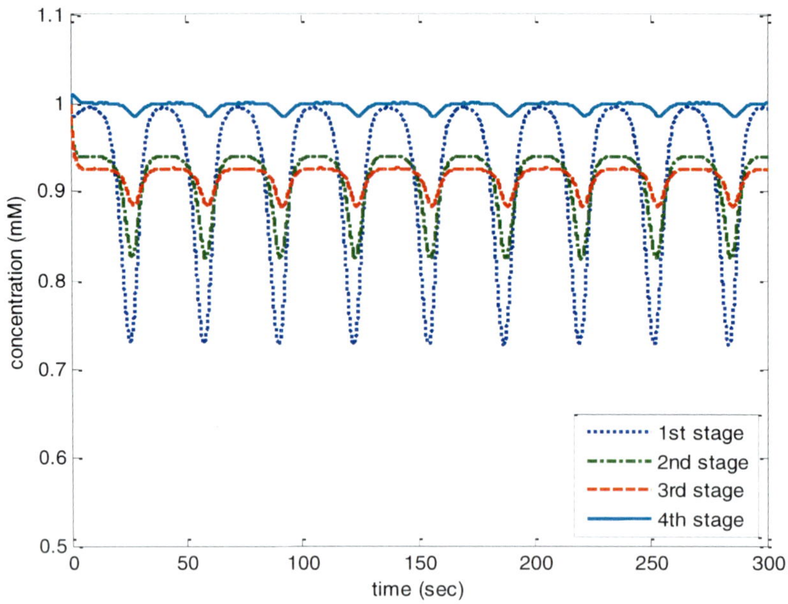

(b)

Figure 27.A PWM with $D = 100\%$. (a) I/O characteristic curve of designed genetic waveform-shaping circuit in each stage; (b) Response of the designed PWM signal in each stage.

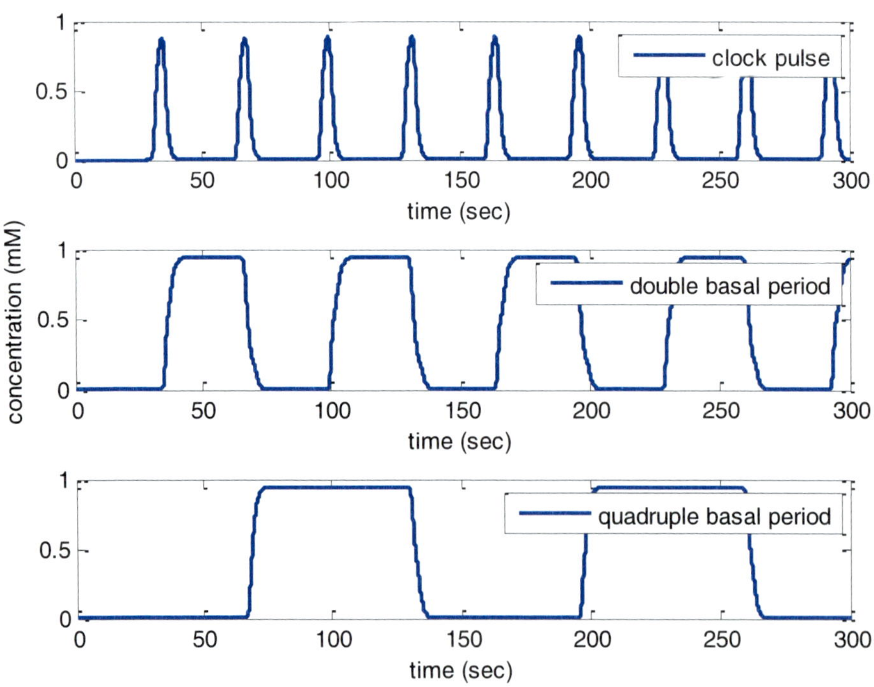

Figure 28. Response of the synchronous genetic counter for the clock signals with double and quadruple basal periods.

To design the clock signals with double and quadruple basal period, suppose that $\delta = 2$, all synthesis and decay rates are 1, all Hill constants are 0.5, all Hill coefficients are 4 in (49), x_{CLK_1} is the clock pulse generated from (53) and the high level DC signal is synthesized in (55). The concentration responses of the designed clock signals with double and quadruple basal periods are shown in Figure 28. State change of the genetic JK flip-flop occurs when the clock pulse goes from 0 to 1. For the clock signals with five-fold basal period, suppose that all variables remain the same to the above example; x_{CLK_1} and x_{CLK_2} are, respectively, the clock pulses generated from (53) and (54), and the DC signal is synthesized by (55). The concentration response of the designed clock signal with five-fold basal period is generated, see Figure 29.

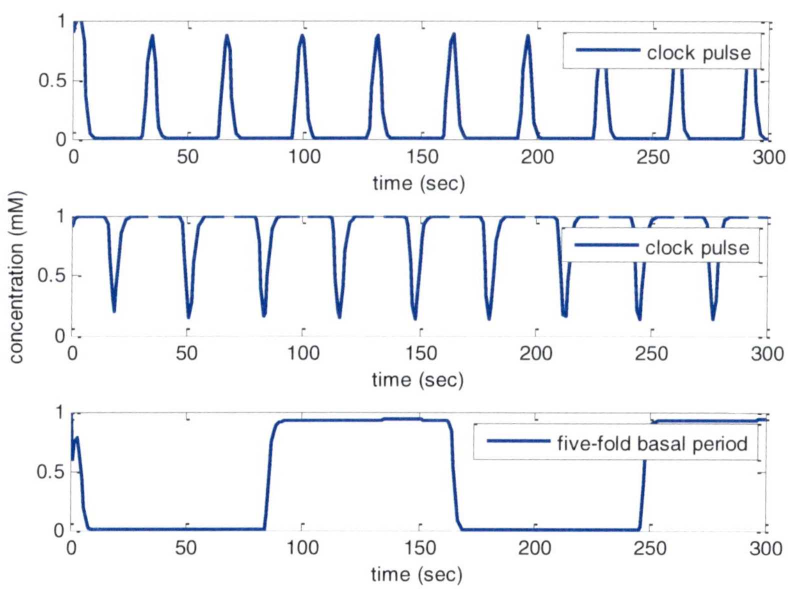

Figure 29. Response of the synchronous genetic counter for the clock signal with afive-fold basal period.

Conclusion

This chapter introduces a RSGA-based genetic logic gate design. The RSGA with real coding combines the advantages of RGA and SGA and is capable of simultaneously solving the parameter and structure optimization problems. As a useful application, a class of genetic logic gates described by the genetic transcriptional model with CRIF is constructed via the RSGA to search its cheaper structure. A genetic counter circuit with a clock pulse generator anda genetic oscillator is synthesized by assembling these genetic logic gates based on the topology of the digital sequential logic circuits to generate a clock signal whose frequency is an inverse integral multiple to that of the genetic oscillator. For the clock pulse generator design, an analogous electronic waveform-shaping circuit with several cascaded buffers shapes logic high/low levels of an oscillation input into a PWM output with various duty cycles. By regulating the threshold level of the buffer, a clock pulse with its frequency consistent to the genetic oscillator is generated. The synchronous genetic counter circuit is triggered by the clock pulse to realize the function of frequency synthesizer. The results show the effectiveness of the RSGA for genetic logic gate designs.

ACKNOWLEDGMENT

This research was sponsored by National Science Council, Taiwan, ROC under the Grant NSC-101-2221-E-005-015-MY3.

REFERENCES

[1] M. Gen and R. Cheng. Genetic Algorithms and Engineering Optimization, Wiley, New York, 2000.

[2] D.E. Goldberg. Real-coded genetic algorithms, virtual alphabets and blocking, *Complex Systems,* 5:139-167, 1991.

[3] K.S.Kang, K.F.Man and D.W. Gu.Structured genetic algorithm for robust H_∞ control system design, *IEEE Transactions on Industrial Electronics,* 43(5): 575-582, 1996.

[4] C.C. Laiand C.Y. Chang.A hierarchical genetic algorithm based approach for image segmentation, in *Proceedings of the IEEE International Conference on Networking, Sensing and Control, Taipei, Taiwan,* pp. 1284-1288, 2004

[5] C.W. Tsai, C.H. Huang and C.L. Lin. Structure-specified IIR filter and control design using real structured genetic algorithm, *Applied Soft Computing,* 9: 1285-1295, 2009.

[6] C.L. Lin, C.H. Huang and C.W. Tsai. Structure-Specified Real Coded Genetic Algorithms with Applications, *Advanced Knowledge Based Systems: Model, Applications & Research, India,* pp. 160-187, 2010.

[7] C.W. Tsai, C.L. Lin and C.H. Huang. Microbrushless DC motor control design based on real-coded structural genetic algorithm, *IEEE/ASME Transactions on Mechatronics,* 16: 151-159, 2011.

[8] N.E.Buchler, U.Gerland and T.Hwa. On schemes of combinatorialtranscription logic, *PNAS,* 100(9): 5136-514, 2003.

[9] A.E.Mayo, Y.Setty, S.Shavit, A.Zaslaver and U.Alon. Plasticity ofthe cis-regulatory input function of a gene, *PLoS Biology,* 4(4): 555-561, 2006.

[10] B.Kaplan, A.Bren, E.Dekel and U.Alon. The incoherent feed-forwardloop can generate non-monotonic input functions for genes, *Molecular Systems Biology,* 4(203): 1-9, 2008.

[11] B.Wang, R.I.Kitney, N.Joly and B.Buck. Engineering modular andorthogonal genetic logic gates for robust digital-like syntheticbiology, *Nature Communications,* 2(508): 1-9, 2011.

[12] Y.Setty, A.E.Mayo, M.G.Surette and U.Alon.Detailed map of acis-regulatory input function, *PNAS,* 100(13): 7702-7707, 2003.

[13] A.Kinkhabwala and C.C.Guet.Uncovering cis-regulatory codes usingsynthetic promoter shuffling, *PLoS ONE,* 3(4): 1-10, 2008.

[14] J.Zhang, Z.Yuan and T.Zhou.Combinatorial regulation: characteristicsof dynamic correlations, *IET System Biology,* 3(6): 440-452, 2009.

[15] A.M.Chen and T.S. Zhou. Sensitivity analysis of a cis-regulatory inputfunction, in *Proceedings of the International Symposium on Optimization and Systems Biology,* pp. 325-332, 2008.

[16] L.Bintu, N.E.Buchler, H.G.Garcia, U. Gerland, T. Hwa, J. Kondev, T. Kuhlman and R. Phillips.Transcriptional regulationby the numbers: applications, *Current Opinion in Genetics & Development,* 15(2): 125-135, 2005.

[17] B.S. Chen and P.W. Chen.GA-based design algorithms for the robust synthetic genetic oscillators with prescribed amplitude, period and phase, *Gene Regulation and Systems Biology,* 4: 35-52, 2010.

[18] B.S. Chen, C.Y. Hsu and J.J. Liou.Robust design of biological circuits: evolutionary systems biology approach, *Journal of Biomedicine and Biotechnology,* 2011: 1-14, 2011.

[19] Y.C. Chang, C.L. Lin and T. Jennawasin.Design of synthetic genetic oscillators using evolutionary optimization, *Evolutionary Bioinformatics,* 9: 137-150, 2013.

[20] C.H. Chuang, C.L. Lin, Y.C. Chang, T. Jennawasin and P.K. Chen.Design of synthetic biological logic circuits based on evolutionary algorithm, *IET Systems Biology,* 7(4): 89-105, 2013.

[21] C.H. Chuang and C.L. Lin. A novel synthesizing genetic logic circuit: frequency multiplier, *IEEE/ACM Transactions on Computational Biology and Bioinformatics,* 11(4, pp 1-12, 2014.

[22] C.H. Chuang and C.L. Lin.Synthesizing genetic sequential logic circuit with clock pulse generator, *BMC Systems Biology,* 8(63): 1-15, 2014.

In: Advances in Evolutionary Algorithms Research
Editor: Gregor Papa

ISBN: 978-1-63463-849-4
© 2015 Nova Science Publishers, Inc.

Chapter 4

MULTI-OBJECTIVE OPTIMIZATION OF BIOBUTANOL PRODUCTION: CONTINUOUS FERMENTATION COUPLED WITH A VACUUM SEPARATION UNIT

Aida S. Rohani, Jules Thibault* and Poupak Mehrani
Department of Chemical and Biological Engineering
University of Ottawa, Canada

ABSTRACT

To produce butanol more economically from acetone-butanol-ethanol (ABE) fermentation, it is required to operate the process under optimal conditions. In this chapter, multi-objective optimization was used to determine Pareto-optimal solutions of a continuous ABE fermentation coupled with a vacuum separation unit. The Pareto-optimal solutions, based on four decision variables and three objective functions, were then ranked using the Net Flow Method (NFM) and were compared to the continuous fermentation process without the vacuum separation unit. It was found that for the best solution, the selective removal of solvents enhanced butanol specific productivity (gButanol/(L.h.gBiomass)) and its average concentration (gButanol/L). An optimal substrate conversion of 96% was obtained for the vacuum fermentation compared to 83% for the non-integrated process where the inlet feed sugar concentrations were 150 and 55 g/L, respectively. Two additional multi-objective optimization cases were investigated in order to find the best set of objective functions for optimizing vacuum fermentation. Results show that higher amounts of microorganisms in the fermenter led to an improvement in the butanol yield (gButanol/gSugar consumed), butanol concentration (gButanol/L), and butanol productivity (gButanol/L.h) values.

Keywords: Multi-objective optimization, Pareto domain, Net Flow Method, ABE fermentation, vacuum fermentation, biobutanol

* Corresponding Author address: 161 Louis Pasteur St., Ottawa, Ontario, Canada, K1N 6N5
Email: Jules.Thibault@uottawa.ca.

NOMENCLATURE

ϕ_1	Dilution rate [h^{-1}]
ϕ_2	Inlet feed sugar concentration [g/L]
ϕ_3	Biomass retention factor [m^3.h/m^3.h]
ϕ_4	Evaporation rate factor [m^3.h/m^3.h]
A	Acetone
AA	Acetic acid
B	Butanol
BA	Butyric acid
BBA	Combined Butanol and butyric acid
Con_S	Sugar conversion [mmol/mmol]
C_i	Concentration of species i [mmol/L]
c_k	Concordance index of objective function k
$C[]$	Global concordance index
$C_{B(avg)}$	Butanol average concentration [g/L]
E	Ethanol
F_n	Stream volumetric flowrate [m^3/h]
i	Denotes species: A, AA, B, BA, BBA, E, S
k	Index for objective function
MW_i	Molecular weight of species i [g/mmol]
n	Stream number
r_i	Production rate of species i [mmol/L/h]
r_X	Biomass growth rate [g/L.h]
P_B	Butanol productivity [g_B/L.h]
SP_B	Butanol specific productivity [g_B/L.h. g_X]
S	Sugar
V	Fermenter volume [m^3]
X	Biomass concentration [g/L]
Y_B	Butanol yield [g/g]

INTRODUCTION

In recent years, the production of biofuels such as bioethanol, biobutanol and biodiesel have attracted significant attention. This accrued interest is mainly driven by factors such as limited supply of fossil fuels, increasing and fluctuating price of oil, and concerns over greenhouse gas emissions from fossil fuels leading to climate change. Amongst liquid biofuels, butanol produced from biomass has attracted special attention with its potential to be an alternative environmentally-sustainable fuel for petroleum gasoline due to its highly similar physical properties as well as its energy content.

The process for the production of butanol from biomass is commonly known as acetone-butanol-ethanol (ABE) fermentation. The economics of ABE production is directly influenced by the type of fermenter used (batch, continuous, fed-batch, etc.), the solvent recovery technique, the extent of sugar conversion, solvent yield, solvent concentration, and productivity. In the ABE fermentation process, butanol toxicity to the fermenting microorganisms results in product inhibition and limits the final butanol concentration in the broth. This in turn results in the cost of butanol recovery to be high, and more energy than the energy content of butanol may be required for its recovery [1, 2]. Therefore, by increasing butanol concentration in the final broth, significant energy saving can be attained.

To partly alleviate product inhibition, the concentration of solvent products in the broth should be maintained below the inhibition level by removing a portion of these products [3]. To achieve this objective, several methods have been investigated in literature: pervaporation [4], liquid-liquid extraction [5, 6], gas stripping [7-9], reverse osmosis [10], and adsorption [11, 12]. Another technique to remove the volatile solvents in the fermentation broth is vacuum fermentation during which the fermenter or a separate unit connected to the fermenter is kept under vacuum conditions via a vacuum pump.

This technique was first used by Cysewski and Wilke [13] in ethanol fermentation in order to reduce ethanol inhibition of the yeast. They demonstrated that by performing the process under vacuum, rapid and complete fermentation of concentrated sugar solutions was possible. The higher boiling point of butanol (118°C) over that of water (100°C) could lead to believe that water is more volatile and, therefore, vacuum fermentation cannot be used in ABE fermentation. However, using computational simulation, Mariano et al., [14] have shown the technical feasibility of vacuum fermentation integrated with butanol fermentation. Water and butanol form an azeotropic mixture and thus butanol can be boiled off at temperatures lower than the individual boiling point of butanol and water. Therefore, at typical butanol concentrations present in the fermentation broth, butanol is significantly more volatile than water and, as a result, butanol concentration in the vapour phase would be much higher than the one in liquid fermentation broth.

To improve the economic viability of a fermentative process, it is paramount to first find the process optimal operating conditions. In this study, the mathematical modeling of a continuous fermentation process was performed to determine the operating variables of a large-scale bioreactor for the production of butanol that would optimize a set of objective functions.

Multi-objective optimization (MOO) has been applied in many complex chemical engineering processes where the simultaneous optimization of more than one objective function is required. When a precise kinetic model of a process is available, multi-objective optimization enables examining the different decision variables without performing costly and time consuming experiments in order to evaluate the desired objective criteria. It is therefore possible to determine from the model the optimal process design. This chapter illustrates the application of multi-objective optimization to determine the optimal operating conditions of a continuous fermentation process coupled with a vacuum separation unit.

To compare the advantage of using such a system, a comparison with the same process, but without the vacuum fermentation unit was also performed.

The impact of a selected set of objective functions including butanol specific productivity, butanol productivity, butanol yield, butanol average concentration in the outlet streams, and sugar conversion was investigated by considering two additional optimization scenarios for the vacuum fermentation.

PROCESS DESCRIPTION

ABE Fermentation Process

The ABE fermentation is usually carried out using bacteria such as *Clostridium acetobutylicum* or *Clostridium biejerinkii*. For most strains, the inhibition concentration of acetone, butanol, and ethanol solvents is approximately 20 g/L, with a butanol concentration of 13 g/L or less [15]. This inhibition means that the fermentation process essentially ceases after the solvent concentration reaches this limit, resulting in a low butanol concentration [16]. It has been demonstrated that the continuous fermentation mode provides some advantages over batch mode where higher productivities can be achieved by maintaining a higher biomass concentration in the fermenter [15, 17]. Moreover, with relatively high dilution rates, a cell retention system must be used to prevent the washout phenomenon, the condition where culture is not able to sustain itself through the fermenter due to high dilution rates [9]. The fermentation is performed at atmospheric pressure and 37°C. The fermentation process is usually initiated in batch mode and, then at a suitable time, it is switched to continuous mode of operation where eventually steady-state operation is achieved. In continuous fermentation, a feed stream containing fermentable sugar and nutrients enters the fermenter where sugar is converted into desired products by the microorganisms. To maintain steady-state operation, an equivalent stream of the fermentation broth must exit the fermenter.

The fermentation process evaluated in this work is schematically represented in Figure 1. This system is used for both the standard continuous fermentation and the fermentation coupled with a vacuum separation unit. In the latter case, a stream (Stream 2), which is withdrawn from the fermentation broth, passes through a heat exchanger to add the necessary latent heat of vaporization to sustain the desired rate of evaporation prior to entering the vacuum flash unit where a fraction of the inlet stream is vaporized. The flash unit operates at 37°C with a pressure in the vicinity of 7 kPa which corresponds to the boiling point of the fermentation broth at 37°C. Because ABE solvents are more volatile than water in the fermentation broth, the vaporized stream (Stream 8) is more concentrated with these solvents. It is therefore possible to partly remove butanol and therefore reducing its inhibition. In order to create vacuum, a condenser is used to condense and separate the solvents in Stream 8 in addition to a vacuum pump. It is assumed that all the volatile solvents that were evaporated are recovered in the condenser (Stream 3) and the vapour stream leaving the condenser carries negligible amounts of solvents. The liquid stream leaving the vacuum unit is pumped and sent to a cell retention unit where part of the liquid permeates through a membrane. The retentate stream is then split into two streams: a purge stream to maintain the biomass concentration constant and a recycle stream to the fermenter. Under steady-state, the flow rate of feed stream must equal that of the four streams exiting the fermentation system (i.e., $F1 = F3 + F5 + F7 + F9$). In the case of a standard continuous fermentation, the vacuum separation unit and the heat exchanger are simply bypassed. The performances of both configurations were optimized and compared in this chapter.

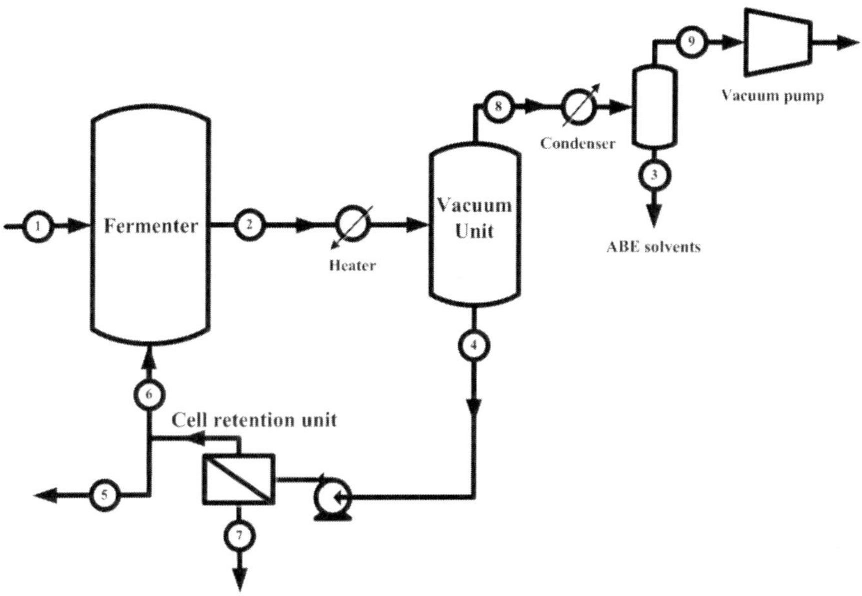

Figure 1. Schematic of a continuous fermenter equipped with a cell retention and a vacuum unit. 1 (Feed stream); 2 (Stream to the vacuum unit); 3 (Solvent condensate); 4 (Broth stream out of the vacuum unit); 5 (Bleed stream); 6 (Recycle stream back to the fermenter); 7 (Permeate stream from cell retention unit); 8 (Vacuum unit vapour stream); 9 (Vapour stream out of condenser/separator).

ABE Fermentation Kinetic Model

The kinetic model used to simulate the continuous fermentation is based on a model proposed by Mulchandani and Volesky [18]. They proposed a model to calculate the solvent (acetone, butanol and ethanol) production rate, the production rates of butyric acid and acetic acid, the growth of biomass, and the consumption of sugars in *Clostridium acetobutylicum* culture for a continuous production. Their experiment was run for 150 h and the cells were retained inside the fermentation vessel. In the current investigation, it is assumed that the fermentation will proceed under steady state for a much longer time period such that a portion of the cells must exit the fermenter (Stream 5 in Figure 1) to maintain a constant biomass concentration. It is assumed that the continuous kinetic model of Mulchandani and Volesky remains valid. In addition, their model was developed on the basis of the following assumptions: substrate limitation and butanol and butyric acid inhibition. The kinetic model proposed by Mulchandani and Volesky [18], which has been slightly modified for minor omissions, is presented in the following equations. The model contains a product inhibition factor *F(I)* that is a function of the combined concentration of butanol and butyric acid.:

$$\begin{aligned} F(I) &= \exp(-\,0.01BBA) && BBA \leq 8 \text{ g/L} \\ F(I) &= -\,0.153BBA + 2.16 && 8 \leq BBA \leq 13.9 \text{ g/L} \end{aligned} \tag{1}$$

The term BBA corresponds to the total concentration of butanol and butyric acid. The cell growth rate (r_x) is based on the Monod equation [19]:

$$r_x = \mu_m \frac{C_S}{C_S + K_S} F(I) X \tag{2}$$

The substrate consumption rate (r_s) is expressed as:

$$-r_S = k_3 \mu X F(I) + k_4 X F(I) + k_1 \frac{C_S}{C_S + K_S} \frac{BA}{BA + K_{BA}} X + k_2 \frac{C_S}{C_S + K_S} \frac{AA}{AA + K_{AA}} X \tag{3}$$

The following two equations represent the rate of acid production, including acetic acid and butyric acid, which are considered as intermediate metabolites. The latter are progressively reduced to acetone and butanol, respectively, as shown in equations (6) and (7):

$$r_{AA} = k_8 [k_3 \mu_m \frac{C_S}{C_S + K_S} F(I) X + k_4 F(I) X] - k_9 \frac{C_{AA}}{C_{AA} + K_{AA}} \frac{C_S}{C_S + K_S} X \tag{4}$$

$$r_{BA} = k_5 [k_3 \mu_m \frac{C_S}{C_S + K_S} F(I) X + k_4 F(I) X] - k_6 \frac{C_{BA}}{C_{BA} + K_{BA}} \frac{C_S}{C_S + K_S} X \tag{5}$$

$$r_A = k_{10} [k_3 \mu_m \frac{C_S}{C_S + K_S} F(I) X + k_4 F(I) X] + k_{15} \frac{C_{AA}}{C_{AA} + K_{AA}} \frac{C_S}{C_S + K_S} X \tag{6}$$

$$r_B = k_7 [k_3 \mu_m \frac{C_S}{C_S + K_S} F(I) X + k_4 F(I) X] + k_{14} \frac{C_{BA}}{C_{BA} + K_{BA}} \frac{C_S}{C_S + K_S} X \tag{7}$$

Ethanol production (r_E) is solely based on substrate consumption:

$$r_E = k_{11} [k_3 \mu_m \frac{C_S}{C_S + K_S} F(I) X + k_4 F(I) X] \tag{8}$$

The change in concentration of all species in the fermenter is obtained by an overall mass balance around the fermenter with constant volume (Figure 1) as shown in equation (9).

$$\frac{dC_i}{dt} = \frac{1}{V} \left[F_1 C_{i,1} + F_6 C_{i,6} - F_2 C_{i,2} + r_i V \right] \tag{9}$$

where C_i stands for the product concentration for each species: butanol, ethanol, acetone, butyric acid, acetic acid, and sugar. A similar mass balance can be written for biomass as follows:

$$\frac{dX}{dt} = \frac{1}{V} \left[F_6 X_6 - F_2 X_2 + r_X V \right] \tag{10}$$

where

$$F_1 = F_3 + F_5 + F_7 + F_9 = D\ V \tag{11}$$

$$F_2 = 20F_1 \tag{12}$$

$$F_6 = F_4 - F_5 - F_7 \tag{13}$$

It is assumed that the feed stream contains no biomass. All the kinetic constants in the aforementioned equations can be found in Mulchandani and Volesky [18]. For completeness, the table of constants in the kinetic model is given in Appendix I. The set of differential equations was solved by finite differences and mass balances were solved at each integration time step. Visual Basic for Applications (VBA) program was used as the simulation platform and the required thermodynamic information was obtained by calling Honeywell UniSim® software from VBA.

Multi-Objective Optimization

Optimization plays a major role in process modeling, design, and operation of chemical processes. To improve the process performance, profitability, and safety, it is required to operate the process under optimal conditions. Process optimization is often complex and nonlinear, and usually requires optimizing simultaneously several, often conflicting, process objective functions. It is possible to combine numerous objective functions into a single objective criterion where each objective is assigned a weighting factor with risk, however, of not achieving the most desired optimal solution [20, 21]. To overcome single objective optimization shortcomings, multi-objective optimization can be used [22].

The aim of this chapter was to model, simulate and optimize a continuous ABE fermentation process integrated with a vacuum separation unit to selectively remove a portion of the solvents and reduce product inhibition. In such a case, changing the operating conditions such as vacuum pressure in the separation unit, dilution rate, initial sugar concentration, and evaporation rate have a direct impact on the objective functions of interest such as butanol specific productivity, butanol productivity, butanol yield, butanol average concentration in the outlet streams, and sugar conversion. Two scenarios were defined and evaluated: the first scenario compared the standard fermentation with the vacuum fermentation configuration, and in the second scenario, the choice of the set of objective functions in the multi-objective optimization were evaluated for the vacuum fermentation configuration.

Pareto Domain

In a typical multi-objective optimization problem, where optimal decisions are made in the presence of two or more conflicting objectives, there is more than one optimal solution. Multi-objective optimization usually proceeds by circumscribing the Pareto domain with a large number of non-dominated solutions. The concept of dominance can be described by comparing two solutions: a solution A is non-dominated by solution B if at least one of the objective functions of A is not worse than that of B and it is better with respect to at least one objective. Moreover, if all the objective function values of A are better than those of B, then solution B is considered a dominated solution with respect to solution A. Several techniques used to generate the Pareto domain have been proposed and applied for chemical engineering processes [23]. In this investigation, the Dual Population Evolutionary Algorithm (DPEA) was used to obtain the Pareto domain for each fermenter configuration [24]. The procedure used can be summarized as follows:

1) A set of input values (decision variables) is randomly generated within their pre-determined range of variation to create an initial population of solutions (M). A certain fraction of the points for each decision variable was chosen on the boundary of the pre-determined range to insure the whole domain is well covered. Then, the objective functions are calculated for each set of input values of the population. In the Pareto domain, each point (solution) is defined based on its sets of decision variables and associated objective functions.
2) The objective functions are compared pairwise to calculate the number of times each solution is dominated. All non-dominated solutions, N_0, and a portion (survival fraction, F_S – 0.3 in this investigation) of the dominated solutions (M - N_0) are kept, resulting in N solutions retained for the next generation.

$$N = N_0 + INT\ [F_S(M - N_0)] \tag{14}$$

3. Then (M - N) new solutions are generated to replace the discarded points in the population. To generate new points, two solutions from the N retained solutions are randomly chosen (onc from the dominated solutions and one from the non-dominated solutions) and by a linear random interpolation between their decision variables a new vector of decision variables is generated. The objective functions are calculated for the new set of decision variables.

These three steps are repeated until the desired number of non-dominated solutions is generated. Many other methods are available to circumscribe the Pareto domain, but all methods use essentially the same procedure to come up with a sufficiently well defined Pareto domain. Based on various tests performed, the method used in this investigation converges more rapidly for a large number of points and provides a well defined Pareto domain covering the whole domain of the decision variable space.

Net Flow Method

For many simple problems having only few objectives, decision makers can choose the optimal solution strictly based on the Pareto domain. However, for more complex problems, a ranking algorithm can be used to determine the optimal region of operation. In this study, the Net Flow Method (NFM) was used for ranking all solutions of the converged Pareto domain.

NFM uses knowledge from an expert or decision maker to perform this ranking based on the following four sets of ranking parameters:

1. The relative importance of each objective function is expressed by a set of normalized relative weights W_K:

$$\sum_{K=1}^{n} W_K = 1 \tag{15}$$

2. The range of variation of each criterion for which the decision maker is not able to prefer one objective function of a given solution over the same objective function of another solution is called the indifference threshold (Q_K). Every two objective functions placed in this range are considered to be indiscernible with respect to each other.

3. The minimum difference between two values for a given criterion that the decision maker starts to prefer between two values is called the preference threshold (P_K). Above this threshold, priority is given to the larger value if a criterion is to be maximized and to a smaller value for a minimization problem.

4. The difference between two values of a criterion which is considered too high to be acceptable refers to the veto threshold (V_K). A solution is banned relative to another if the veto threshold is violated for at least one objective function in a solution.

For each objective function, the following relationship exists between the three thresholds:

$$0 \leq Q_K \leq P_K \leq V_K$$

These NFM parameters give the importance that each criterion has to the eyes of the decision maker. Based on the relative weights and the three thresholds, each solution is given a score. The whole Pareto domain is then ranked based on these scores. The NFM algorithm to perform the ranking executes as follows:

1. First, for each two solutions of i and j in the Pareto domain, the difference between the values of F_k of each objective function (K) is calculated by the following equation, the difference is calculated for all the solutions (M) in Pareto domain pairwise:

$$\Delta_K[i,j] = F_K(i) - F_K(j) \begin{cases} i \in [1, M] \\ j \in [1, M] \\ k \in [i, n] \end{cases} \tag{16}$$

2. The concordance index $c_K\,[i, j]$ is then calculated for each objective function for every pair of solutions in the Pareto domain using equation (17).

$$c_K[i,j]=\begin{cases}1 & \text{if } \Delta_K[i,j]\le Q_K\\ \dfrac{P_K-\Delta_K[i,j]}{P_K-Q_K} & \text{if } Q_K<\Delta_K[i,j]\le P_K\\ 0 & \text{if } \Delta_K[i,j]>P_K\end{cases} \tag{17}$$

Based on the indifference and preference thresholds for a given objective function (K), the concordance index measures the strength of the argument when the value of a criterion for solution i ($F_K(i)$) is at least as good as the same value ($F_K(j)$) in solution j. For differences below the indifference threshold, the concordance index equals unity while for differences over the preference threshold it equals zero. For a difference value between Q_K and P_K, the concordance index varies linearly between 0 and 1.

3. To determine the global concordance index, the weighted sum of individual concordance indices is calculated for each two solutions.

$$C[i,j]=\sum_{K=1}^{n}W_K c_K[i,j] \quad \begin{cases} i\in[1,M]\\ j\in[1,M]\end{cases} \tag{18}$$

4. Then the discordance index (D_K) is calculated based on the preference and veto thresholds of each criterion for a pair of solutions.

$$D_K[i,j]=\begin{cases}0 & \text{if } \Delta_K[i,j]\le P_K\\ \dfrac{\Delta_K[i,j]-P_K}{V_K-P_K} & \text{if } P_K<\Delta_K[i,j]\le V_K\\ 1 & \text{if } \Delta_K[i,j]>V_K\end{cases} \tag{19}$$

The discordance index measures the strength of the argument for the solutions when the value of a criterion for solution i ($F_K(i)$) is significantly worse than the same value ($F_K(j)$) in solution j. For differences below the preference threshold, the discordance index equals zero while for differences over veto threshold it equals unity. For the difference values varying between Q_K and V_K, it varies linearly between 0 and 1.

5. The global concordance and discordance values are used to show the performance of each pair of solutions in the Pareto domain. Considering all objective functions, the quality of solution i relative to solution j is calculated by the following equation:

$$\sigma[i,j]=C[i,j]\left(\prod_{K=1}^{n}[1-(D_K[i,j])^3]\right) \quad \begin{cases} i\in[1,M]\\ j\in[1,M]\end{cases} \tag{20}$$

when $\sigma[i,j]$ is close to zero, it indicates that solution j outranks solution i. If the value is close to 1 then solution i either outranks solution j or both solutions are in each other's vicinity.

6. At the end, the final ranking is done by summing up all the individual outranking elements for each solution in the Pareto domain.

$$\sigma_i = \sum_{j=1}^{M} \sigma\,[i,j] - \sum_{j=1}^{M} \sigma\,[j,i] \tag{21}$$

The first term compares the performance of the solution *i* relative to other solutions while the second term compares the performance of other solutions relative to solution *i*. After scoring each solution as it was indicated above solutions are sorted from highest to lowest. The solution with the highest ranking value is the solution that suits the decision-maker problem best. A more detailed description of Net Flow Method can be found in the literature [24-26].

DEFINITIONS OF OBJECTIVE FUNCTIONS AND DECISION VARIABLES

Standard versus Vacuum Fermentation

To evaluate the benefits of incorporating a vacuum separation unit in the fermentation process, the standard continuous ABE fermentation process (Case 1) was optimized and compared with the continuous fermentation coupled with a vacuum solvent removal unit (Case 2) also under optimal conditions. Both cases consisted of three objective functions, with three and four decision variables, respectively. All three objective functions needed to be maximized:

Case 1:

$$f_1(\phi_1,\phi_2,\phi_3) = SP_B$$
$$f_2(\phi_1,\phi_2,\phi_3) = C_{B(avg)}$$
$$f_3(\phi_1,\phi_2,\phi_3) = Con_S$$

Case 2:

$$f_1(\phi_1,\phi_2,\phi_3,\phi_4) = SP_B$$
$$f_2(\phi_1,\phi_2,\phi_3,\phi_4) = C_{B(avg)}$$
$$f_3(\phi_1,\phi_2,\phi_3,\phi_4) = Con_S$$

Table 1 presents the definition of all objective functions and decision variables used in this chapter. In both Cases 1 and 2, the three objective functions are the maximization of butanol specific productivity, average butanol concentration, and sugar conversion. The butanol specific productivity is the butanol productivity divided by the cell concentration which serves at the same time to prevent the biomass from reaching very high values. On the other hand, the unit term added to the cell concentration in the denominator is a soft constraint to prevent the biomass reaching very small values in order to create a very high butanol specific productivity. The decision variables used were the dilution rate (ϕ_1), sugar concentration in the feed (ϕ_2), biomass retention factor (ϕ_3), and evaporation rate factor (ϕ_4). The biomass retention factor is obtained by adjusting the bleed stream flow ratio ($F_5/(F_5+F_7)$). To satisfy the steady-state mass balance, the evaporation rate factor for Case 2 was expressed as a fraction of Stream 2 and was manipulated by changing the vapour fraction of the vacuum unit. Since the vacuum unit did not exist in standard fermentation, ϕ_4 was not used as a decision variable in Case 1. The Pareto-optimal solutions for both cases were ranked by the Net Flow Method to find the best point. The NFM relative weights and thresholds used for each case are presented in Table 2.

Table 1. Definition of objective functions and decision variables with their lower and upper bounds

	Parameters	Definitions
Objectives Functions	Butanol specific productivity, SP_B (g_B/L.h.g_x)	$\frac{1}{V}\frac{[C_{B,3}MW_BF_3 + C_{B,4}MW_B(F_7+F_5)]}{X+1}$
	Average butanol concentration, C_B (g/L)	$\frac{C_{B,3}MW_BF_3 + C_{B,4}MW_B(F_7+F_5)}{F_1}$
	Sugar conversion, Con_S (fraction)	$1-\frac{C_{S,7}(F_7+F_5)}{C_{S,1}F_1}$
	Butanol yield, Y_B (g/g)	$\frac{C_{B,3}MW_BF_3 + C_{B,4}MW_B(F_7+F_5)}{C_{S,1}F_1MW_S - C_{S,7}(F_7+F_5)MW_S}$
	Butanol productivity, P_B (g/L.h)	$\frac{1}{V}[C_{B,3}MW_BF_3 + C_{B,4}MW_B(F_7+F_5)]$
Decision Variables	Dilution rate, ϕ_1 (h^{-1})	$\frac{F_1}{V}$ $0.01 \le \phi_1 \le 0.8$
	Inlet feed sugar concentration, ϕ_2 (g/L)	$C_{S,1}MW_S$ $5 \le \phi_2 \le 150$
	Biomass retention factor, ϕ_3 (m^3.h/m^3.h)	$\frac{F_5}{F_7+F_5}$ $0.05 \le \phi_3 \le 1$
	Evaporation rate factor, ϕ_4 (m^3.h/m^3.h)	$\frac{F_8}{F_2}$ $0 \le \phi_4 \le 0.04$

Two Additional Vacuum Fermentation Cases

It will be shown in the results that vacuum fermentation (Case 2) leads to higher values of all three objective functions when compared to the standard fermentation (Case 1). It will also be shown that the decision variables for the best Pareto-optimal solutions for Case 2 were mostly concentrated around the maximum sugar concentration set at 150 g/L. Since the sugar feedstock and pre-treatment methods are generally fixed in industrial ABE fermentation plants, sugar concentrations in the feed stream are almost invariant, thus it was decided for the remaining case studies to keep the sugar concentration in the inlet feed stream at 150 g/L. As a result, the inlet sugar feed concentration is excluded from the decision variable set. Two additional case studies were conducted for the continuous vacuum fermentation configuration to examine the choice of the objective functions on the performance of the fermentation unit. Cases 3 and 4 are defined as follows:

Case 3:

$$f_1(\phi_1,\phi_3,\phi_4) = SP_B$$
$$f_2(\phi_1,\phi_3,\phi_4) = Y_B$$
$$f_3(\phi_1,\phi_3,\phi_4) = Con_S$$

Case 4:

$$f_1(\phi_1,\phi_3,\phi_4) = P_B$$
$$f_2(\phi_1,\phi_3,\phi_4) = Y_B$$
$$f_3(\phi_1,\phi_3,\phi_4) = Con_S$$

Table 2. Net Flow Method parameters used to rank the Pareto-optimal solutions for Cases 1-4

Mode	Criteria	Relative Weights	Thresholds		
			Indifference	Preference	Veto
Case 1	SP_B	0.4	0.05	0.1	0.2
	$C_{B(avg)}$	0.2	1	2	6
	Con_S	0.4	0.05	0.1	0.3
Case 2	SP_B	0.4	0.05	0.1	0.2
	$C_{B(avg)}$	0.2	2	5	12
	Con_S	0.4	0.05	0.1	0.3
Case 3	SP_B	0.4	0.05	0.1	0.2
	Y_B	0.2	0.005	0.01	0.03
	Con_S	0.4	0.05	0.1	0.3
Case 4	P_B	0.4	2	3	7
	Y_B	0.2	0.005	0.01	0.03
	Con_S	0.4	0.05	0.1	0.3

Results and Discussion

The Pareto domain for each case study was obtained by determining 1000 Pareto-optimal solutions using the DPEA genetic algorithm. These 1000 solutions were then ranked using the Net Flow Method based on the relative weights and threshold values presented in Table 2. The plots of the three objective functions for the ranked Pareto domains for Cases 1 and 2 are presented in Figures 2 and 3. In all plots related to the Pareto domain, the red dot represents the best Pareto-optimal solution. The black, medium grey and light grey regions represent the best 5%, the next 45% and the last 50% ranked solutions, respectively. Figures 2 and 3, for Cases 1 and 2, clearly show the trade-offs that exist between the three objective functions. An increase in the butanol average concentration was accompanied by a decrease in its specific productivity. For Case 1, the trade-off is even more striking between the butanol specific productivity and sugar conversion where an increase in specific productivity is accompanied by a drastic reduction in sugar conversion. A possible explanation is that at low dilution rates, a greater proportion of sugar fed to the fermenter is consumed and, as a result, a higher average butanol concentration is achieved. On the other hand, at low dilution rates, a smaller overall amount of butanol is produced, resulting in lower specific productivity.

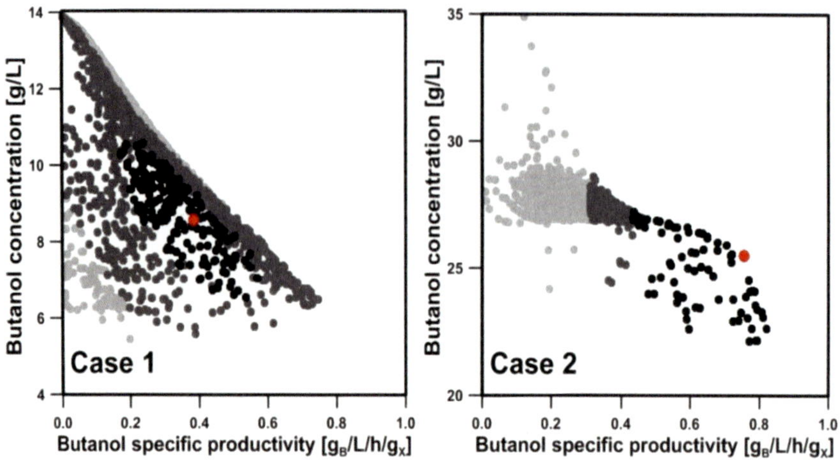

Figure 2. Plot of butanol average concentration versus butanol specific productivity for Cases 1 and 2.

The comparison of Cases 1 and 2 in Figure 3 indicates that the sugar conversion remains fairly high over a wider range of specific productivity for fermentation coupled with a vacuum separation unit. The values of all objective functions and the decision variables as well as few important selected variables for the best ranked Pareto-optimal solutions for both cases are reported in Table 3. Values associated with the highest-ranked Pareto-optimal solution in Table 3 indicate that most of the key factors determining the profitability of an ABE fermentation plant are superior when a vacuum separation unit is used. In Case 2, the average concentration of butanol by combining the three output streams (F_3, F_5, F_7) is 25.9 g/L which represents a three-fold increase compared to that of Case 1. High butanol concentration in the final fermentation broth is greatly advantageous since it will result in lower separation costs for butanol recovery from the dilute broth. It was demonstrated by Philips and Humphrey [27] that as butanol concentration increases from 10 g/L to 40 g/L, the ratio of energy input over the energy available in recovered butanol decreases from 1.5 to 0.25. Moreover, due to the higher average butanol concentration and higher dilution rate, the butanol specific productivity was increased by 75% for Case 2, when compared to Case 1.

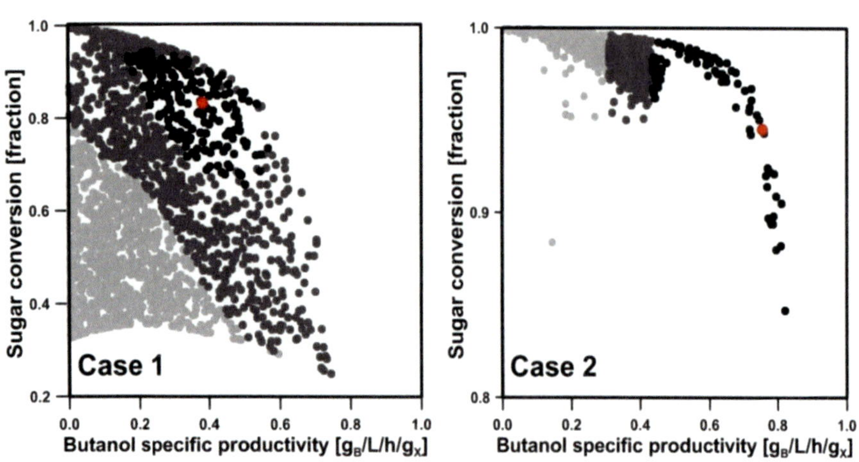

Figure 3. Plot of sugar conversion versus butanol specific productivity for Cases 1 and 2.

Higher biomass leads to higher conversion of sugars to butanol and because of the selective removal of solvents from the fermenter, inhibition was partly mitigated and thus the butanol production could progress further. An inhibition factor of unity in equation (1) represents no inhibition in fermentation and as the factor decreases, butanol and butyric acid toxicity increases, which eventually lead to biomass growth cessation when the factor reaches zero.

In Case 2, due to the reduced solvent inhibition compared to that of Case 1, biomass concentration is higher which means higher butanol concentration is attainable. With respect to decision variables, Figure 4 shows the plots of the inlet feed sugar concentration as a function of dilution rate for Cases 1 and 2.

The highest ranked solution for the standard fermentation has a feed sugar concentration of 55 g/L and a dilution rate of 0.63 h^{-1} whereas for Case 2 they are 150 g/L and 0.75 h^{-1}, respectively.

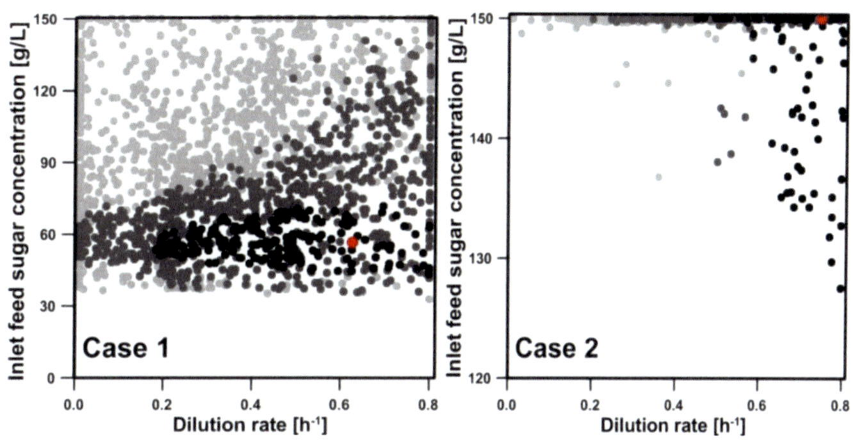

Figure 4. Plot of inlet feed sugar concentration versus dilution rate for Cases 1 and 2.

The significant difference in the inlet feed sugar concentration between the standard and the vacuum fermentation is due to the lowered butanol toxicity in the fermenter because of the partial extraction of solvents from the fermentation broth in the latter case. When butanol concentration is maintained at a concentration lower than its inhibiting level in Case 2, the inlet sugar concentration is 2.7 times greater than the one in Case 1. The results are consistent with previous experimental results presented by Mariano et al., [28].

Even though the inlet sugar concentration is higher in Case 2, the sugar conversion is higher than in Case 1 due to the higher sugar consumption rates associated with lower butanol concentration in the fermenter. Since the butanol specific productivity is directly proportional to the dilution rate, the best 5% ranked Pareto-optimal solutions for Case 2 have higher dilution rates. In Cases 1 and 2, however, the butanol yield is relatively low at 0.18 g/g. Therefore, in Case 3 the average butanol concentration was replaced by the butanol yield as one of the three objective functions whereas the other two objective functions (butanol specific productivity and sugar conversion) remained unchanged. Also, based on the optimal decision variables in Case 2, the inlet feed sugar concentration was set at 150 g/L for Case 3. Figure 5 shows the plots of the three objective functions for Case 3. In general, the butanol yield decreased with increasing butanol specific productivity, and the best 5% ranked solutions (black region) was divided into two parts: a part with high butanol yield and low specific productivity, and the other with low butanol yield and high specific productivity. The best optimal solution for Case 3 is located at specific productivity of 0.74 $g_B/L/h/g_X$, butanol yield of 0.18 g/g, and sugar conversion of 95%. As it is depicted in Figure 5, except for the butanol yield value, the other two objective functions, namely the specific productivity and sugar conversion, have approximately reached their maximum values. A possible reason for low butanol yield of the best ranked solution is the low relative weight of butanol yield (only 20%) in the ranking algorithm when compared to other two objective functions (the relative weights are 40% for butanol specific productivity, and 40% for sugar conversion) in NFM (Table 2). Thus for economic reasons, a decision maker might change the relative weights to obtain a higher butanol yield at the expense of lower productivity.

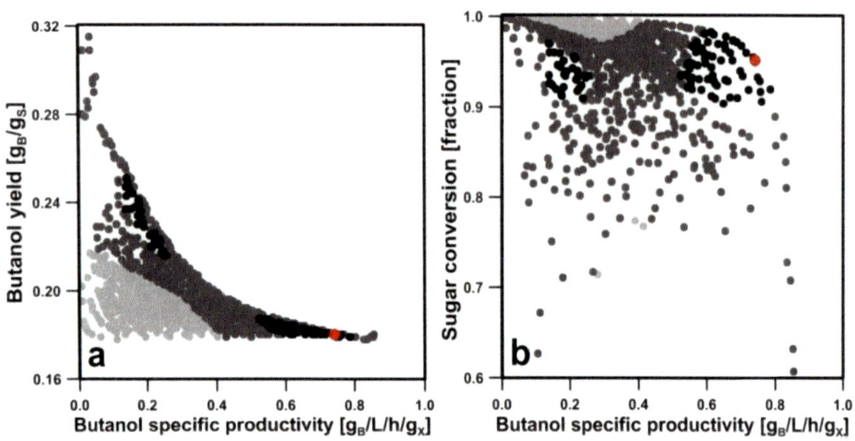

Figure 5. Plots of objective functions for Case 3. (a) Butanol yield versus butanol specific productivity; and (b) Sugar conversion versus butanol specific productivity.

The summary of results in Table 3 shows that the change of butanol average concentration to butanol yield as an objective function in Case 3 did not influence the yield value for the best solution in Case 3. Other calculated parameters in Case 3 are also very close to those in Case 2. Hence, changing one of the objective functions in Case 3 did not significantly affect the final results. In the first three cases, the specific productivity was used as one of the objective functions. The specific productivity is defined as the mass of butanol produced per unit volume and unit time divided by the biomass concentration. The motivation to divide the productivity (g/L/h) by the biomass concentration is to indirectly place a constraint on the biomass concentration. Thus, in Case 4, the specific productivity was replaced by the productivity as one of the three objectives whereas the other two objectives were the butanol yield and sugar conversion. The plots of the objective functions for Case 4 are presented in Figure 6. For this case study, the best Pareto-optimal solution was obtained at the highest productivity and a relatively higher value of the yield while sugar conversion remained close to that in the previous vacuum fermentation cases.

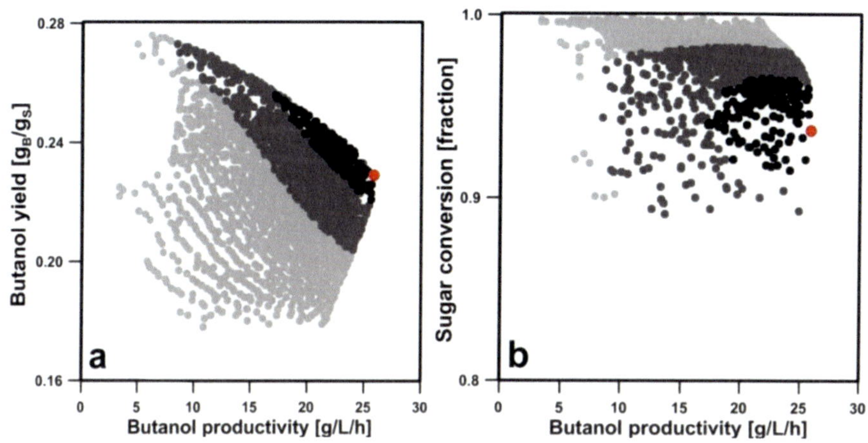

Figure 6. Plots of objective functions for Case 4. (a): Butanol yield versus butanol productivity; and (b): Sugar conversion versus butanol productivity.

In Case 4, the butanol productivity reached 26.4 g/L/h while the specific productivity decreased to 0.19 $g_B/L/h/g_X$. Using the butanol specific productivity as an objective function attempts to have the highest possible butanol productivity while placing a constraint on the biomass concentration in the fermenter. Since the butanol productivity is not divided by the biomass concentration, the biomass concentration in the fermenter can reach much higher values. Results of Figure 6 show that the butanol yield for the best solution in Case 4 is 0.23 g/g which represents an increase of 28% compared to those in Cases 2 and 3. In Case 4, the sugar conversion remained approximately the same as in Cases 2 and 3. In Case 4, the average butanol concentration for the optimal solution was 32.3 g/L which implies an improvement of 25% when compared to those in Cases 2 and 3. The average ABE concentration also increased from 41.1 g/L in Cases 2 and 3 to 56 g/L in Case 4. This is due to the fact that the concentrations of the fermentation intermediates (acetic acid and butyric acid) decreased in the fermenter in Case 4 (Table 3). Lower acid concentration in the fermenter is beneficial since decreased acid concentrations means more intermediates were converted into the solvents of interest. Moreover, the presence of acids in the fermentation broth contributes to higher inhibition levels. Biomass concentration in Case 4 is 139 g/L which is more than 5 times higher than that in other vacuum fermentation cases.

This significant increase in biomass concentration in Case 4 resulted in higher butanol average concentration and productivity. Nevertheless, in order to maintain high biomass concentrations within the fermenter, more substrate is needed. It is interesting to note that the evaporation flow rate was much less for Case 4 than for Cases 2 and 3, and yet the optimal point shows higher yield and productivity and similar sugar conversion. The dominating factor was in the definition of the productivity. With the specific productivity involving a soft constraint on the biomass, the biomass concentration was kept low and, as a result, the rate of formation of butanol was reduced. This study points to the importance of choosing carefully the objective criteria for the determination of the optimal operating point. It is important to note that the reason for choosing the specific productivity as an objective function in Cases 1-3 was to increase the fermentation efficiency by maintaining a low amount of microorganism in the fermenter. However, there is a trade-off between high butanol concentration and low biomass concentration. In Cases 2 and 3, the biomass retention factor was close to 1 (F_7 is very low compared to F_5) which implies that it could be possible to eliminate the cell retention unit. Removing the cell retention unit would lead to a cost reduction in the fermentation process. In this case, the biomass concentration would simply be controlled by the bleed flow rate F_5. The evaporation rate in Case 4 (50.8 m^3/h) decreased and the butanol concentration in the condensate increased from 36.83 g/L (in Cases 2 and 3) to 166 g/L (in Case 4). Thus, the energy consumption for solvent condensation in Case 4 can be reduced while the average butanol concentration was improved. High dilution rates resulted in higher productivities and higher evaporation rates. Consequently, for all three cases for vacuum fermentation (Cases 2-4), the dilution rate for the best Pareto-optimal solution is higher than 0.8 h^{-1}.

Table 3. Summary of decision variables and objective functions associated with the best Pareto-optimal solutions for Cases 1-4

Parameters	Case 1	Case 2	Case 3	Case 4
Butanol specific productivity (g_B/L.h.g_X)	0.42[a]	0.75[a]	0.741[a]	0.19
Butanol productivity (g/L.h)	5.8	20.6	20.6	26.4[a]
Butanol yield (g/g)	0.18	0.18	0.18[a]	0.23[a]
Butanol concentration (avg) (g/L)	8.18[a]	25.9[a]	25.71	32.3
ABE concentration (avg) (g/L)	13.27	41.21	41.01	56
Acetic acid concentration in the fermenter (g/L)	2.24	6.3	6.3	2.06
Butyric acid concentration in the fermenter (g/L)	2.03	5.8	5.8	2.7
Butanol concentration in the condensate (g/L)	-	36.83	36.83	166
Butanol concentration in the fermenter (g/L)	8.18	2.67	2.67	10.4
Inhibition factor	0.6	0.866	0.866	0.153
Sugar conversion (%)	83[a]	96[a]	95[a]	95[a]
Inlet feed sugar concentration (g/L)	55[b]	150[b]	150	150
Residual Sugar (g/L)	9.4	17.8	19.52	12.09
Cell retention ratio (m^3.h/m^3.h)	0.2[b]	0.98[b]	0.93[b]	0.05[b]
Biomass concentration (g/L)	12.9	27.4	26.9	139
Dilution rate (h^{-1})	0.63[b]	0.75[b]	0.8[b]	0.8[b]
Stream 3 flow rate (m^3/h)	-	220.4	214.3	50.8
Stream 5 flow rate (m^3/h)	56.8	96.5	97.9	13.46
Stream 7 flow rate (m^3/h)	227.2	2.3	7.8	256.1

[a] Objective functions
[b] Decision variables

CONCLUSION

The aim of this chapter was to illustrate the application of multi-objective optimization for the production of butanol in a continuous fermentation process with and without the incorporation of a vaccum separation unit. Three scenarios of the fermentation process coupled with a vacuum separation unit were analysed and compared to the optimization results obtained with the standard continuous fermentation. After performing process simulation, obtaining the Pareto domain for both configurations, and ranking the Pareto-optimal solutions with the Net Flow Method, the optimal operating region was identified. Higher butanol productivities and average butanol concentrations were observed in the vacuum fermentation compared to the standard continuous fermentation. However, butanol yield values were found to be fairly low in standard and vacuum fermentation cases. It was also shown that the biomass concentration in the fermenter has some impact on the butanol yield values. Moreover, higher sugar consumption in the vacuum fermentation was observed which will undoubtedly affect the butanol production economics. An economic analysis of all different scenarios is currently underway. Investigating three vacuum fermentation cases with a distinct set of objective functions in each case showed that the selection of the objective criteria can have a major impact on the determination of the optimal operating points.

REFERENCES

[1] Ezeji, T.C., Qureshi, N., & Blaschek, H.P. Bioproduction of butanol from biomass: from genes to bioreactors. *Current Opinion in Biotechnology*. 18: 220–227, 2007.

[2] Mariano, A.P., Costa, C.B., Angelis, D.F., Filho, F.M., Atala, D.I.P, Maciel, M.R.W., Filho, R.M. Optimization strategies based on sequential quadratic programming applied for a fermentation process for butanol production. *Appl Biochem Biotechnol*. 159, 366-381, 2009.

[3] Groot, W., Lans, R., & Luyben, K. Technologies for butanol recovery integrated with fermentations. Appl. Microbiol. Biotechnol. 32: 305-308, 1991.

[4] Groot, W., Oever, C., & Kossen, N. Pervaporation for simultaneous product recovery in the butanol/isopropanol batch fermentation. *Biotechnol. Lett*. 6: 709-714, 1984.

[5] Evans, P., & Wang, W. Enhancement of butanol fermentation by Clostridium *acetobutylicum* in the presence of decanololeyl alcohol mixed extractants. Appl. Environ. Microbiol. 54: 1662-1667, 1988.

[6] Roffler, S., Blanch W., & Wilke, W. In-situ recovery of butanol during fermentation. *Bioproc. Eng*. 2: 181-190, 1987.

[7] Bailey, J., & Ollis, D. Biochemical Engineering Fundamentals, 2nd Ed., McGraw-Hill, 1986.

[8] Ezeji, T.C., Qureshi, N., & Blaschek, H.P. Production of butanol by *Clostridium beijerinckii* BA101 and in-situ recovery by gas stripping. *World. J. Microbiol. Biotechnol*. 19: 595-603, 2003.

[9] Groot, W., Lans, R., & Luyben, K. Batch and continuous butanol fermentation with free cells: integration with product recovery by gas stripping. *Microbiol. Biotechnol*. 32: 305-308, 1989.

[10] Qureshi, N, & Blaschek, H. Recent advances in ABE fermentation: hyper-butanol producing *Clostridium beijerinckii* BA101. *J. Ind. Microb. Biotechnol*. 27: 287-291, 2001.

[11] Abdehagh, N., Tezel, T.H. & Thibault, J. Adsorbent screening for biobutanol separation by adsorption: kinetics, isotherms and competitive effect of other compounds. *Adsorption*. 19: 1263-1272, 2013.

[12] Garcia, A., Iannotti, E., & Fischer, J. Butanol fermentation liquor production and separation by reverse osmosis. *Biotechnol. Bioeng*. 28: 785–791, 1986.

[13] Cysewski, & G., Wilke, C. Rapid ethanol fermentations using vacuum and cell recycle. *Biotechnol. Bioeng*. 19: 1125-1143, 1977.

[14] Mariano, A.P., Costa, C.B., Angelis, D.F., Filho, F.M., Atala, D.I.P, Maciel, M.R.W., & Filho, R.M. Dynamics and control strategies for a butanol fermentation process. *Chem. Eng. Res. Des.*88: 562-571, 2010.

[15] Jones, D., & Woods, D. Acetone-butanol fermentation revisited. *Microbiol. Rev.* 50: 484-524, 1986.

[16] Mariano, A.P., Qureshi, H., Filho, R.M., & Ezeji, T. Assessment of in situ butanol recovery by vacuum during acetone butanol ethanol (ABE) fermentation. *J. Chem. Technol. Biotechnol.* 87: 334-340, 2012.

[17] Qureshi, N., Schripsema, J., Leinhardt, J., & Blaschek, H. Continuous solvent production by *Clostridium beijerinckii* BA101 immobilized by adsorption onto brick. *World. J. Microb. Biot.* 16: 377-382, 2000.

[18] Mulchandani, A., & Volesky, B. Modelling of the acetone-butanol fermentation with cell retention. *Can. J. Chem. Eng.* 64: 625-631, 1986.

[19] Monod, J. The growth of bacterial cultures. *Annu. Rev. Microbiol.* 3: 371-394, 1949.

[20] Bonilla-Petriciolet, A., & Rangaiah, G.P. *Introduction. In multi-objective optimization in chemical engineering: developments and applications* (Rangaiah, G. P., & Bonilla-Petriciolet, A., Ed.) John Wiley & Sons Ltd, Oxford, UK, pp. 3-16, 2013.

[21] Chankong, V. & Haimes, Y. *Multi-objective decision making theory and methodology.* North Holland series in system science and engineering. Mathews, USA, 1983.

[22] Doumpos, M., & Zopounidis, C. *Multi-criteria decision aid classification methods.* Applied Optimization, Kluwer Academic, 2002.

[23] Jaimes, A.L., & Coello, C.A. Multi-objective evolutionary algorithms: A review of the state-of-the-art and some of their applications in Chemical Engineering (Rangaiah, G.P.,ed.), *Multi-objective optimization: Techniques and applications in Chemical Engineering*, Singapore: World Scientific Publishing Co. Pte. Ltd., pp. 61-90, 2009.

[24] Halsall-Whitney, H., & Thibault, J. Multi-objective optimization for chemical processes and controller design: approximating and classifying the Pareto domain. *Comput. Chem. Eng.*, 30: 1155-1168, 2008.

[25] Thibault, J. Net Flow and rough sets: two methods for ranking the Pareto domain (Rangaiah, G.P., Ed.) *Multi-objective optimization: Techniques and applications in Chemical Engineering*, Singapore: World Scientific Publishing Co. Pte. Ltd., pp. 189-236, 2009.

[26] Thibault, J., Filho, R., Dias, M., Junqueira, T., Cavalett, O., Jesus, C., Rossell, C., & Bonomi, A. Simulation and multi-objective optimization of vacuum ethanol fermentation. *2nd International Conference on Simulation and Modeling Methodologies, Technologies and Applications*, 79-86, 2012

[27] Philips, J., & Humphrey, A. Microbial production of energy: liquid fuels. *Biotechnol. Bioprocess. Eng.* 1: 26-28, 1984.

[28] Mariano, A.P., Keshtkar, M., Atala, D.I.P., Filho, F., Maciel, M., Filho, R.M., & Stuart, P. Energy requirements for butanol recovery using the flash fermentation technology. *Energy Fuels.* 25: 2347-2355, 2011.

APPENDIX I

List of model constants [18]

Constants	Values
μ_m	0.35 [h^{-1}]
k_1	0.35[mmol/g/h]
k_2	0.59 [mmol/g.h]
k_3	89.0 [mmol/g]
k_4	0.45 [mmol/g/h]
k_5	0.11
k_6	0.5 [mmol/g/h]
k_7	0.39
k_8	0.19
k_9	0.9 [mmol/g.h]
k_{10}	0.22
k_{11}	0.059
k_{14}	2.0 [mmol/g/h]
k_{15}	2.2 [mmol/g/h]
k_s	21.14 [mmol/L]
k_{AA}	10.10 [mmol/L]
k_{BA}	15.9 [mmol/L]

In: Advances in Evolutionary Algorithms Research
Editor: Gregor Papa
ISBN: 978-1-63463-849-4
© 2015 Nova Science Publishers, Inc.

Chapter 5

PARALLEL IMPLEMENTATION OF SCALARIZATION APPROACHES FOR MULTI-OBJECTIVE OPTIMIZATION PROBLEMS

Eren Akça[1,*], Ökkeş Tolga Altınöz[2] and Asım Egemen Yılmaz[1,2]
[1]HAVELSAN A.S., Ankara, Turkey
[2]Ankara University, Electrical and Electronics Engineering, Ankara, Turkey

ABSTRACT

The aim of solving the multi-objective optimization problem is to find all possible trade-off solutions as accurate and as fast as possible. Since there is an infinite number of solutions desired to be obtained for continuous problems, this process is infeasible due to insufficient computation power. Hence, only a set of solutions can be collectable. From many possible multi-objective optimization architectures, the solution set can be formed with the simplest approach, which is the scalarization approach. The scalarization approaches are only the functions that take the evaluation values of each objective as parameters of the function, and convert the multi-objective optimization problem into a single objective problem. The idea of scalarization is simple, but the necessity of running multiple single objective algorithms for each possible solution makes this approach time consuming when compared to other multi-objective approaches. However, since the single objective algorithms are needed to implement each possible solution candidate on objective space without sharing any knowledge between each run, the scalarization can easily parallelize for faster execution. Hence, in this chapter, the parallel implementation of scalarization approach is explained in details, and the performance of the algorithm is presented with well-known benchmark problems.

Keywords: Multi-objective optimization, parallel implementation, CUDA, GPU, particle swarm optimization

* Corresponding author: HAVELSAN A.S., Ankara, Turkey, Email: eren.akca@havelsan.com.tr.

INTRODUCTION

The problem for determining the best possible solution set with respect to multiple objectives is referred to as a multi-objective (MO) optimization problem. There are many approaches for the solution of these kinds of problems. The most straightforward approach, the so-called "scalarization" or "aggregation", is based on combining the objectives in order to obtain a single-objective [1].

The solution of the MO optimization problem is a set that contains trade-off solutions [2]. On the other hand, the problem instance defined via the scalarization technique yields a single solution. In order to find another trade-off solution, the parameters throughout the scalarization process shall be varied, and the resulting problem instance (which is different than the previous one) shall be solved. In the particular case in which the problem is bi-objective (with the objective functions f_1 and f_2) and the weighted-sum method is applied, the aggregated objective function is $w_1f_1+(1-w_1)f_2$, where the weight w_1 is a real number between 0 and 1. By varying this weight, a new single-objective problem instance (and a new solution) is obtained. Obviously, for this simple case, the parameter setup of the "scalarization scheme" consists of only the weight w_1. For a higher number of objectives and different scalarization techniques, the scalarization scheme might address a parameter set with multiple elements.

Scalarization techniques were popular in 1980s and early 1990s, prior to the development of powerful multi-objective optimization algorithms such as the Non-Dominated Sorting Genetic Algorithm (NSGA) [3], NSGA-II [4] or Vector Evaluated Genetic Algorithm (VEGA) [5], etc. After the development of these powerful and successful multi-objective optimization algorithms, scalarization techniques were considered to be old-fashioned, and they were abandoned. By the time, especially after the evolution and rapid development of multi-core architectures in 2000s, researchers have started to reconsider and revisit the scalarization techniques since these techniques are usually suitable for parallelization when carefully implemented.

In the last decade, engineers have applied parallelization techniques and libraries in order to decrease the cost of a study/project and the execution time of the parallelized algorithms. Currently, two major parallelization techniques can be mentioned:

a) Distributed computing [6] via the Message passing Interface (MPI), in which the algorithm is divided/duplicated into sub-codes, and then these codes transferred to the distributed computational units. Each unit executes relatively tiny piece of the code, then they transfer the response to the main computer. There is not any restriction related to the distance between computation units, so that any unit could be installed elsewhere (e.g., even in another country and/or continent),
b) Multicore processing [7]; for which parallel processing units are on a single device such as personal computer, workstation or server. Then the code is executed on different cores of on-board devices like Central Processing Units (CPUs) and/or General Purpose Graphic Processing Units (GPUs).

There are two main architectures (CPU and GPU) in a personal computer device. The tasks assigned to these two units differ from each other. The CPU is composed of only a few number of very fast cores, which have the ability to execute relatively complex operations.

On the other hand, GPU consists of a large number of slow cores that are able to execute fundamental operations. When considering the scalarization approach for multi-objective optimization as a parallelization problem, it is desired to execute the single objective optimization algorithm many times. Therefore, the number of parallel execution units is crucial for this kind of problem.

In this chapter, with a similar motivation, we demonstrate how these approaches can be parallelized and implemented on the GPU via the Compute Unified Device Architecture (CUDA) framework.

PARALLELIZATION

Fundamentals of Parallel Programming with CUDA

The researchers familiar with the C/C++ programming language used to desire a programming language or framework letting them write parallel codes easily. For this purpose in 2007, NVidia [8] introduced a software framework called CUDA. By means of this, a sequential function code can be converted to a parallel kernel by using the libraries and some prefix expressions. By this way, the programmers do not need to learn a new programming language. They are able to use their previous know-how related to C/C++, and they can enhance this knowledge with some basic expressions introduced by CUDA. However, without the knowledge about the CUDA software and the parallel architecture hardware, it is not possible to write efficient codes. CUDA programming begins with the division of the architectures. It defines the CPU as a host and the GPU as a device. The parallel programming actually is the assignment of duties to parallel structure and collection of the results by the CPU. In summary, the codes are written for CPU on C/C++ environment, and these codes include some parallel structures. A host executes these codes, and a host commands device for the executed code. When the device executes the code, the host waits until the job is finished, then a new parallel duty can be assigned, or the host can collect results from the finished job. Thus, a device becomes a parallel computation unit. Hence, parallel computing relies on the data movement between host and device. Although both host and device are very fast computation units, the data bus is slower. Therefore, in order to write an efficient program, the programmer must keep his/her code for minimum data transfer between the host and the device. The GPU has stream multiprocessors (SMs). Each SM has 8 stream processors (SPs), also known as cores, and each core has a number of threads. In Tesla architecture there are 240 SPs, and on each SP has 128 threads, which is the kernel execution unit. The bodies of threads are called groups. The groups are performed concurrently with respect to the core size. If the GPU architecture has two cores, then two blocks of threads are executed simultaneously. If it has four cores, then four blocks are executed concurrently. Host and device communicate via data movement. The host moves data to the memory of the GPU board. This memory is called global memory, with access from all threads and the host. The host can also access constant and texture memories. However, it cannot access shared memory, which is a divided structure assigned for every block. The threads within the block can access their own shared memory. The communication of the shared memory is faster than the global memory. Hence, a parallel code must contain data transfers to shared memory more often, instead of global memory. In this chapter, random numbers are needed to execute the algorithm. Hence, instead of the *rand*() function of the C/C++ environment, CURAND library of the CUDA pack has been employed. In addition, the CUDA Event is preferred for accurate measurement of the execution time.

The Scalarization Approach: Weighted Sum Example

As stated in the previous section, the main aim in a multi-objective optimization problem is to find a set of trade-off solutions. The optimality of a particular solution is determined via the definition of "domination" in the Pareto space. In Figure 1, the pictorial descriptions of the domination and the set of non-dominated solutions (i.e., the Pareto Front) are given for a simple bi-objective problem.

In order to obtain a set of solutions for a bi-objective optimization problem via the weighted-sum method (for which the aggregated objective function $w_1f_1+(1-w_1)f_2$ is constructed), the weight w1 shall be varied between 0 and 1 in a systematical manner; and a new solution shall be found for each value of w_1. Even though this approach seems to be simple and well-working, it fails especially when the Pareto front is concave (totally or between two particular points in the Pareto Space). In order to illustrate this, let us try to understand the main idea beneath the weighted-sum approach. As seen in Figure 2, the aggregated objective function $w_1f_1+(1-w_1)f_2$ corresponds to a line in the Pareto space (particularly the f_1f_2 plane). Throughout the optimization process, in which $c= w_1f_1+(1-w_1)f_2$ is minimized, the corresponding line is shifted by preserving its slope. Eventually, the solution obtained is nothing but the intersection of the corresponding line with the Pareto front curve (which is considered to be convex, for the time being) as seen in Figure 3.

As seen in Figure 2, the slope of the line is determined by the weight, and altering this parameter will yield a different line. As seen in Figure 3, altering the weight would yield a different solution (in case the Pareto front is convex).

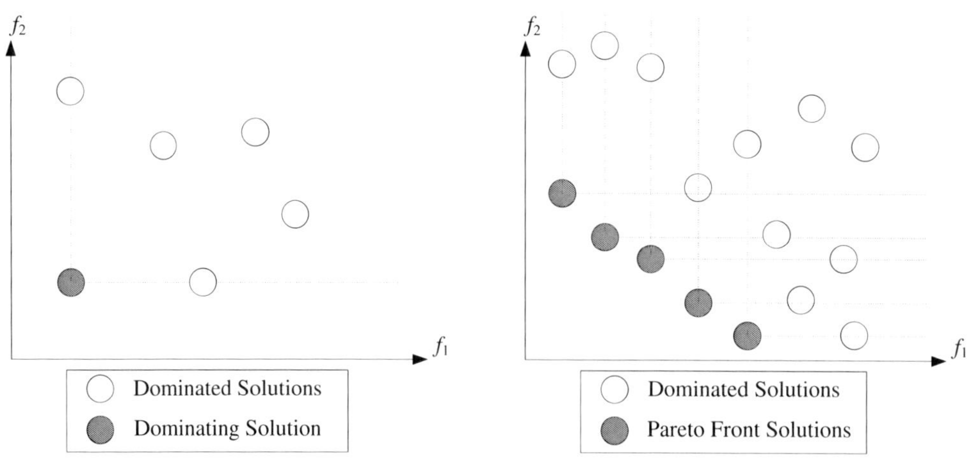

Figure 1. Pictorial descriptions of domination and the Pareto Front.

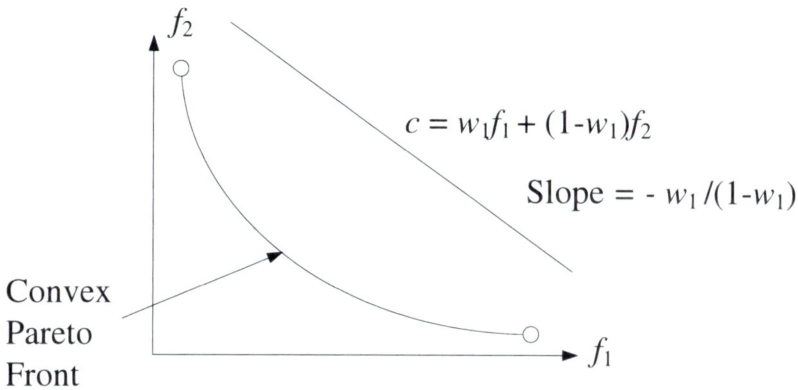

Figure 2. Pictorial description of the solution via the weighted sum approach for convex Pareto Front.

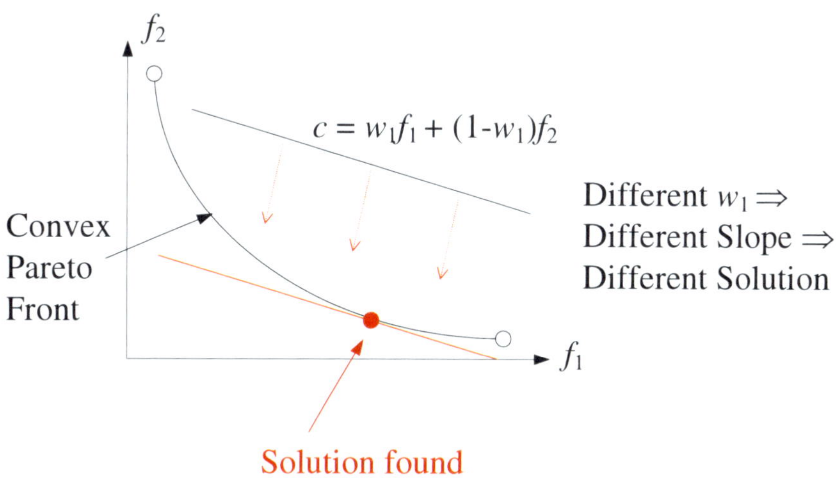

Figure 3. Pictorial description of how different solutions can be found by altering the weight in the weighted sum approach for convex Pareto Front.

On the other hand, let us consider the case for which the Pareto front is concave between two points A and B as seen in Figure 4. In this case, the point B becomes a solution. In case the weight is altered as seen in Figure 5, the point A is found as an alternative solution. Unfortunately, in such a case, even if the weight is altered in its whole range, no points on the Pareto front other than A and B can be found by this approach [9]. Without a topological proof, this can be observed pictorially by intersecting different-slope lines with this concave Pareto front in Figures 4 and 5.

Since it is impossible to know whether the Pareto front is convex or concave in real life problems, the weighted-sum approach cannot be applied confidently. Hence, in this chapter, we consider other well-known scalarization methods. The next sub-section is devoted to the description of this method.

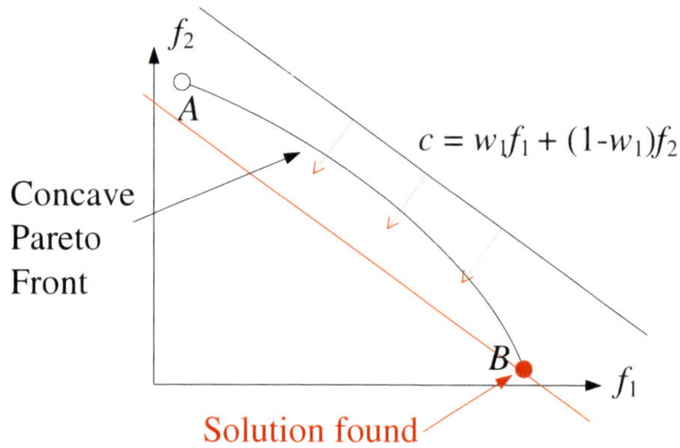

Figure 4. Pictorial description of the solution via the weighted sum approach for concave Pareto Front (where the point B is found as the solution).

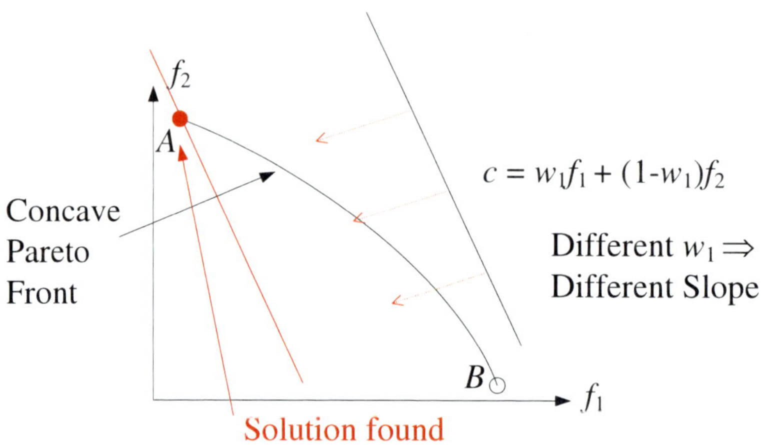

Figure 5. Pictorial description of the solution by altering the weight in the weighted sum approach for concave Pareto Front (where the point A is found as the alternative solution).

Parallel CUDA Implementation of the Scalarization Approach

The main idea of our parallel implementation throughout this chapter is illustrated in Figure 6. Each scalarization scheme is handled in a separate thread; after the relevant solutions are obtained, they are gathered in a centralized manner to constitute the Pareto front from which the human decision maker picks a solution according to his/her needs. This approach ensures that the number of solutions that can be found in parallel is limited by the capability of the GPU card used. If the problem is a mission-planning problem as in our case, the two objectives might be "minimizing the overall mission completion time" and "minimizing the overall mission risk"; and the Pareto front is a plethora of various alternative mission plans with different overall completion time and risk values. In this case, the planner (or the commander) will pick up a solution (i.e., a mission plan to be executed) by using his/her own initiative. Regardless of the choice, it will be certain that the particular picked solution will be non-dominated.

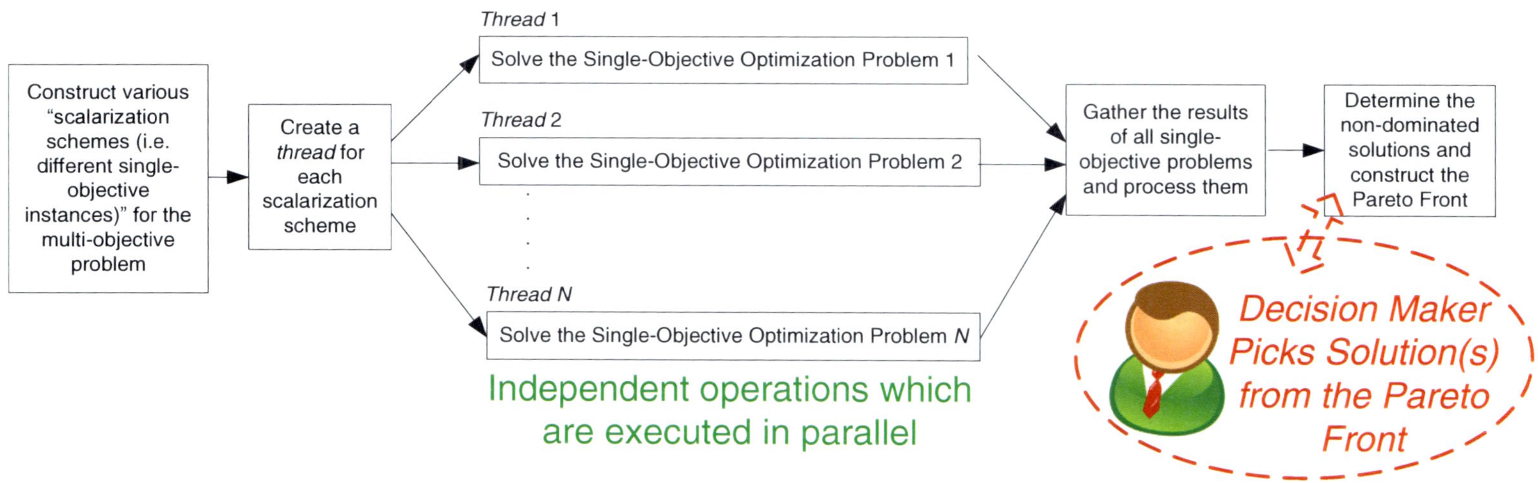

Figure 6. Pictorial description of the parallel CUDA implementation of the desirability-function based approach.

As a part of this chapter, we implemented Particle Swarm Optimization [10] as a single objective optimization algorithm. The parallel CUDA implementation was compared to the sequential code.

It was seen that both implementations (sequential and parallel) were able to find similar solutions but in different elapsed times. As seen in Figure 7, if the number of Pareto front solutions increases, the advantage of the parallel CUDA appears dramatically.

Figure 7 gives the performance comparison of different GPU architectures against CPU sequential implementation. When the results are investigated for the professional type GPU architectures, the number of solutions has a slightly lower effect on execution time. However, for a mobile GPU, the difference between a good CPU is almost none. However, it is also believed that, instead of expensive and advanced CPU, the researcher can reach almost same performance with a low-level mobile GPU device. Nevertheless, the researcher must consider the fact that the codes are run sequentially on the CPU. It is also possible to convert sequential codes to run on different cores of the CPU.

Overall, these results show how efficient the parallel CUDA implementation will be in case the decision maker in a multi-objective optimization problem requires numerous Pareto solutions.

Implementation

Fundamentals of Scalarization Methods

Generally a standard multi-objective optimization problem can be formulated as follows:

$$\min \quad F(\bar{x}) = \{f_1(\bar{x}), f_2(\bar{x}), \ldots, f_m(\bar{x})\}$$

Where there are m objectives, which should be minimized. Any solution candidate is represented as a decision variable $\bar{x} = \{x_1, x_2, \ldots, x_n\}$, and n is the dimension of the problem. The task of the multi-objective optimization algorithm is to find an approximation of the Pareto optimal set, which is defined as the set of all optimal points. A Pareto optimal solution of the multi-objective problem is a solution such that there is no other solution that gives better result for all objectives.

The weighted sum method is the oldest method for scalarization approach. The definition of the weighted sum ([11],[12]) method is mathematically displayed as:

$$f_{eq}(\bar{x}) = \sum_{i=1}^{m} w_i f_i(\bar{x})$$

where w_i is the weight for each objective i and the sum of weights equals to one. If the shape of Pareto front is convex (for minimization problems), this approach can be applied to such problems.

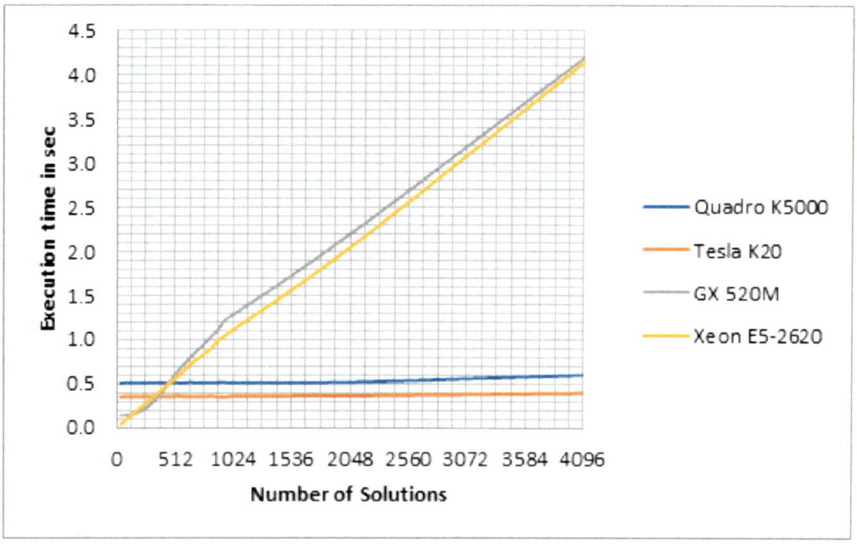

Figure 7. Comparison of the sequential and the parallel CUDA implementations.

The Tchebycheff-method is defined to find every Pareto-optimal solution regardless of the shape of the problem on objective space, either convex or concave. Tchebycheff method is originally based on L_P weighted of multiple objectives, which are defined as:

$$f_{eq}(\bar{x}) = \left(\sum_{i=1}^{m} w_i \left| f_i(\bar{x}) - u_i \right|^p \right)^{1/p}$$

where (similarly) w_i's are the weights and sum of them equals to one, and u is the ideal point which corresponds to the minimum value of each objective, namely $u_i = \min(f_i(x))$. The L_2 scalarization method and L-inf (also known as generalized Tchebycheff) [13] are respectively defined as:

$$f_{eq}(\bar{x}) = \left(\sum_{i=1}^{m} w_i \left| f_i(\bar{x}) - u_i \right|^2 \right)^{1/2}$$

$$f_{eq}(\bar{x}) = \max\left(w_i \left| f_i(\bar{x}) - u_i \right| \right)$$

In general cases, due to the computation power necessity to obtain ideal point at the each execution, the formulation is changed as:

$$f_{eq}(\bar{x}) = \max\left(w_i \left| f_i(\bar{x}) \right| \right)$$

In this chapter, by considering these three well-known scalarization methods, the performance of parallel algorithm with respect to execution time is demonstrated on benchmark functions. In the next section, benchmark problems are defined and explained.

Benchmark Problems

In this chapter, ten benchmark problems with different complexity and Pareto shape are selected to present the performance of the methods. Table I gives the mathematical formulation of the problems. The performance comparison is performed not only on the accuracy of the results, but also, more importantly, on the execution time. As given in Table 1 the complexity of the benchmark problems is given from the simplest to problems that are more complex. The reason behind is that as the complexity of the function increases, the single processors have to accomplish much more calculations. And since the single processors on a GPU have a lower capacity than CPU, it will be a good comparison not only for the number of solutions in solution space, but also for the problem complexity.
Table I presents three columns. The first column gives the names of benchmark problems. The reader can access some information about the function by searching with a presented function name. Second column is for the mathematical formulation of the function. As the order of row increases, the complexity of the function also increases. The last column defines the range of the decision variables.

Results and Discussions

In Figure 7 the execution speed of the parallel code against the sequential code is demonstrated for different GPU architectures. In this section, the results obtained from parallel execution of different scalarization methods are graphically demonstrated and discussed.

Seven benchmark problems are considered for three different scalarization methods. Each single objective problem was solved with the particle swarm optimization algorithm. The parameters of the algorithm were selected as follows;

Number of members in population = 64
Maximum number of iterations = 100 (for ZDT problems) and 1000 (for UF problems)
$c_1 \& c_2 = 1.49$
$k = 0.78$
Problem Dimension = 10 (for ZDT) and 30 (for UF)

Two types of problem are considered in this chapter. The ZDT problems are relatively simple and have the least complex mathematical formulations. However, the shape of their Pareto front is convex, concave and discrete. Since the ZDT presents simple calculations, another class of complex benchmark problems is needed. Therefore, UF functions are employed for this task.

Figure 8 gives the graphical distribution of the solutions on objective space for different scalarization methods. The weighted sum method finds the solution especially concentrated on the upper side (f_2 axis) of objective space. All scalarization approaches can find the Pareto front.

Table I. Benchmark Problems

Func. Name	Mathematical Description	Decision Variable Range
ZDT1	$f_1(x) = x_1, g = 1 + \frac{9}{n-1}\sum_{i=2}^{n} x_i, f_2(x) = g\left(1 - \sqrt{\frac{f_1}{g}}\right)$	$0 \le x_i \le 1$
ZDT2	$f_1(x) = x_1, g = 1 + \frac{9}{n-1}\sum_{i=2}^{n} x_i, f_2(x) = g\left(1 - \left(\frac{f_1}{g}\right)^2\right)$	$0 \le x_i \le 1$
ZDT3	$f_1(x) = x_1 \quad g = 1 + \frac{9}{n-1}\sum_{i=2}^{n} x_i$ $f_2(x) = g\left(1 - \sqrt{\frac{f_1}{g}} - \frac{x_1}{g}\sin(10\pi x_1)\right)$	$0 \le x_i \le 1$
UF1	$f_1(x) = x_1 + \frac{2}{\lvert J_1\rvert}\sum_{i\in J_1}\left[x_i - \sin\left(6\pi x_1 + \frac{i\pi}{n}\right)\right]^2$ $f_2(x) = 1 - \sqrt{x_1} + \frac{2}{\lvert J_2\rvert}\sum_{i\in J_2}\left[x_i - \sin\left(6\pi x_1 + \frac{i\pi}{n}\right)\right]^2$ $J_1 = \{i \mid i \text{ is odd and } 2 \le i \le n\}, J_2 = \{i \mid i \text{ is even and } 2 \le i \le n\}$	$0 \le x_1 \le 1$ $-1 \le x_{i-1} \le 1$
UF2	$f_1(x) = x_1 + \frac{2}{\lvert J_1\rvert}\sum_{i\in J_1}[y_i]^2, f_2(x) = 1 - \sqrt{x_1} + \frac{2}{\lvert J_2\rvert}\sum_{i\in J_2}[y_i]^2$ $yi = \begin{cases} xi - \left[0.3x_1^2\cos\left(24\pi x_1 + \frac{4i\pi}{n}\right) + 0.6x_1\right]\cos\left(6\pi x_1 + \frac{i\pi}{n}\right) & i \in J_1 \\ xi - \left[0.3x_1^2\cos\left(24\pi x_1 + \frac{4i\pi}{n}\right) + 0.6x_1\right]\sin\left(6\pi x_1 + \frac{i\pi}{n}\right) & i \in J_2 \end{cases}$	$0 \le x_1 \le 1$ $-1 \le x_{i-1} \le 1$
UF3	$f_1(x) = x_1 + \frac{2}{\lvert J_1\rvert}\left(\left[4\sum_{i\in J_1} y_i^2\right] - \left[2\prod_{i\in J_1}\cos\left(\frac{20y_i\pi}{\sqrt{i}}\right)\right] + 2\right)$ $f_2(x) = 1 - \sqrt{x_1} + \frac{2}{\lvert J_2\rvert}\left(\left[4\sum_{i\in J_2} y_i^2\right] - \left[2\prod_{i\in J_2}\cos\left(\frac{20y_i\pi}{\sqrt{i}}\right)\right] + 2\right)$ $y_i = x_i - x_1^{\left(0.5\left(1+\frac{3(i-2)}{n-2}\right)\right)}$	$0 \le x_i \le 1$

Table I. (Continued)

Func. Name	Mathematical Description	Decision Variable Range
UF4	$f_1(x) = x_1 + \frac{2}{\lvert J_1 \rvert}\sum_{i\in J_1} h[y_i]$, $f_2(x) = 1-(x_1)^2 + \frac{2}{\lvert J_2 \rvert}\sum_{i\in J_2} h[y_i]$ $y_i = x_i - \sin\left(6\pi x_1 + \frac{i\pi}{n}\right), h[t] = \frac{t}{1+e^{2t}}$	$0 \le x_1 \le 1$ $-2 \le x_{i-1} \le 2$

For Figure 9, which is given for ZDT2 problem, as expected, the weighted sum method only determines the boundaries of the Pareto front since the shape of the problem is concave. Also L_2 method presents solution on Pareto front with and unequally spaced solutions. Among them L_{inf} is the best approach for this problem, since it performs almost equally spaced solutions.

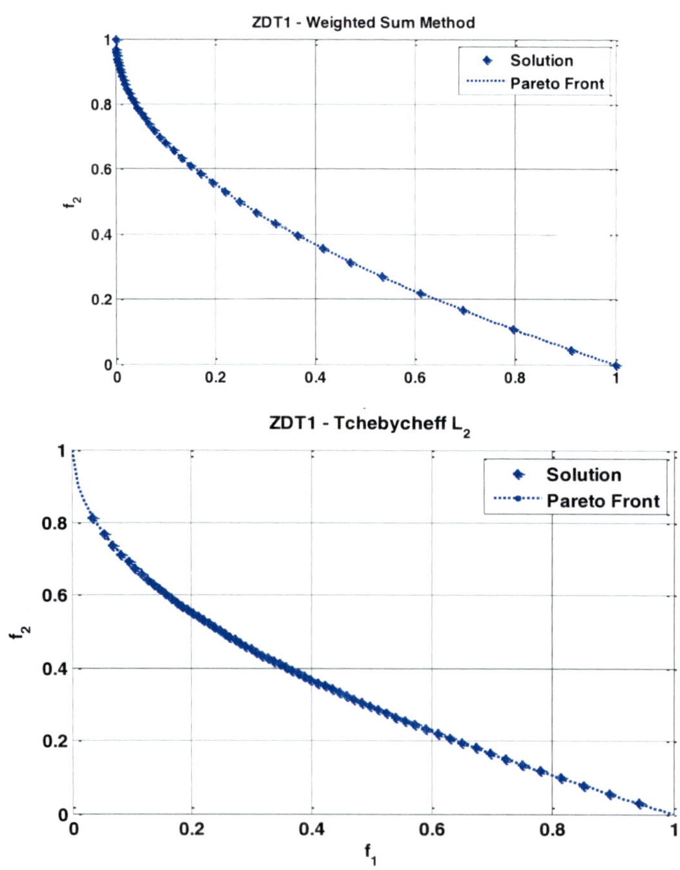

Figure 8. (Continued).

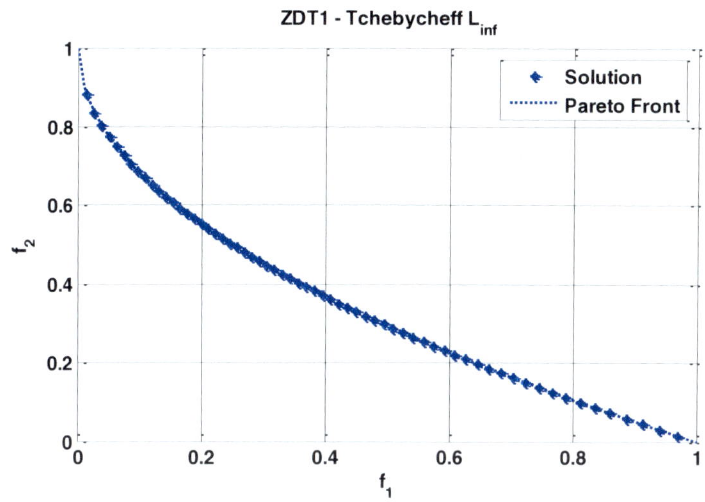

Figure 8. Comparison of the scalarization approaches on ZDT1 function.

Figure 10 displays the results of scalarization approaches on ZDT3 problem such that the shape of Pareto front is in a discrete manner when compared with the shapes of the other benchmark problems. The weighted sum method presents that at least one solution can be detected for each separate part of Pareto front. Among all scalarization approaches, only the weighted sum is able to find a solution at each part of the discrete Pareto front. Even though L_2 and L_{inf} show worse performance than the weighted sum with respect to distribution of the solutions on Pareto front, the performance of L_2 and L_{inf} can be enhanced with the calculation of the ideal vector at each iteration. When the graphical description of L_{inf} is investigated, it is seen than since the (0,0) is taken as an ideal point of this chapter, only the upper side of the Pareto front (upper side of f_2=0 line) is detected.

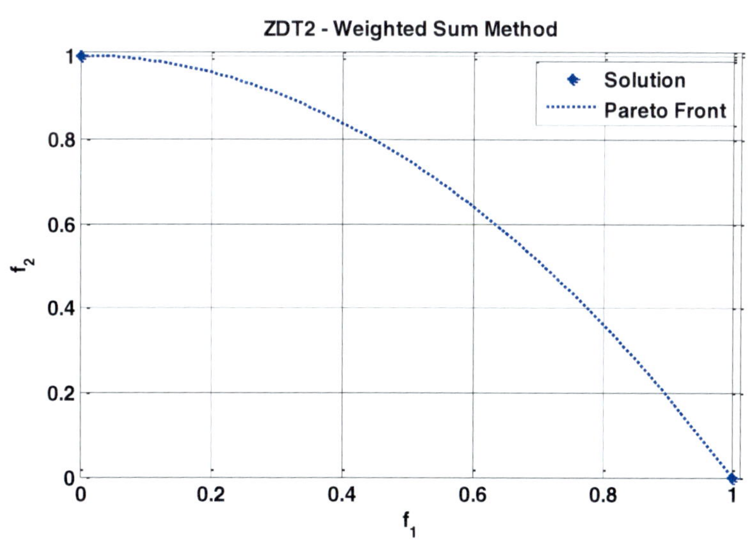

Figure 9. (Continued).

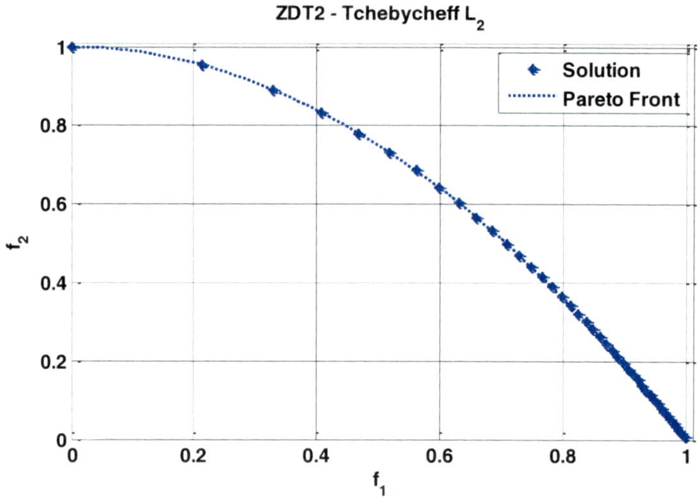

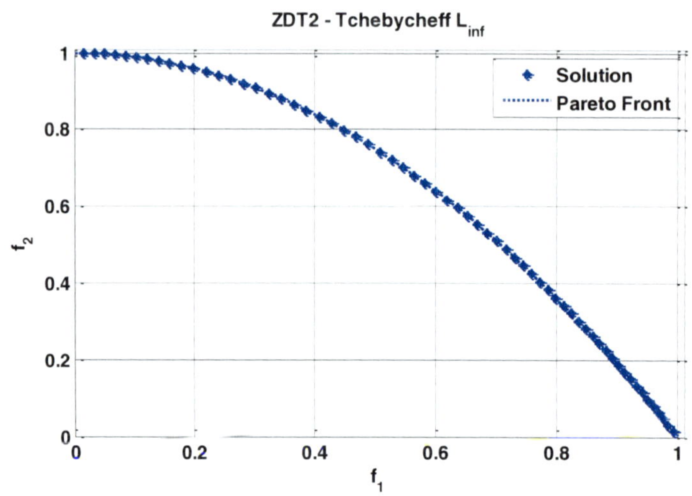

Figure 9. Comparison of the scalarization approaches on ZDT2 function.

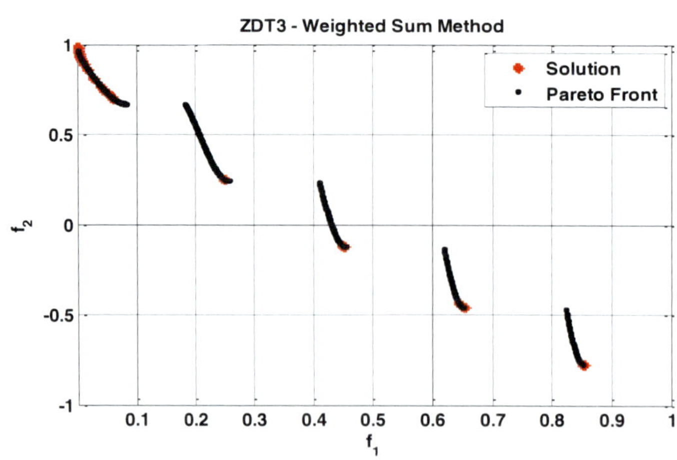

Figure 10. (Continued).

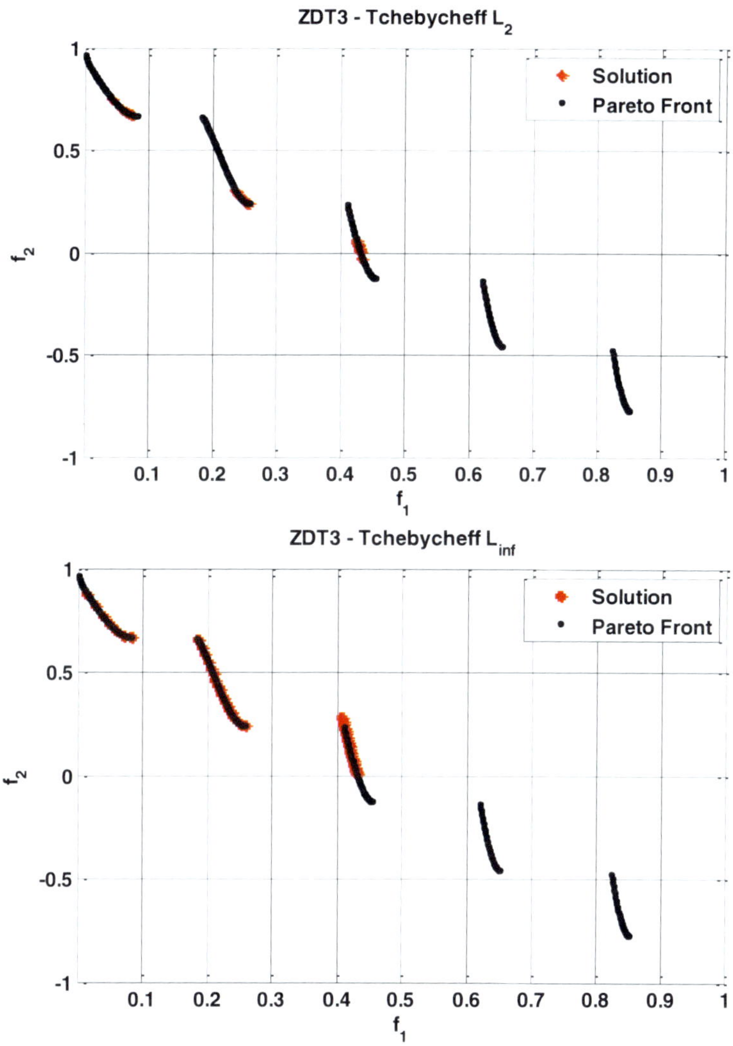

Figure 10. Comparison of the scalarization approaches on ZDT3 function.

Until this point, only three multi-objective benchmark problems with simple mathematical formulation are evaluated with a parallel particle swarm optimization. The results prove the advantages and disadvantages of the scalarization approaches considered in this chapter. From now on, four multi-objective optimization algorithms, which have relatively complex mathematical calculations, will be discussed. Since the complexity and dimension of the benchmark problems increase with UF functions, the maximum number of iterations is increased from 100 to 1000. In addition, the dimension of problem increases from 10 to 30.

The complexity of the problem became the cause for unexpected results for UF1 for given single objective parameters such as the number of members in population and the maximum number of function evaluations. At its current state, the performance of the weighted sum method outperforms against L_2 and L_{inf} methods. According to the results, none of the approaches can reach to Pareto front.

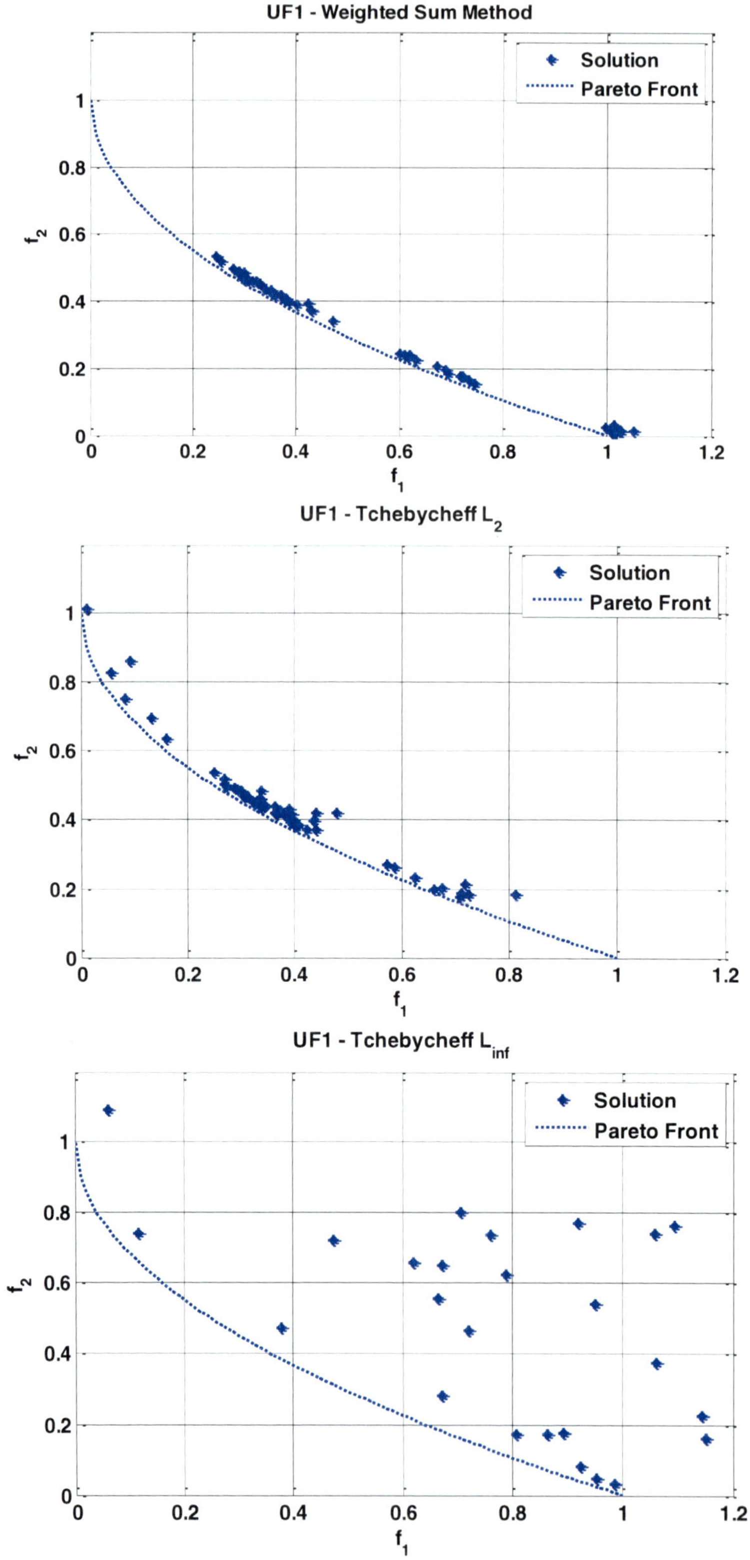

Figure 11. Comparison of the scalarization approaches on UF1 function.

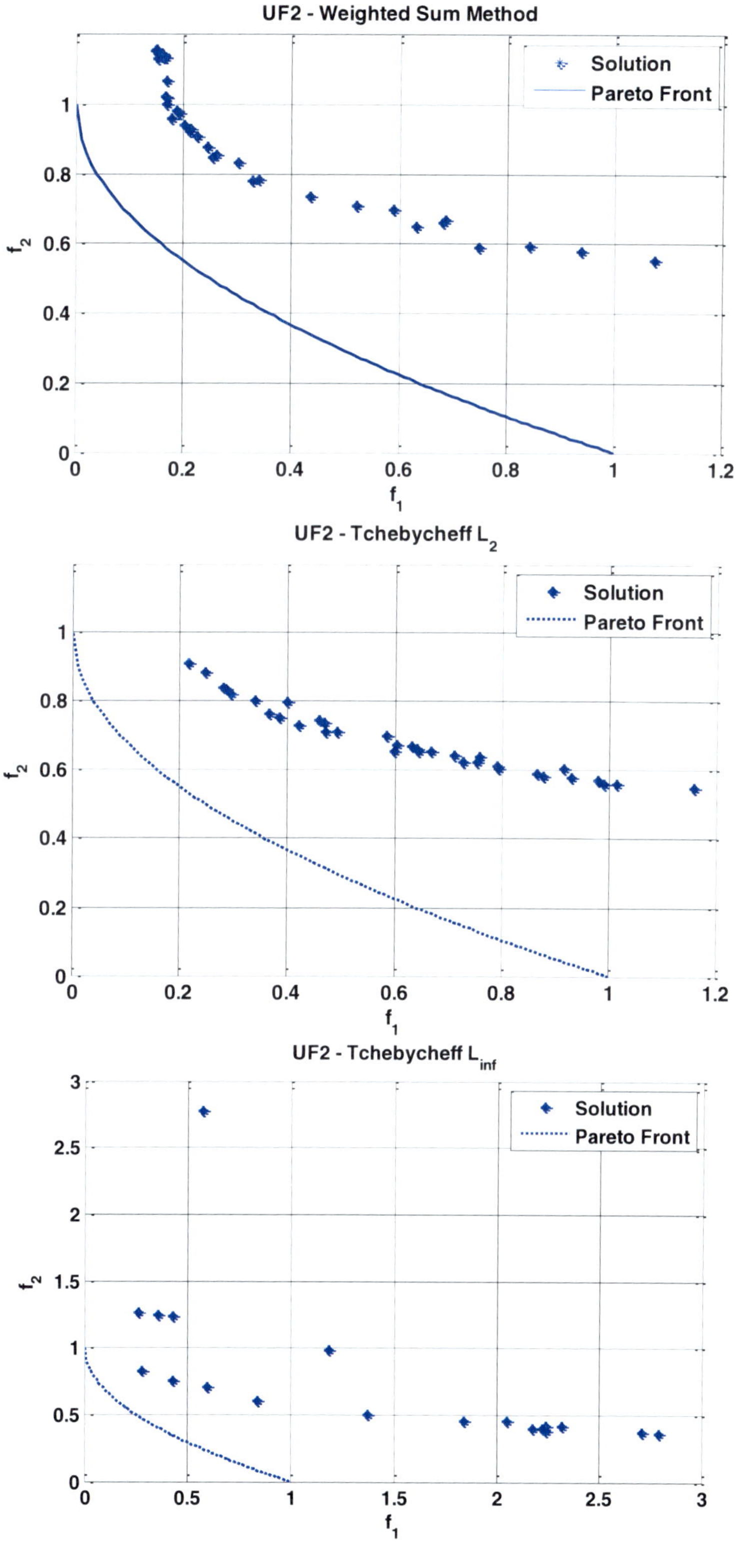

Figure 12. Comparison of the scalarization approaches on UF2 function.

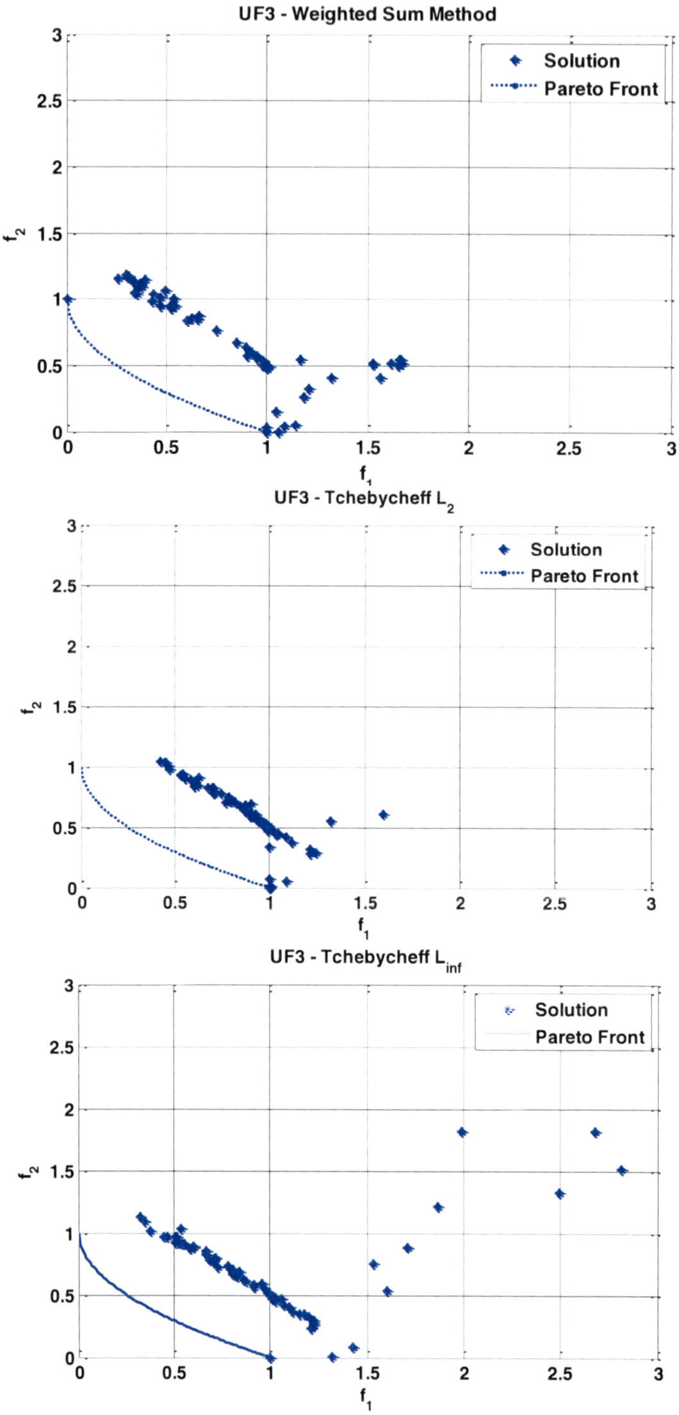

Figure 13. Comparison of the scalarization approaches on UF3 function.

Similar to the results concluded from UF1 function, the performance of scalarization approaches for UF2 can be evaluated the same as for UF1. However, the performances of these approaches differ for both UF3 and UF4. For all UF benchmark problems, it is certain that none of these approaches can represent Pareto front.

As seen in Figure 13, which is given for representing the performance of scalarization approaches for UF3, none of the approaches can find Pareto front and the performance of them is almost the same.

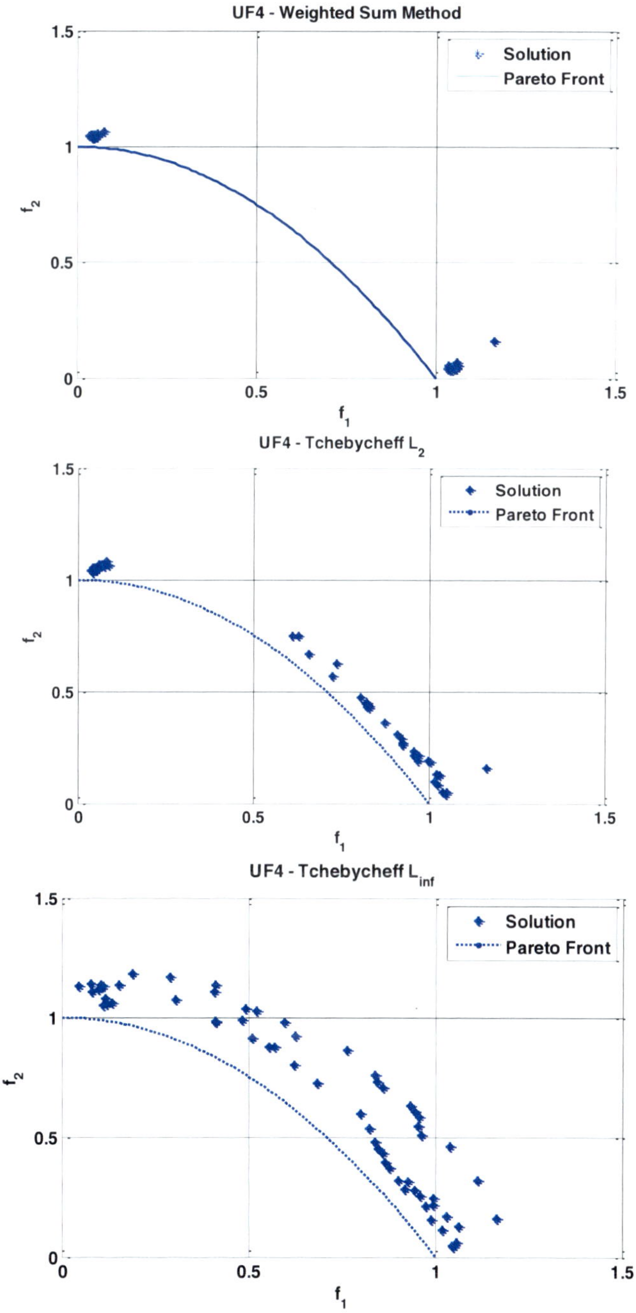

Figure 14. Comparison of the scalarization approaches on UF4 function.

For UF4, which has the concave shaped Pareto front, the weighted sum method presents almost the same performance for ZDT2. However, it is not possible to mention about L_2 and L_{inf} with the same manner. L_2 and L_{inf} could not detect Pareto front, also L_{inf} gives the layered results such that two layers of solutions are graphically demonstrated on objective space. If non-dominated search algorithms run as a post-program of the system, the upper layer solutions are deleted from solution set.

CONCLUSION

In this chapter, scalarization approaches are converted to a parallel form and they are implemented on the GPU board. More specifically, the computation of the objective and the fitness functions for the individuals in the particle swarm optimization can perform concurrently on GPUs. The impact of such a modification in the implementation might not be drastic for the simple benchmark problems (ZDT) since they usually consist of computationally cheap functions. But in case of computationally expensive functions (UF), the advantage of utilization of the streams is expected to be quite dramatic.

Finally, in this chapter we have demonstrated that it is possible to achieve up to 8-16 times faster GPU implementations for the multi-objective problems via a careful and intelligent CUDA implementation. Further improvements in the implementation shall be made in the near future. Moreover, we have verified the claims in [10] and demonstrated the efficiency of the proposed approach.

ACKNOWLEDGMENT

This chapter was made possible by grants from the Turkish Ministry of Science, Industry and Technology (Industrial Thesis – San-Tez Programme; with Grant Nr. 01568.STZ.2012-2) and the Scientific and Technological Research Council of Turkey - TÜBİTAK (with Grant Nr. 112E168). The authors would like to express their gratitude to these institutions for their support.

REFERENCES

[1] Marler, R; Arora, S. "Transformation methods for multi-objective optimization," Engineering Optimization, vol. 37, no. 1, 551-569, 2009.

[2] Trautmann, H; Mehmen, J. "Preference-based Pareto optimization in certain and noisy environments," Engineering Optimization, vol. 41, no. 1, 23-38, 2009.

[3] Srinivas, N; Deb, K. "Multi-Objective function optimization using non-dominated sorting genetic algorithms," Evolutionary Computation, vol. 2, no. 3, 221–248, 1995.

[4] Deb, K; Pratap, A; Agarwal, S; Meyarivan, T. "A fast and elitist multi-objective genetic algorithm: NSGA-II," IEEE Transactions on Evolutionary Computation, vol. 6, no. 2, 182–97, 2002.

[5] Schaffer, JD. "Multiple objective optimization with vector evaluated genetic algorithms," In: Proceedings of the international conference on genetic algorithm and their applications, 93-100, 1985.
[6] Arora, S; Barak, B. Computational Complexity – A Modern Approach, Cambridge, 2009.
[7] Altinoz, OT; Yilmaz, AE; Ciuprina, G. "Comparison of particle swarm optimization on various GPUs designed for add-on graphic boards," International Symposium on Computing in Science and Engineering, 297-301, 2013.
[8] NVIDIA Corporation, "CUDA dynamic parallelism programming," NVIDIA, 2012.
[9] Burachik, RS; Kaya, CY; Rizvi, MM. "A new scalarization technique to approximate Pareto fronts of problems with disconnected feasible sets," Journal of Optimization Theory and Applications, vol. 162, no. 2, 428-446, 2014.
[10] Altinoz, OT; Yilmaz, AE; Ciuprina, G. "A Multi-objective Optimization Approach via Systematical Modification of the Desirability Function Shapes," in Proc. 8th International Symposium on Advanced Topics in Electrical Engineering, 1-6, 2013.
[11] Gass, S; Saaty, T. "The Computational Algorithm for the Parametric Objective Function," Naval Research Logistics Quarterly, vol. 2, no. 2, 39–45, 1955.
[12] Zadeh, L. "Optimality and Non-Scalar-Valued Performance Criteria," IEEE Transactions on Automatic Control, vol. 8, no. 8, 59–60, 1963.
[13] Miettinen, K. Nonlinear Multi-objective Optimization. Norwell, MA, Kluwer, 1999.

In: Advances in Evolutionary Algorithms Research
Editor: Gregor Papa
ISBN: 978-1-63463-849-4
© 2015 Nova Science Publishers, Inc.

Chapter 6

DEVELOPING LED ILLUMINATION OPTICS DESIGN

David Kaljun[1,*] and Janez Žerovnik[1,2]
[1]Faculty of Mechanical Engineering,
University of Ljubljana, Slovenia
[2]Institute of Mathematics, Physics and Mechanics,
Ljubljana, Slovenia

ABSTRACT

The fast development in LED technology dictates the pace at which the manufacturers of LED luminaires have to adopt existing or develop new products. To speed up the development process they have to implement new methods and techniques. In this chapter we discuss an extension of the work. The goal of the main research is finding a fast method for building lighting systems with given target light distributions. One of the initial steps in achieving the goal is to approximate the measured input data to function models. For that we use several versions of genetic algorithms and local search algorithms. The algorithms are tested on 100 artificial lenses. Results show that all of the algorithms find practically useful approximations. Statistical test are performed to highlight the best and worse algorithms.

Keywords: LED illumination, light distribution, genetic algorithm

INTRODUCTION

When facing an NP-hard optimization problem as the one described below, heuristic approaches are usually needed to compute practical solutions. It is well known that best results are obtained when a special heuristics is designed and tuned for each particular problem. This means that the heuristics should be based on considerations of the particular problem and perhaps also on properties of the most likely instances. On the other hand, it is

[*] E-mail: david.kaljun@fs.uni-lj.si.

useful to work within a framework of some metaheuristics which can be seen as general strategies to attack an optimization problem.

Metaheuristics usually make fewer assumptions about the problem, so they are more agile and may be used on a broader spectrum. On the other hand, they do not guarantee that a globally optimal solution can be found in every instance. They search for a so called near optimal solution, because in most cases we also have no approximation guarantee [1].

We adapt the approach from the paper [2] and implement two variations of a genetic algorithm, three variations of local search and a random sampler. In [2] we evaluated the relative performance of these algorithms when they were ran on real lenses. Now we extend the experimental study [2] on a dataset of artificial instances that are generated so that we know optimal solutions.

The chapter is organized as follows. The next section will briefly describe the engineering problem. Section 3 provides an insight into the analytical model, Section 4 describes the algorithms and provides the experiment setup. Section 5 shows the results of the experiment. Conclusions are given in Section 6.

THE ENGINEERING PROBLEM

With the arrival and mass production of high power - high efficacy white Light Emitting Diodes (LEDs), the world of illumination entered a phase of revolution. The LEDs at the basics enable lower energy consumption, never before seen housing design freedoms and of course a revolution in the optics system design, which will be described in detail further down. The latter in turn enables the optics designer to build a lighting system that delivers the light to the environment in a fully controlled fashion. The many possible designs lead to new problems of choosing the optimal or at least a very good design depending on possibly different goals such as optimization of energy consumption, production cost, and, last but not least, the light pollution of the environment.

Nevertheless the primary goal or challenge of every luminaire design process is to design a luminaire with an efficient light engine. The light engine consists of the source, which in this case are LEDs, and the appropriate secondary optics. The choice of the secondary optics is the key in developing a good system while working with LEDs. For designing such a system nowadays technology provides two options. The first option is to have the know-how and the resources to design a specific lens to accomplish the task. However, the resources coupled with the development and production of optical elements may be enormous. Therefore a lot of manufactures are using the second option that means to use ready-made lenses. These lenses are produced by specialized companies in the world who offer different types of lenses for all of the major brands of LEDs. The trick here is to choose the best combination of lenses to get the most efficient system. The current practice in the development process is a trial and error procedure, where the developer chooses a combination of lenses, and simulates the system via Monte Carlo ray-tracing methods. The success heavily depends on the engineers' intuition and experience, but also needs sizeable computation resources for checking the proposed design.

Namely, the usual practical situation is that we have the light distributions given by large dataset of points in the space with (desired or measured) light intensity. These so called photometries are provided in standard formats. There are two main digital photometric data formats. The IESNA (.ies) format used mainly in the USA and the European ELUMDAM (.ldt) file format. Both formats transfer data in almost the same way. The only difference is in the coding of the luminaire general information data. The IESNA format uses special key words in the first rows of the file to incorporate the information about the manufacturer name, date, product name/number, laboratory test information etc. There is no limit to the number of information rows.

After the last code word the information in the rows bellow is specified in the standard and is not allowed to be written differently. In contrast the ELUMDAT file format has a fixed and specified content in every row from the beginning till the end. Also, it is not allowed to skip any rows because the file format depends on the row number count. In both standards, the radiation pattern data is the same. Basically the radiation pattern is described with spatial vectors in spherical coordinates which all have a common source point that in fact is the fixed origin point of the measurement. Every vector has three components, the azimuthal angle, the polar angle and the luminous intensity. The number of vectors depends on the complexity of the pattern and the demanded accuracy. In general a minimum of 3312 (46 polar on 72 azimuthal) vectors are provided. The radial distance at every vector is determined as the luminous intensity at that angle set. The luminous intensity is measured absolutely but in most cases normalized with the luminous flux. This step is done to enable the comparison between radiation patterns with different absolute values (important for visual chart plot comparison).

As the standard file formats offer data in a fashion that is not very suited for automatic optimization a natural avenue of research related to the second approach is to replace the trial and error method by a more efficient design method based on analytical and algorithmic tools. For this aim, a theoretical framework is needed. Among the first known theoretical results is the analytical model [3] that was proposed for LEDs without secondary optics. The idea inspired by [3] is to fit the data from the standard photometric files with suitable functions that in turn provide a construction of a light engine which approximates the target light distribution.

Moreno and Sun proposed an analytical model to describe the far field radiation pattern of a LED without secondary optics. It was shown that most radiation patterns could be modeled with the sum of two types of functions, the Gaussian type and the cosine-power type. All presented cases were modeled with the maximum sum of 3 functions. Moreno and Sun fitted photometric data of a LED without secondary optics. The data was similar to the standard, but obtained from the LED's datasheet graphs. It was shown in [4] that slightly modified model of Moreno and Sun can be successfully applied to measured data of a LED with secondary optics. The application of the model allows us to further pursuit the research of developing a fast and reliable computation method to aid in the design process of a light engine that consists of an array of LEDs and different secondary optics.

MODEL AND EVALUATION FUNCTION

With so many different LED's that have different radiation patterns and many different secondary optics which can be placed over these LED's to control the light distribution, finding the right combination of a LED - lens combo is presumably a very complicated and challenging task. Consequently, providing a general analytical model for all of them is also likely to be a very challenging research problem. Therefore [4] restricts attention to LED-lens combinations that have symmetrical spatial light distributions. This yields an analytical model in two dimensions, so it describes a curve rather a surface. We use the model [4] that can be formally be given as [5]

$$I(\theta; \boldsymbol{a}, \boldsymbol{b}, \boldsymbol{c}) = I_{max} \sum_{k=1}^{K} * \ a_k * \cos(\theta - b_k)^{c_k}$$

θ is the polar angle and the parameters $\mathbf{a} = (a_1, a_2, \ldots, a_k)$, $\mathbf{b} = (b_1, b_2, \ldots, b_k)$, $\mathbf{c} = (c_1, c_2, \ldots, c_k)$ have values in the intervals: $a_i \in [0, 1]$, $b_i \in [-90, 90]$, $c_i \in [0, 100]$; $i = (1,2,\ldots,k)$. To evaluate a parameter set we have to define the goodness of fit to the measured data. Folowing [3], this is chosen to be minimizing the root mean square error (RMS).

$$RMS(\boldsymbol{a}, \boldsymbol{b}, \boldsymbol{c}) = \sqrt{\frac{1}{N} \sum_{i=1}^{N} [I_m(\theta_i) - I(\theta_i, \boldsymbol{u}, \boldsymbol{b}, \boldsymbol{c})]^2}$$

In practical application, for a sufficiently accurate fit the RMS value must be less than 5% [3]. On the other hand, current standards and technology allows up to 2% noise in the measured data. Therefore, the target results of the fitting algorithms are at less than 5% RMS error, but at the same time there is no practical need for a solution with less than 1% or 2% RMS error.

Experimental Study Overview

Although the minimization problem defined above is conceptually simple, it is on the other hand likely to be computationally hard. In other words, it is a min square error approximation of a function for which no analytical solution is known. The experiment in [2] was set-up to test the algorithms' performance on different real life LED-lens combinations. We have chosen a set of real available lenses to be approximated. The set was taken from the online catalogue of one of the biggest and most present manufacturer in the world Ledil Oy Finland [6]. The selection from the broad spectrum of lenses in the catalogue was based on the decision that the used LED is of the XP-E product line from the manufacturer Cree [7]. The second criteria was that the lenses have a symmetric spatial light distribution. All of the chosen lenses were approximated with all algorithms. To ensure that algorithms' results could be compared the target error was set to 0% and the runtime was limited in terms of basic steps that are defined as one generation of a feasible solution in the local search and an adequate operation for genetic algorithms. This implies that the wall clock runtime was also roughly the same for all algorithms.

We address the optimization problem as a discrete optimization problem. Natural questions that may be asked here is why use heuristics and why discrete optimization heuristics on a continuous optimization problem. First, application of an approximation method is justified because there is no analytical solution for the best approximation of this type of functions.

Moreover, in order to apply continuous optimization methods such as the Newton method, we usually need a good approximation in order to assure convergence. Therefore a method for finding a good starting solution before running fine approximation based on continuous optimization methods is needed. However, in view of the at least 2% noise in the data, these starting solutions may in many cases already be of sufficient quality! Nevertheless, it may be of interest to compare the two approaches and their combination in future work, although it is not of practical interest for the engineering problem regarded here. When considering the optimization problem as a discrete problem, the values of parameters to be estimated will be $a_i \in \{0, 0.001, 0.002, \ldots, 1\}$, $b_i \in \{-90, -89.9, -89.8, \ldots, 90\}$, and $c_i \in \{0, 1, 2, \ldots, 100\}$. Hence, the discrete search space here consists of $N_t = 1000^3*1800^3*100^3 \approx 5.83*10^{24}$ tuples $t = (a_1, a_2, a_3, b_1, b_2, b_3, c_1, c_2, c_3)$. In the experiments, all the heuristics were tested on all instances of the dataset. The time limit for a run is set to be 4 million steps where a step is defined to be equivalent of one iteration of a basic local search heuristics. In other words, iterative improvement would visit 4 million feasible solutions. The time for other heuristics is estimated to be comparable, and will be explained in detail later. The CPU time per algorithm and lens was measured to be approximately 16 minutes on the Intel Core I7-4790K @ 4.4 Ghz and 16 GB of RAM. The code is not fully optimized. The overall runtime of the experiment was substantially lowered by use of parallelization. We ran the experiment on 6 of the 8 available CPU threads.

The Algorithms

In the experiment we use six different algorithms. Three of them are well known standard algorithms of local search, two are genetic algorithms which will be explained in detail bellow and one is a random sampling algorithm that we use to exclude trivialities.

Local Search Heuristics

Among the three local search type algorithms are a basic steepest descend algorithm with a fixed neighborhood that we address in the results section with the abbreviation **SD**, an iterative improvement with a fixed neighborhood that is addressed as **IF** and an iterative improvement with variable neighborhood which is addressed as **IR**. Because the algorithms are well known we will not discuss the interworking. For more details we refer to [2, 5].

We only briefly recall the definitions of neighborhoods. The first neighborhood has a fixed step size. Given the step sizes d_a, d_b and d_c a neighbor is obtained by adding or subtracting the appropriate step size to each parameter. Hence, there are 2^9 neighbors.

In the second variable size neighborhood, a neighbor is generated by adding a random number from the interval [-(step_size), +(step size)] to each parameter. Note that in this case a solution has an infinite number of neighbors, therefore only iterative improvement can be implemented for this neighborhood.

Genetic Algorithm

The genetic algorithms used in the experiment and described below mimic the evolutionary behavior. The algorithms are the same as in [2], and are explained in some detail below.

The standard genetic algorithm (**SGA**), uses three genetic operators: selection, cross-breeding and mutation. The selection [8] operator works as a kind of a filter where fitter individuals in a population get to have higher weights as the less fit individuals. The weights are then transmitted to the cross-breeding operator in the way that the individuals with higher weights are more likely to be chosen as parents as opposed to the others. In fact the choosing mechanism is programed so that the first 60 % of the generated children population have at least one parent that is randomly chosen from the best 30 % in the parent generation. The second parent is randomly chosen from the whole parent population. Both parents of the remaining 40 % children generation are taken randomly from the entire parent generation. The cross-breeding or crossover operator [8, 9, 10, 11] is where a population is created by generating new solutions. These are created by randomly combining and crossing parameters from two parent solutions that were chosen as explained above. The crossing is done via cross point so that every parent pair produces a pair of children. The cross point is chosen randomly and the children are generated in the following rule: choose randomly a cross point CP, write the parents as $P_1 = (P_1^{bCP}, P_1^{aCP})$ and $P_2 = (P_2^{bCP}, P_2^{aCP})$ and combine $C_1 = (P_1^{bCP}, P_2^{aCP})$, $C_2 = (P_2^{bCP}, P_1^{aCP})$. Here P_n^{aCP} are all of the parents parameters that are after the CP and P_n^{bCP} are all of the parents parameters that are before the CP. The last operator in every generation is the self-adapting mutation [8, 10, 12] operator which finalizes the individuals in the new population. The mutation operates in the following manner: in the randomly chosen individual, a random number of parameters are chosen to be changed (mutated) which is done by adding a randomly chosen value for $da_1 = da_2 = da_3 = [-0.01, -0.009, -0.008, \ldots, 0.01]$, for $db_1 = db_2 = db_3 = [-0.25, 0.24, -0.23, \ldots, 0.25]$ and $dc_1 = dc_2 = dc_3 = [-2.5, -2.4, -2.3, \ldots, 2.5]$ to the current parameter value.

SGA algorithm begins with the generation and calculation of the initial population (the zero population). Next it sorts the population entities from the fittest to the least fit and applies weights. After the sorting process the algorithm generates the next generation with the use of the crossover operator. This is then submitted to mutation with the adaptive mutation operator. When the new generation is fully formed the algorithm begins the process from the point of selection. It continues to do so until the last generation is finalized. The number of generations to be generated is calculated as the quotient of the maximal number of iterations minus the population size and the population size $N_G = (T_{max} - N_P) / N_P$.

Preliminary results [2, 5], have shown that genetic algorithms gave some encouraging results in particular in combination with local search. That is why we developed an adapted standard genetic algorithm, which is named the hybrid genetic algorithm and addressed as **HGA.** The hybrid genetic algorithm works in the same way as the standard one, but with an extra operator before the crossover. It starts with generating the initial solution and sorts the entities in the current solution from the fittest to least fit. Then, instead of directly cross breading the new generation it first runs the iterative improvement with fixed neighborhood algorithm on 10 best entities of the current generation which in turn get locally optimized (enhanced) for a number of iterations. This also changes the choosing of the parents as we only optimize 10 best solutions we now chose from this 10 solutions in the first part of the cross bread instead of the 30 % best solutions. After that the HGA operates in the same way as the standard genetic algorithm does.

For the number of generations to be executed on HGA algorithm, the calculation is a bit more complicated, because it has to include the iterations of the local search. The formula can be written as $N_G = (T_{max} - N_P) / (N_P + 10*N_{iter})$. More about the algorithms can be found in [2].

Experimental Parameters

As previously mentioned the experiment was conducted as an extension to the experiment presented in [2]. We use the same algorithms as in [2] but on a larger set of artificial instances. This should provide more conclusive results as the sample size is 100 and the way the instances were generated guaranteed a uniform distribution of parameters on the above described discrete intervals. In the model we take K=3, which means that we will have a sum of three functions and therefore nine parameters. We then generated 100 instances (artificial lenses) to be approximated. The parameter values a_i, b_i, and c_i were generated independently from a uniform random distribution using the MT19937 random generator implemented in C++ code to ensure randomization and portability of the code. This also ensured that the optimal solution (with RMS=0) exists.

To fully compare the genetic algorithm performance to the local search algorithms we locked the total amount of computation iterations (one computation iteration in our case is the evaluation of the RMS error at the given coefficient values) to four million. As the performance of genetic algorithms heavily depends on the population size and the number of generations, we choose different population sizes and calculated the number of generations and local search iterations needed to achieve the desired four million calculation iterations as close as possible (minor deviations can occur due to restriction of evaluating a whole generation). The combinations of the genetic algorithm are given in Table 1.

Experimental Results

As the number of test instances here is 100, it would be impractical to present them all. Instead, we present maximum, minimum, average and median value for every algorithm.

For the statistical comparison, we use the Wilcoxon Signed rank test, which compares different pairs of algorithms with each other to evaluate the difference in performance.

The results are presented in 5 groups, one for each genetic algorithm combination as can be observed in Table 1, and one for the local search algorithms. At the end of the section we will present an additional comparison of the best algorithms from each group.

First, we compare the standard genetic algorithms. In Table 2 and Figure 1 we present the maximum, minimum, average and median results of the RMS error achieved by these algorithms.

With the exception of SGA 0 all of the algorithms on all instances found a useful solution that was lower than the limit of 5%. In fact, they found a much lower maximum value. Also, all of them found very low minimum RMS being the lowest achieved by the SGA 4 algorithm with 0.0037 %.

Table 1. Parameter combinations for genetic algorithms used in the experiment

Algorithm	No. pop.	No. gen.	No. loc. Sea. Iter.
SGA 0	1000	3999	NA
SGA 1	5000	799	NA
SGA 2	10000	399	NA
SGA 3	50000	79	NA
SGA 4	100000	39	NA
HGA 0 0	1000	40	10000
HGA 1 0	5000	38	10000
HGA 2 0	10000	36	10000
HGA 3 0	50000	26	10000
HGA 4 0	100000	20	10000
HGA 0 1	1000	20	20000
HGA 1 1	5000	19	20000
HGA 2 1	10000	19	20000
HGA 3 1	50000	16	20000
HGA 4 1	100000	13	20000
HGA 0 2	1000	10	40000
HGA 1 2	5000	10	40000
HGA 2 2	10000	10	40000
HGA 3 2	50000	9	40000
HGA 4 2	100000	8	40000

Table 2. RMS error in % achieved by the SGA algorithms over 100 instances

	SGA 0	SGA 1	SGA 2	SGA 3	SGA 4
MAX	5.365180	2.908000	3.067230	2.331810	1.718750
MIN	0.323957	0.102185	0.107640	0.050105	0.003733
AVG	1.477545	1.106519	0.948480	0.659030	0.517301
MEDIAN	1.251805	1.050562	0.89192	0.510524	0.469515

Table 3. Asymptotic significances of Wilcoxon Signed rank test for results of SGA * at four million calculating operations

	SGA 1	SGA 2	SGA 3	SGA 4
SGA 0	0.00008212	0.00000012	0	0
SGA 1		0.00026422	0	0
SGA 2			0	0
SGA 3				0.00021476

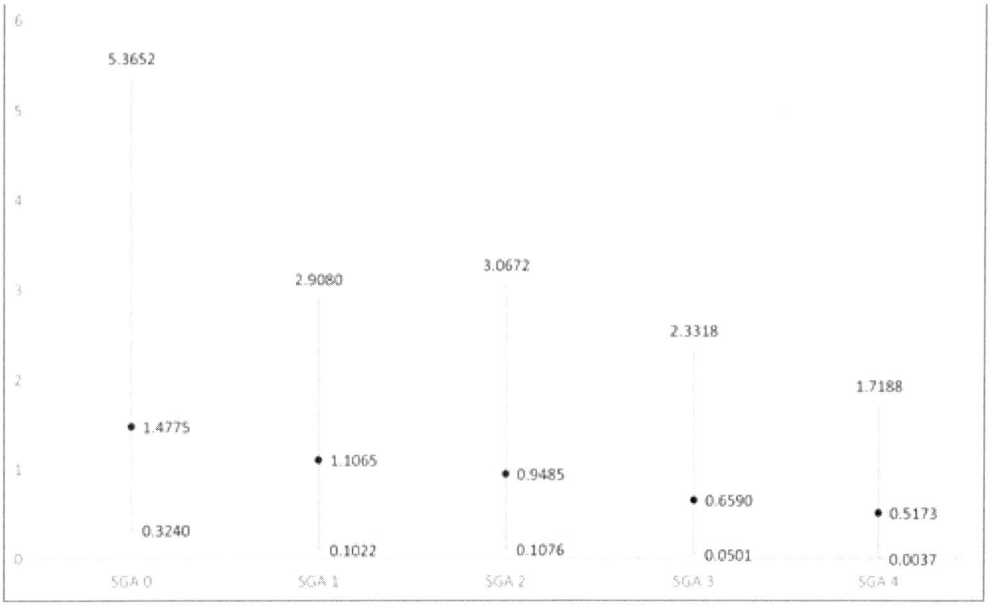

Figure 1. Graphical representation of the RMS error in % achieved by SGA algorithm over 100 instances.

Table 4. RMS error in % achieved by the HGA * 0 algorithms over 100 instances

	HGA 0 0	HGA 1 0	HGA 2 0	HGA 3 0	HGA 4 0
MAX	1.630800	1.767550	2.25839	2.272840	2.446410
MIN	0.017571	0.004770	0.006818	0.027234	0.002782
AVG	0.661746	0.732596	0.735788	0.696882	0.708434
MEDIAN	0.651472	0.677504	0.671136	0.635083	0.634843

The same can be observed on the average values where the SGA 4 algorithm again prevails. Finally, we apply the Wilcoxon statistical test. The test tells us whether there is a significant difference between the compared algorithms. It does that by testing the null hypothesis *"The median of differences between variables (=algorithms) equals 0"* [13]. Hence, for the algorithms to differ the hypothesis has to be rejected, in other words the value of the asymptotic significance has to be less or equal to 0.05. Based on the data from Table 3 we can see that all of the algorithms differ, which means that there has to be a clear winner of the group. Based on the fact that all of SGA algorithms differ from each other and on the average and median values we can conclude that the algorithm SGA 4 that has the lowest values is the best of the SGA group. This is in accordance with the findings from [2], where the same test was done with real lenses.

The second group consists of the HGA * 0 algorithms. In Table 4 and Figure 2 we present the RSM values in %, and in Table 5 the results of the statistical test are presented. In contrast to SGA algorithms here the statistical test shows large asymptotic significance values which in turn means that the algorithms do not differ significantly. We could deduce a similar conclusion if we look at the RMS data. It shows that despite the max values are different the average and median values are all inside the range of 0.1 %. To identify the best algorithm we took a look at the standard deviation value. From these information we deduced that the best algorithm was the HGA 0 0 which has the lowest average, median and standard deviation value. But we also have to note that the differences here are minimal and the algorithm choice in this case would not largely impact the overall performance of the end application. In the third group we present the HGA * 1 algorithms.

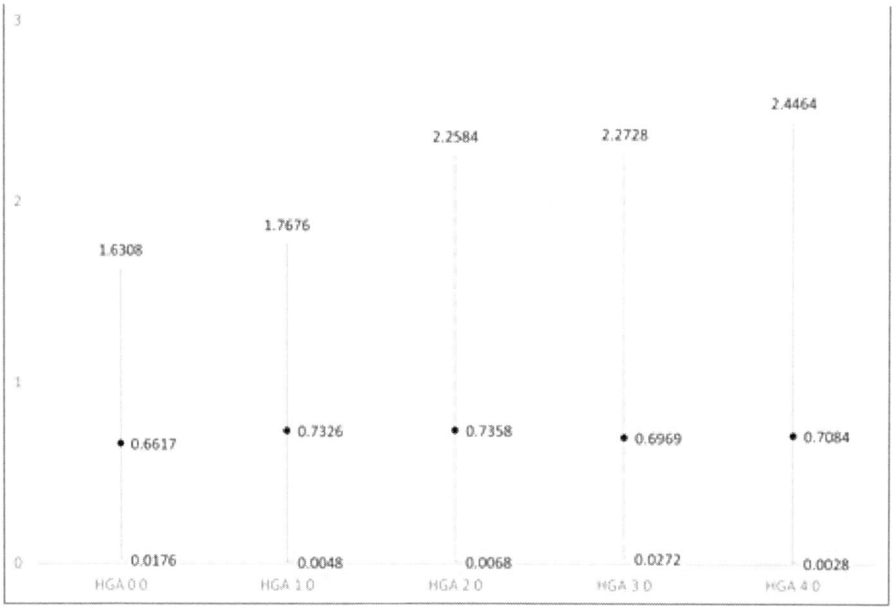

Figure 2. Graphical representation of the RMS error in % achieved by HGA * 0 algorithm over 100 instances.

Table 5. Asymptotic significances of Wilcoxon Signed rank test for results of HGA * 0 at four million calculating operations

	HGA 1 0	HGA 2 0	HGA 3 0	HGA 4 0
HGA 0 0	0.41	0.163	0.344	0.193
HAG 1 0		0.637	0.269	0.51
HGA 2 0			0.482	0.718
HGA 3 0				0.521

Table 6. RMS error in % achieved by the HGA * 1 algorithms over 100 instances

	HGA 0 1	HGA 1 1	HGA 2 1	HGA 3 1	HGA 4 1
MAX	1.572750	3.113550	1.654000	2.464530	2.255290
MIN	0.006365	0.004550	0.008269	0.020331	0.043900
AVG	0.684496	0.716657	0.644145	0.703564	0.712973
MEDIAN	0.698412	0.678058	0.642333	0.687333	0.625510

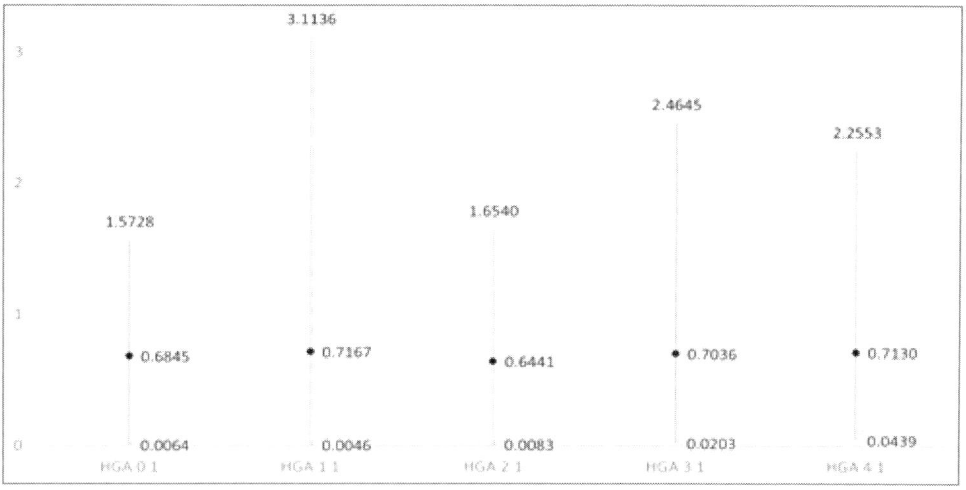

Figure 3. Graphical representation of the RMS error in % achieved by HGA * 1 algorithm over 100 instances.

Table 7. Asymptotic significances of Wilcoxon Signed rank test for results of HGA * 1 at four million calculating operations

	HGA 1 1	HGA 2 1	HGA 3 1	HGA 4 1
HGA 0 1	0.718	0.53	0.854	0.302
HAG 1 1		0.187	0.999	0.575
HGA 2 1			0.153	0.109
HGA 3 1				0.759

Table 6 and Table 7 present the RMS and asymptotic significance values and Figure 3 presents the RMS values in a graphical way.

As in the previous group the compared algorithms do not differ significantly. The asymptotic significance values are very high, and the average, median, max and min values are relatively close on all algorithms. The only exception is algorithm HGA 11 with a max value of 3.1136 %. Again, we take a look at the standard deviation value and when considering them all we see that the HGA 2 1 has the lowest average, median, standard deviation value and the second lowest min, max value. This puts it affront of the other algorithm by a margin.

The last group of genetic algorithms consists of the HGA * 2 algorithms. The RMS and test results are presented in Table 8 and Table 9. Figure 4 graphically presents the RMS values.

The statistical and RSM data for the last group point in a similar direction as the previous two. Again, there is no significant difference between the algorithms, and pretty much all of them are at the same quality level. Again, we have the RMS and median values inside a small range. If we take all of them into account and add the standard deviation values we can see that the HGA 02 algorithm may be selected as the best one. But again the differences are very small.

Table 8. RMS error in % achieved by the HGA * 2 algorithms over 100 instances

	HGA 0 2	HGA 1 2	HGA 2 2	HGA 3 2	HGA 4 2
MAX	1.663370	1.854240	1.768980	2.742130	2.222220
MIN	0.015795	0.037211	0.032755	0.024480	0.007560
AVG	0.699864	0.760561	0.770468	0.750164	0.768006
MEDIAN	0.713316	0.665750	0.717848	0.682404	0.679477

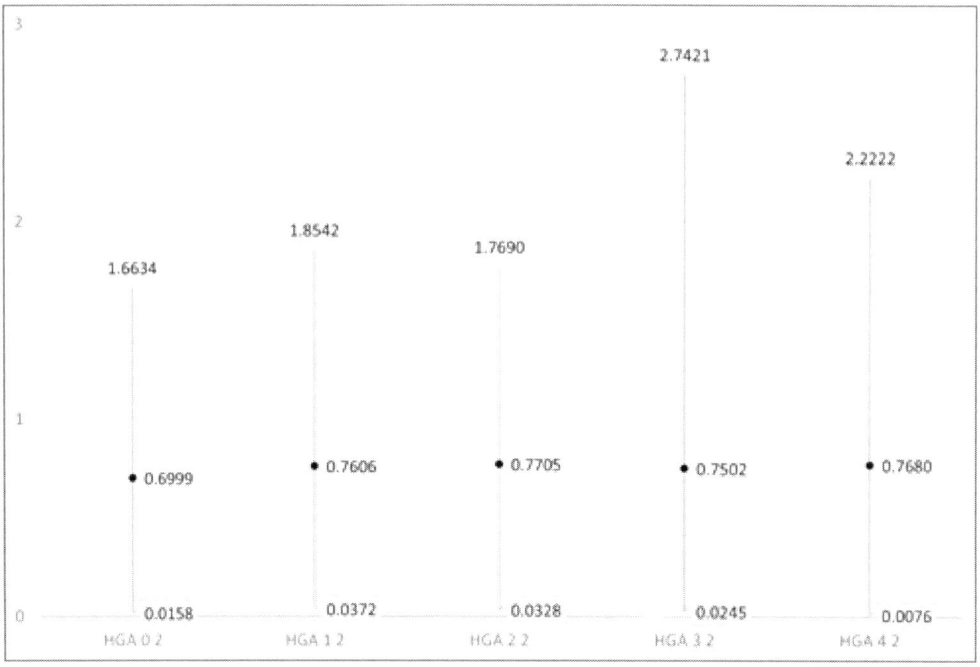

Figure 4. Graphical representation of the RMS error in % achieved by HGA * 2 algorithm over 100 instances.

Table 9. Asymptotic significance of Wilcoxon Signed rank test for results of HGA * 2 at four million calculating operations

	HGA 1 2	HGA 2 2	HGA 3 2	HGA 4 2
HGA 0 2	0.142	0.133	0.726	0.109
HAG 1 2		0.918	0.449	0.843
HGA 2 2			0.289	0.862
HGA 3 2				0.503

Besides the genetic algorithms we have also run three local search algorithms and the trivial algorithm RAN that simply generates and evaluates random solutions. The next two tables and one figure present the RMS and statistical test results for the local search algorithms.

Table 10. RMS error in % achieved by the local search algorithms over 100 instances

	SD	IF	IR	RAN
MAX	49.95040	33.26150	6.227830	8.660520
MIN	0.003880	0.018580	0.518872	0.603101
AVG	3.292490	1.541263	1.436479	2.441579
MEDIAN	1.521062	0.646586	1.194790	2.137840

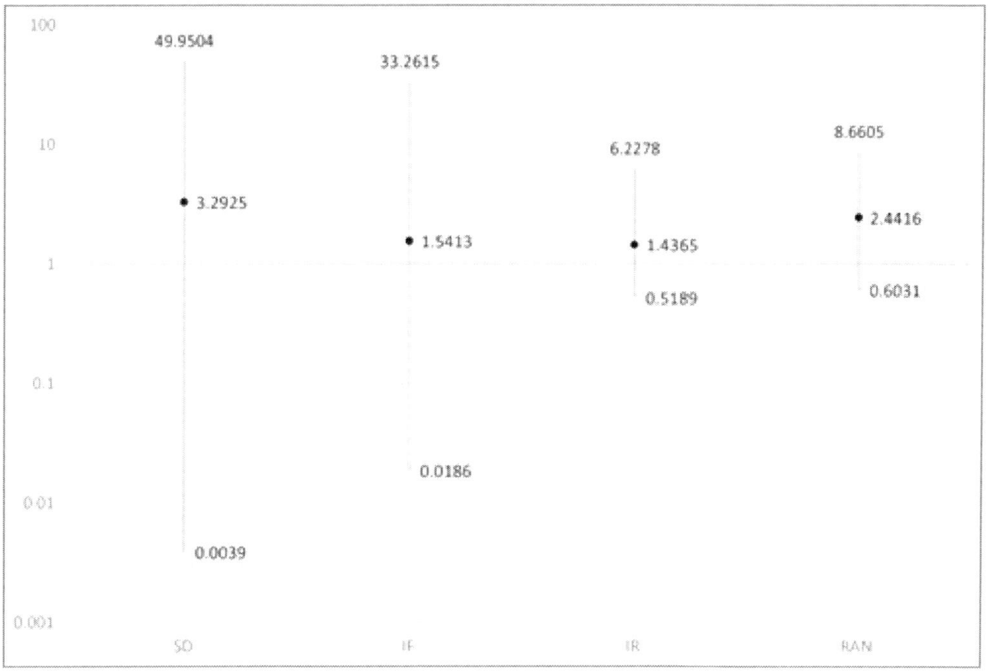

Figure 5. Graphical representation of the RMS error in % achieved by the local search algorithm over 100 instances.

Table 11. Asymptotic significance of Wilcoxon Signed rank test for the results of Local search algorithms at four million calculating operations

	IF	IR	RAN
SD	0	0.00119997	0.8878926
IF		0.00000003	0
IR			0

The results for the local search algorithms are not as homogenous as they were in the genetic algorithm groups. We can observe that the SD and IF algorithm have very high maximum errors, but also on the other hand they have the lowest minimal errors. As for the median value the IF is the clear winner. From the statistical point of view, we see that there is no significant difference between SD and RAN. The other pairs differ from each other. Based on the data the favorites are IF and IR. But with IF having the median value almost 50% lower than IR, the IF algorithm can be chosen as the winner in this group. Before we move to the comparison of the group winners, let us briefly discuss a possible hypothesis on why the IF and SD algorithms have such high maximum values. The SD and IF algorithms have a common fixed starting point and a neighborhood defined with a fixed step, which was chosen on the experience gained from real lenses. Because the parameters for the artificial lenses were chosen independent they could result in a combination that is nearly impossible to find from the fixed starting position with a fixed neighborhood step. A possible reason why none of the other algorithms had such problems may be that none of them has a neighborhood defined with a fixed step, and the genetic algorithms also have multiple starting points. Consequently, these algorithms are less sensitive to the choice of initial solution.

To conclude the results section we compare the wining algorithms from all sections with each other. Table 12 shows the RMS values of the winning algorithms, Figure 6 shows a graphical representation of the same data and Table 13 shows the statistical test results. The statistical test implies that SGA 4 significantly differs from all algorithms. This can be observed in Table 12 where we can see that SGA 4 achieves by far the best min, average and median value.

Table 12. RMS error in % achieved by the wining algorithms over 100 instances

	SGA 4	HGA 0 0	HGA 2 1	HGA 0 2	IF
MAX	1.718750	1.630800	1.654000	1.663370	33.26150
MIN	0.003733	0.017571	0.008269	0.015795	0.018580
AVG	0.517301	0.661746	0.644145	0.699864	1.541263
MEDIAN	0.469515	0.651472	0.642333	0.713316	0.646586

Figure 6. Graphical representation of the RMS error in % achieved by the wining algorithms over 100 instances.

Table 13. Asymptotic significance of Wilcoxon Signed rank test for the results of the wining algorithms at four million calculating operations

	HGA 0 0	HGA 2 1	HGA 0 2	IF
SGA 4	0.001	0.006	0	0.035
HGA 0 0		0.996	0.278	0.514
HGA 2 1			0.376	0.587
HGA 0 2				0.739

However, all the others have relatively the same average and mean values. According to this data the SGA 4 algorithm, the standard genetic algorithm with a population of 100000 individuals and 39 generations is the overall winner.

Conclusion

We have extended the experimental study done in [2] by comparing the same algorithms on a larger set of test instances. In contrast to the instances based on real lenses, the instances here were randomly generated, which implies that the instance parameters are randomly distributed in the entire search space. Furthermore, it is assured that solutions with RMS=0 exist. We can see that most of the algorithms are immune to the distribution of the instances throughout the search space except the SD and IF algorithms that have some minor trouble. Hence the high max RMS values in Table 10. Performance wise all of the algorithms found in almost all instances an appropriate solution. The genetic algorithms SGA 4 and all of the HGA ** algorithms found appropriate solutions on all instances. The average RMS values in the wining algorithms were around 0.65 %, which is far better than the 5% upper bound. We can conclude that genetic and hybrid genetic algorithms as well as the local search heuristics provide useful solutions. In particular, the genetic algorithms work well on a large set of parameters, however it is observed that large population proved to significantly improve performance of the standard genetic algorithm.

Curiously, none of the algorithms found an ideal solution with 0% RMS error. The reason for this is probably that we operate in a discrete search space and the algorithms simply did not have the right values in their discrete search space. This limitation however motivates future research where we will try to upgrade the algorithms with a continuous optimization method such as the Newton method aiming to pinpoint the exact parameter combination that results in a RMS error of 0%.

We now briefly recall the results from [2], where a similar test was run on real lenses. In the SGA group the SGA 4 and 5 were chosen as the two best algorithms.

In the HGA groups, mostly the algorithms with shorter local searches were chosen as the best one. As here, the differences between the HGA algorithms were not statistically significant, and probably would not affect the performance of the end application. Among the local search type heuristics, the clear winner was the IF algorithm. In the final comparison on the dataset of twelve real lenses [2], HGA 4 1 gave the best results, however the performance was not significantly better that of other HGA's and IF. On realistic dataset HGA 4 1 was significantly better than SGA 5.

We conclude by summarizing the results presented here and the complementary study [2]:

- Standard genetic algorithm SGA, local search, and the hybrid genetic algorithm provide practically useful solutions to the problem. Even the simple algorithm RAN found some very good solutions.
- Depending on the dataset, statistically significant best results are obtained by the standard genetic algorithm SGA on random instances and both hybrid genetic algorithm HGA and local search IF on the realistic dataset.
- Standard genetic algorithm SGA with larger population size performs better than SGA with a smaller population and more generations.
- Hybrid genetic algorithm HGA is very robust against changing the population size and length of the local search operator.
- Local search type heuristics SD and IF are sensitive to the choice of initial solution, which is not the case for the genetic algorithms (standard and hybrid).

REFERENCES

[1] Talbi, E.-G. Metaheuristics: From Design to Implementation. John Wiley & Sons, 2009.

[2] Kaljun, D., and Žerovnik, J. Heuristics for optimization of LED spatial light distribution model. Special Issue of Informatica on Bioinspired Optimization, submited 21.11.2014.

[3] Moreno, I., and Sun, C.-C. Modeling the radiation pattern of LEDs. *Optics Express*, 6(3): 1808-1819, 2008.

[4] Kaljun, D., and Žerovnik, J. Function fitting the symmetric radiation pattern of a LED with attached secondary optic. *Optics Express*, 22(24): 29587-29593, 2014.

[5] Kaljun, D., and Žerovnik, J. (2014). On local search based heuristics for optimization problems. *Croatian Operational Research Review*, 5(2): 317-327.

[6] Ledil Oy. Product search. Retrieved from Ledil: http://www.ledil.com/ (2015, January 14).

[7] Cree. LED Components @ Modules. Retrieved from Cree: http:// www.cree.com/LED-Components-and-Modules, (2014, January 14).

[8] Haupt, R. L., and Haupt, S. E. Practical Genetic Algorithms, 2nd Edition. John Wiley & Sons, 2004.

[9] Aarts, E. H., and Lenstra, J. K. Local Search Algorithms. Chichester: John Wiley & Sons, 1997.

[10] Bäck, T. Evolutionary Algorithms in Theory and Practice: Evolution Strategies, Evolutionary Programming, Genetic Algorithm. Oxford: Oxford Univ. Press, 1996.

[11] Mitchell, M. An Introduction to Genetic Algorithms. The MIT Press, 1996.

[12] Simon, D. Evolutionary Optimization Algorithms. John Wiley & Sons, 2013.

[13] Wilcoxon, F. Individual Comparisons by Ranking Methods. *Biometrics Bulletin,* 1(6): 80-83, 1945.

In: Advances in Evolutionary Algorithms Research
Editor: Gregor Papa
ISBN: 978-1-63463-849-4
© 2015 Nova Science Publishers, Inc.

Chapter 7

DESIGNING MIRRORS FOR ULTRAFAST LASERS

Rafał Biedrzycki[1,*], Jarosław Arabas[1] and Michał Szymański[2]
[1]Institute of Electronic Systems, Warsaw University of Technology, Poland
[2]Faculty of Applied Informatics and Mathematics, Warsaw University of Life Sciences, Poland

ABSTRACT

The chapter reports on a successful application of evolutionary computation techniques to a practical problem. Differential Evolution (DE) and Covariance Matrix Adaptation (CMA-ES) were applied to the computer-aided design of a highly dispersive mirror which was dedicated for use in an ultrafast laser. A complete path of the design process is presented, starting from formulation of the optimization problem to the hardware implementation of the mirror. The best structure of the mirror, which was generated by CMA-ES, was manufactured using epitaxial coating technology. Measurements confirmed that the design requirements were met by the device.

Keywords: CMA-ES, differential evolution, double chirped mirror

INTRODUCTION

According to the No-Free Lunch theorem for optimization [1] it is impossible to draw reliable general conclusions about the superiority of one optimization method over another for all optimization problems.

In other words, each optimization method may yield satisfactory results only for certain problem classes. For this reason, the development of global optimization methods is

* Corresponding author: Rafał Biedrzycki. Institute of Electronic Systems, ul. Nowowiejska 15/19, 00-665 Warsaw, Poland. E-mail: rbiedrzy@elka.pw.edu.pl.

facilitated by sets of standardized benchmark problems. Since problems and experiment conditions are standardized, it is possible to draw conclusions about the efficiency of different optimization methods by comparing their results. In the fields of evolutionary computation, such widely accepted benchmark sets have been developed relatively recently and belong to two families. The first is the set of CEC benchmarks [2] which was started in 2005 and the second is BBOB [3], whose first edition was released in 2009. Statistical analysis of objective function values yielded by different optimization methods for these benchmark sets makes it possible to answer the question: "what optimization method and what set of parameters would be of the first choice when I know a little about the problem class?"

In practical optimization problems, there usually exists some kind of expertise, domain knowledge, good practice or heuristics to define a baseline level of the quality of a solution. It is expected that application of optimization techniques will yield results that will outperform the baseline level. The domain knowledge may also allow for defining initial solutions which can be used as starting points for optimization methods to speed up the optimization process. Hence, practical problems are not of a pure black-box type, as is usually assumed in the optimization competitions based on benchmark sets.

It may also happen that a series of different optimization tasks should be considered in the process of solving a practical problem, since the end user may change the problem definition after looking at the results yielded by the optimization method.

Thus, the picture of a single objective function that does not change over the design process is too idealistic. This chapter illustrates the aforementioned practical issues. An example problem is discussed which consists of the computer-aided design of a mirror that is dedicated to work as a component of an ultrafast laser. In a specified range of wavelength, the mirror is expected to have a very high reflection coefficient.

In addition, a parameter called group delay dispersion (GDD) should be kept in a relatively narrow range of values. The mirror studied in this chapter was produced using semiconductor technology. It is made of interleaving layers of GaAs and AlAs of different thicknesses. The layered semiconductor structure is coated with several layers of anti-reflective dielectric material. The optimization process consists of searching for the set of thickness values of dielectric and semiconductor layers that define a mirror that satisfies the reflectivity and GDD requirements.

The whole design process was comprised of multiple stages which are briefly characterized in Table 1 and are discussed in more detail in the forthcoming sections. All optimization results were obtained under the R environment [4] which was enriched by installation of several specialized packages to perform optimization methods.

Implementations of all methods came with default parameter settings which allowed for optimization to be started without preliminary parameter tuning and gave the impression that the used methods were parameter-less.

Among the tested optimization methods a winner was selected that yielded the best solutions to the considered problem. After some simple parameter tuning, the solution yielded by the winning method became the starting point for the design of a mirror with a different specification of parameters, which was manufactured using semiconductor technology. The characteristics of the manufactured mirror were measured and compared with the model.

Table 1. Stages of the design process discussed in the chapter

	Step	Description	Result
1	Problem analysis.	Specification of the design criteria.	Constraints and goals are defined.
2	Decision on the optimization problem definition.	Visual inspection of results yielded by DE for different objective function definitions.	The objective function is defined.
3	Attempt to generate the design without using domain knowledge.	Optimization with CMA-ES and DE with a random starting point.	Results do not fulfill requirements.
4	Attempt to calculate thicknesses of AR layers.	Optimization of AR (six layers) with DE, using a random starting point, requiring GDD=0, R=0.	The achieved satisfactory solution is denoted AR_0.
5	Attempt to generate the design (semiconductor part) using published analytical method.	Application of the analytical design methodology according to Matuschek [5].	The design, denoted DCM_0, does not satisfy requirements.
6	Attempt to generate the design using domain knowledge.	Optimization with CMA-ES and DE with DCM_0 and AR_0 as the starting point.	Improvement to step 3; optimal solutions are still below requirements.
7	Attempt to tune the basic parameters of DE and CMA-ES.	Change of initial value of the mutation standard deviation σ for CMA-ES and crossover factor CR for DE, with DCM_0 and AR_0 as the starting point.	Optimal solutions satisfy requirements; CMA-ES yields better results than DE.
8	Search for a better starting point.	Optimization with CMA-ES using starting points with alternative specific structures of the semiconductor part of the mirror.	Optimal solutions are satisfactory; the best starting point is SCM.
9	Search for a better optimization method.	Optimization with CMA-ES, DE, Nelder-Mead and BFGS, with SCM and AR_0 as the starting point.	An optimal result is yielded by CMA-ES and is denoted by DCM_1.
10	Reformulation of the optimization problem.	Reduction of the number of AR layers; optimization with CMA-ES taking a modified DCM_1 as the starting point.	Optimal result satisfies the design criteria and is denoted DCM_2.
11	Reformulation of the optimization problem.	Reduction of the number of semiconductor layers; optimization with CMA-ES taking modified DCM_2 as the starting point.	Optimal result satisfies the design criteria and is denoted DCM_3.
12	Production using semiconductor technology.	The semiconductor part of the design DCM_3 is manufactured.	Semiconductor mirror without AR coating.
13	Characterization of the mirror.	Measurements of R and GDD for the manufactured semiconductor part of the DCM_3 mirror.	Agreement between predicted and measured characteristics.
14	Production of the AR coating.	To be completed.	Ready-to-use mirror.

They stayed in good agreement, which validated the simulation model used as a basis for optimization. The measured characteristics also meet the design requirements. At present, the mirror is in the process of deposition of anti-reflective coating. After completion of this phase it is planned that the mirror will be used as a component of an ultrafast laser.

MIRRORS FOR ULTRAFAST LASERS

Ultrafast lasers, which generate optical pulses in the picosecond and femtosecond range, have numerous applications, e.g., in industry [6], biology and medicine [7]. The basic technique that allows for generating ultrashort pulses is mode-locking. We distinguish between active and passive mode-locking, with the latter producing much shorter pulses [8]. The underlying principle of this technique is to induce a fixed phase relationship between the modes inside the resonant cavity. In order to achieve this, all kinds of dispersion appearing in the cavity must be compensated. This can be achieved either by using a prism pair, a grating pair, or a multilayer mirror, also called a chirped mirror (CM) [5].

A CM is a structure that contains an alternating sequence of layers of two different optical materials. The thickness of each pair of layers linearly increases with the layer number. In effect, the light from a range of wavelengths is effectively reflected, and longer wavelengths penetrate the structure deeper than shorter ones.

Thus the delay of reflected light depends on its wavelength. This process can be characterized by the GDD coefficient. Typically, the dependence of GDD on the wavelength is very irregular, which is undesirable. This effect can be reduced in a double chirped mirror (DCM) where the thickness of the layers changes non-linearly. A properly designed DCM should exhibit high reflection in a broad wavelength band together with non-oscillating dependence of the GDD on the wavelength.

In this chapter a semiconductor DCM (SDCM) is considered. Semiconductor materials, GaAs and AlAs, which are used for creating the mirror, have high refractive indexes (about 3.51 and 2.95), which makes it hard to avoid reflection of the light from the mirror surface. For this reason, the SDCM should be additionally covered by an anti-reflective (AR) layer composed of a few layers of dielectric materials.

Therefore, the SDCM production process consists of two technological stages: using molecular beam epitaxy to produce semiconductor layers on a two-inch GaAs substrate and using plasma-enhanced chemical vapor deposition technology to coat the SDCM with dielectric AR layers.

Theoretical Model for Layered Mirrors

A mathematical model of the reflection process assumes that a time-harmonic plane wave falls on the stratified medium, which is schematically depicted in Figure 1. The electric field $E(x)$ satisfies the Helmholtz equation:

$$\frac{d^2E(x)}{dx^2} + \left[\tilde{n}^2(x)k_0^2 - \beta^2\right]E(x) = 0 \tag{1}$$

where $\beta = n_{eff} k_0$ is the propagation constant, $k_0 = 2\pi/\lambda_0$, λ_0 is the free space wavelength and n_{eff} is the effective refractive index.

In the considered case the refractive index profile $\tilde{n}(x)$ is a piecewise constant function since in each layer the refractive index is constant. Therefore, the symbol $\tilde{n}_n$ will be used further where the subscript numerates the layer. In the n-th layer, the field $E(x)$ is a superposition of waves traveling towards the left and the right direction:

$$E(x) = A_n \exp(iK_n x) + B_n \exp(-iK_n x) \tag{2}$$

where $K_n = k_0\sqrt{\tilde{n}_n^2 - n_{eff}^2}$. Note in Figure 1 that the incident wave comes from the left side of the stack and there is no wave that comes from behind the stack, which can be expressed by setting $B_{N+1} = 0$. In addition, without losing generality, it can be assumed that $A_0 = 1$. The values of B_0 and A_{N+1} can be identified as amplitude coefficients of reflectivity and transmission, respectively. The transfer matrix method is a well-known method used in optics [9, 10] and quantum mechanics [11]. Since it has already been accurately discussed in many works, we provide only a brief description of its application in our calculations. The field and its first derivative must be continuous at the interfaces. These relationships allow us to derive a matrix equation of the form:

$$\begin{bmatrix} a_{11} & a_{12} \\ a_{21} & a_{22} \end{bmatrix} \begin{bmatrix} B_0 \\ A_{N+1} \end{bmatrix} = \begin{bmatrix} b_1 \\ b_2 \end{bmatrix} \tag{3}$$

where a_{kl} and b_k are the transfer matrix elements that depend on thicknesses and refractive indexes of layers. The solution of (3) yields the key parameters of DCM:

$$\mathrm{R} = |B_0|^2, \ \mathrm{GDD} = \frac{d^2 \arg B_0}{d\omega^2} \tag{4}$$

where $\omega = 2\pi c/\lambda_0$ denotes the angular frequency, c is the light velocity, R is the reflectivity coefficient, and GDD is the group delay dispersion.

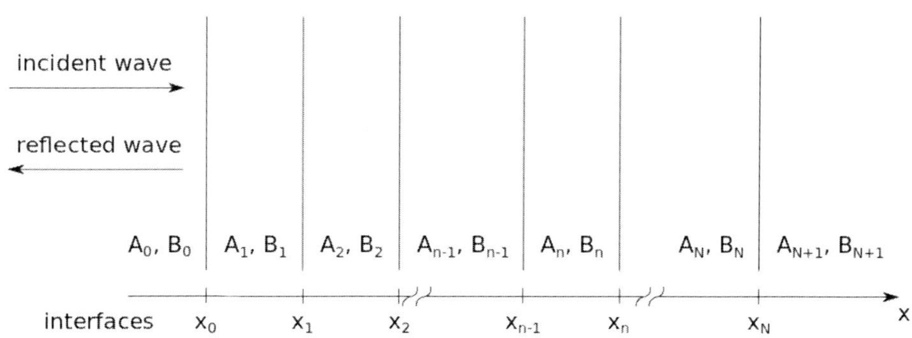

Figure 1. Schematic view of a stratified medium.

Approaches to Designing a DCM

An analytical methodology of designing DCMs has been proposed by Matuschek [5]. He gave example designs of dielectric mirrors yielded by his methodology. He also presented one example design of a semiconductor mirror with GDD= −750 fs^2. In the latter case, the design resulting from analytical solutions was tuned using the BFGS method which yielded the final design. Its theoretical characteristic was in good agreement with the design assumptions in the wavelength band [1.03, 1.08] μm. He reported that a mirror which was manufactured according to the design methodology had GDD values varying from about −400 fs^2 up to −1000 fs^2. Other approaches to the DCM design are based on numerical optimization of the mirror structure. In the majority of approaches, dielectric materials are used to design DCMs. Such materials were used by Yakovlev et al. [12] who applied a memetic algorithm to design a 49-layer $SiO_2/TiO_2/Ta_2O_5$ mirror. The design of a 52-layer structure with GDD ≈ −60 fs^2 and its implementation was reported by Yan-Zhi et al. [13] who applied a needle optimization technique [14]. Another successful DCM implementation was reported by Pervak et al. [15] who used the commercial package OptiLayer to design a dielectric DCM with GDD ≈ −2500 fs^2.

Less popular technology for manufacturing DCMs is based on GaAs/AlAs semiconductor layers, covered by AR coating comprised of several layers of dielectric material. An important advantage of semiconductor technology is its good accuracy of manufacturing the design. The difference of the refractive indexes of GaAs and AlAs is smaller than in the case of dielectric materials; therefore more layers are needed to achieve mirror parameters that are comparable to the dielectric DCMs. More layers introduce more interfaces between layers, which increases the risk of harmful interferences that disrupt the GDD curve. DCMs with a larger number of layers are also harder to optimize.

In [16] an SDCM has been presented whose GDD is a function of wavelength. It contained 65 layer pairs. In [17] an SDCM with GDD = -750 fs^2 in a 40 nm band width around 1055 nm has been reported with 60 pairs of layers.

Unfortunately, most of the articles in this domain do not report important information about the design process such as the objective function formulation, settings of parameters or the starting point, which does not allow for results to be reproduced. The forthcoming text outlines the whole design process of semiconductor DCMs composed of GaAs and AlAs layers with dielectric coating. The design was based on the numerical optimization of a DCM model. The mirror yielded by the described process has been manufactured in the Institute of Electron Technology[1], and the preliminary results have been published in [18].

Preparatory Stages of the Design Process

In the preparatory stages of the design process the objective was to obtain an SDCM with the following parameters: GDD= −2500 ± 100 fs^2, R≥ 0.999 in the wavelength band from λ_l = 1.02 μm to λ_h = 1.04 μm. It was assumed that the AR coating was composed of 3 pairs of SiO_2, TiO_2, and the SDCM was composed of 60 pairs of GaAs and AlAs.

[1] Institute of Electron Technology, Warsaw, Poland.

The thickness of each layer was limited by the range [0, 0.2] μm. It was assumed that when an optimization method generated a point that did not fall into the admissible range of thickness values then the values outside the range were projected onto the closest bound. It was also assumed that all values of layer thickness were acceptable, although from materials science it is known that the thickness of a layer must be a multiple of a characteristic value which is specific for the considered material.

Definition and Properties of the Considered DCM Design Problem

On the basis of the results of black-box optimization competitions (BBOB and CEC), two methods: Differential Evolution DE/local-to-best/1/bin (referred to as DE) [19] and Covariance Matrix Adaptation Evolution Strategy (CMA-ES) [20] were selected for preliminary studies. Their different variants have been on the top of the efficiency rankings and their implementations are easily available as R packages [21, 22].

In the problem formulation it is required that the resulting mirror should satisfy the criteria defined in terms of R and GDD, which makes the design process a bi-criteria optimization problem. It was assumed that both criteria should be aggregated into one objective function.

After a series of preliminary trials the objective function was defined as:

$$q(\mathbf{x}) = a \cdot q_R(\mathbf{x}) + (1 - a) \cdot q_D(\mathbf{x}) \tag{5}$$

where $\mathbf{x}$ is the vector of layer thickness values, q_D and q_R are distances from the target levels of GDD and R:

$$q_D(\mathbf{x}) = b\sum_{\lambda}\left(D_0 - D_\lambda(\mathbf{x},\lambda)\right)^2, q_R(\mathbf{x}) = u\sum_{\lambda}\left(1 - R_\lambda(\mathbf{x})\right)^2 \tag{6}$$

The values of b and u are the scaling factors responsible for the bounding values of q_D and q_R in the range [0, 1], λ is a wavelength sampled from range λ_l, λ_h, D_0 is the required GDD value, $D(\mathbf{x}, \lambda)$ and $R_\lambda(\mathbf{x})$ are the GDD and R values calculated for the wavelength λ. In the case of GDD, its actual value is trimmed to fit into the range [−1000, 1000] according to the formula:

$$D(\mathbf{x},\lambda) = \begin{cases} 1000, \text{if} D_\lambda(\mathbf{x}) > 1000 \\ -1000, \text{if} D_\lambda(\mathbf{x}) < -1000 \\ D_\lambda(\mathbf{x}), \text{otherwise} \end{cases} \tag{7}$$

Symbol a is a weighing coefficient. It is known that optimization of GDD is much harder than R, therefore a was set to 0.01.

During preliminary experiments with CMA-ES and DE it was observed that an acceptable result could not be obtained when the starting point was randomly drawn from the admissible area. Therefore, a reasonable starting point for the semiconductor part of the mirror was generated using the approach introduced by Matuschek [5].

The initial solution was the result of a series of experiments with tuning equation parameters. Finally a design was obtained which satisfied the reflectivity requirements, but it had unacceptable oscillations in GDD. This design is referred to as DCM_0 in the remainder of the text. The initial thickness values of the AR coating, composed of six dielectric layers, were the result of optimization with DE of the objective function (5) assuming the desired values of GDD=0 and R=0. That starting point for the AR part will be called AR_0. DCM_0 together with AR_0 were considered as the starting point and were optimized until a good solution, denoted DCM_1, was found. The objective function is very irregular — sample two-dimensional cross-section contour plots are provided in Figure 2. Each plot was generated by changing the thickness of two selected layers in the optimized DCM_0 design.

Analysis of Figure 2 reveals that the character of the objective function landscape is qualitatively different depending on the dimensions where the cross-section is analyzed. It is more regular at the end of the mirror. It is also visible (cf. plot for layers 61 and 62) that a change of the objective function value, resulting from a change of thickness of a selected layer, can be partially compensated by the change of thickness of its neighbor.

The problem cannot be separated into a series of low-dimensional problems, i.e., it is impossible to divide it into smaller problems and optimize the thickness of a group of layers regardless of all other layers.

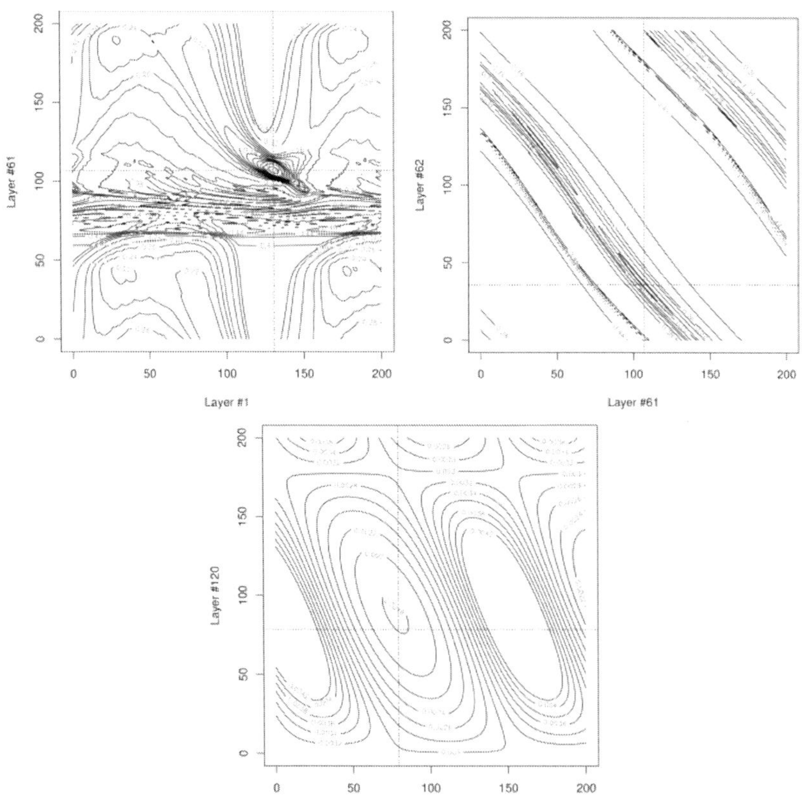

Figure 2. Objective function contour plots obtained by changing thickness values, expressed in nm, of two layers in the optimized DCM_0 solution. Numbers of changed layers are indicated by corresponding axes. Coordinates of the optimal solution are marked by dotted lines.

This is illustrated in Figure 3, where, unlike Figure 2, thicknesses of layers were drawn randomly. Here the optima observed in two-dimensional cross-sections do not match the optimum after the optimization is completed.

Tuning the Optimization Procedure

Although the DCM_0 with AR_0 was a better starting point than random solutions, the design requirements were not satisfied. Therefore crucial parameters of the optimization method needed to be tuned, assuming the DCM_0 with AR_0 as the starting point. The experiments showed that for CMA-ES it is possible to obtain acceptable results after setting the initial value of the mutation standard deviation $\sigma = 0.0003$, and for DE, the crossover factor needed to be set to CR=1, which means that the crossover was switched off. Inspection of the generated solution revealed that some layers were very thin, close to the lower limit. Therefore, it was checked how many infeasible solutions were generated during optimization and how they were corrected. Performed experiments showed that 16 out of 25 independent runs generated no infeasible solutions at all.

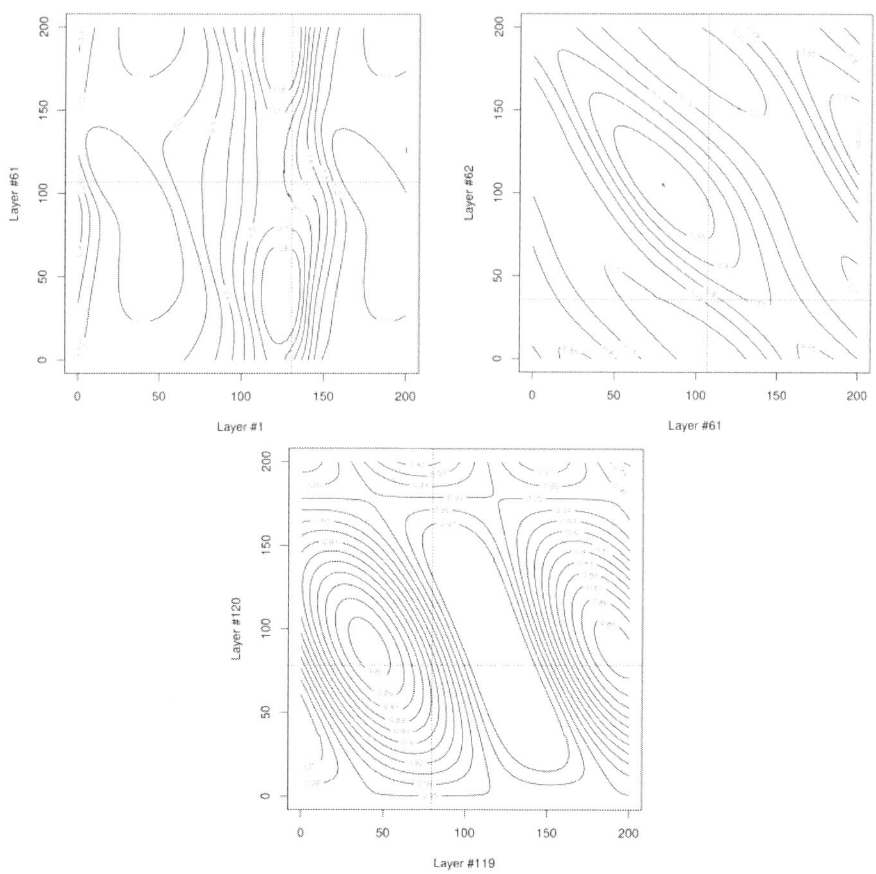

Figure 3. Sample two-dimensional cross-sections of the fitness function for a mirror with randomly drawn layer thickness. Dotted lines mark the thickness values for the optimized DCM_0 design.

In the remaining 9 runs the ratio of generated infeasible solutions was very low when compared to the number of all generated solutions (in most cases it was smaller than 1%). This suggests that the method of constraint handling was not of great importance in the considered problem. After a methodology to generate acceptable solutions was found, the next step was targeted at finding the best solution possible. To achieve this goal, the starting point selection problem was revisited and a broader range of optimization methods was compared. Other starting points for the semiconductor part of the mirror were checked because it was possible that a relatively good starting point calculated from the theory was a trap for the optimizers, being in the basin of attraction of a local optimum. Therefore, in addition to the DCM_0, two other starting points were considered: a Bragg mirror (BM) and a single chirped mirror (SCM). Plots of layer thickness values for the considered alternative starting points are provided in Figure 4.

In the case of the BM, thicknesses of layers of each type were constant (Figure 4a), whereas for the SCM, they linearly increased along with the layer index. In both cases, thickness values stayed in the range 75-85 nm, which was much narrower than the range for the DCM_0 (~0-140 nm) (Figure 4c).

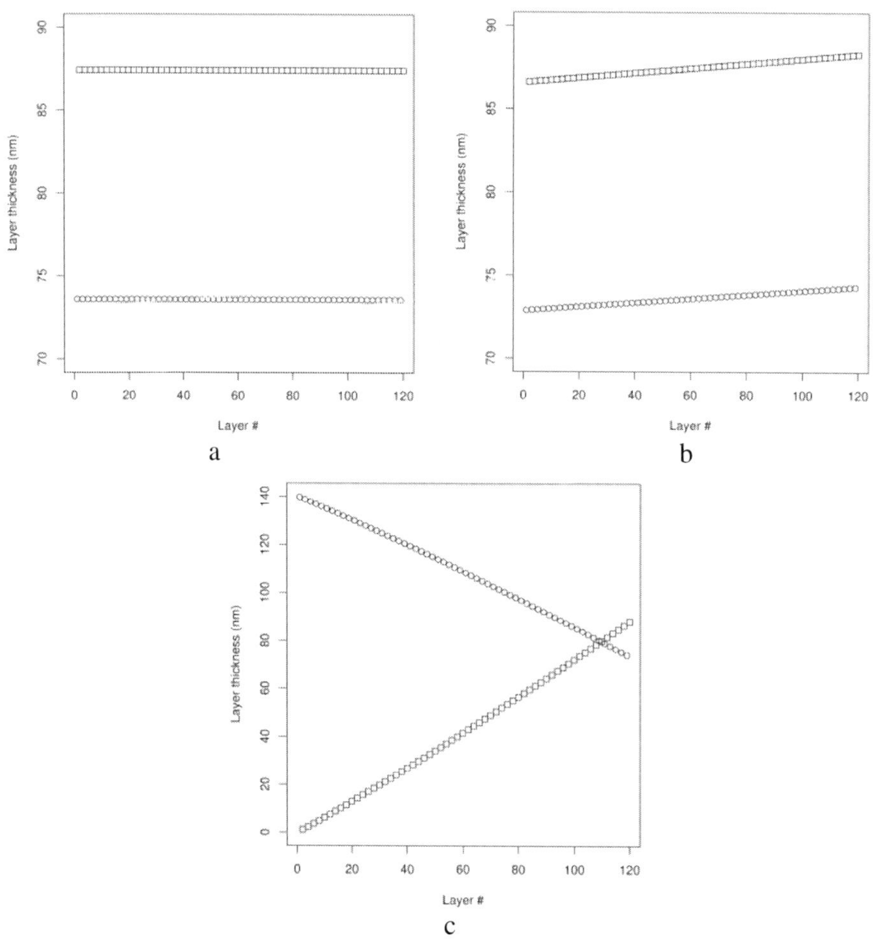

Figure 4. Layer thickness of: a) Bragg mirror, b) single chirped mirror c) DCM_0. The thickness of GaAs is marked by circles; the thickness of AlAs is marked by squares.

In the case of the DCM_0, thicknesses of layers of both type changed almost linearly, but in the opposite direction the thicknesses increased for AlAs layers and decreased for GaAs layers in the function of the layer number. A search for a better starting point was performed using CMA-ES as the only optimization procedure to spare time and effort.

For each starting point, CMA-ES was run 25 times. The achieved objective function values are presented in the form of box-and-whisker plot in Figure 5. According to Figure 5, the results obtained for the DCM_0 as a starting point were characterized with much greater variance in quality than in the case of the BM and the SCM. On average, CMA-ES started from the SCM and the BM yielded results of comparable quality; however, the results for the SCM were less variable. Therefore, it was concluded that the SCM was the best starting point for performing the optimization of mirror designs.

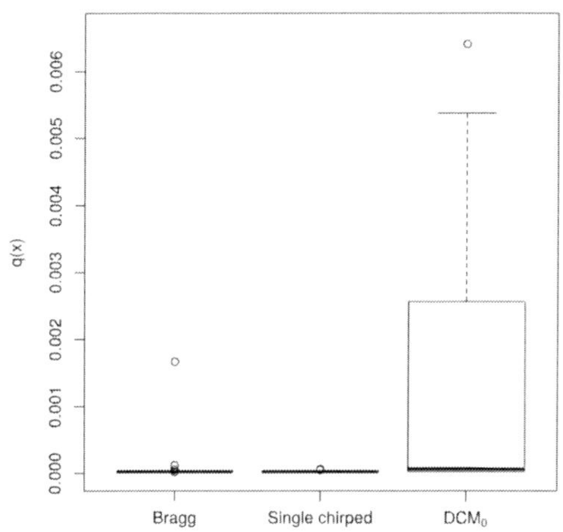

a

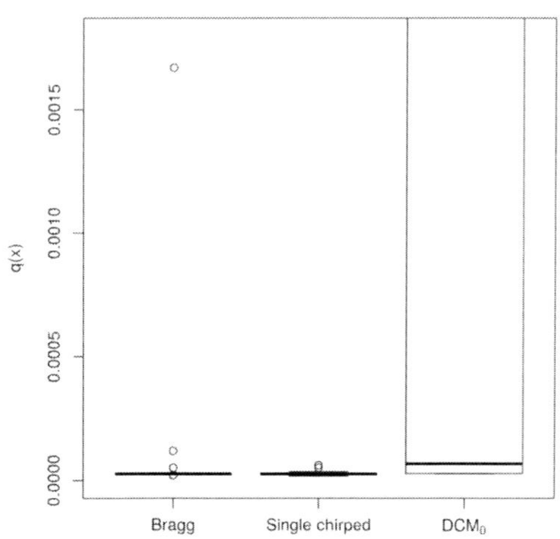

b

Figure 5. Comparison of objective function values achieved from different starting points, a) original plot, b) changed y-axis scale for easier inspection of results obtained when the starting point was the Bragg or the single chirped mirror.

After completing the experiments to determine the most suitable starting point, the problem of selecting the most appropriate optimization method was revisited. The significant influence of the starting point on the quality of the final result might suggest that, effectively, a kind of local optimization was performed by both CMA-ES and DE. This provided inspiration to check if some other local optimization method could yield competitive results. This hypothesis was verified by including two popular local optimization techniques: a version of the variable metric method, called L-BFGS-B [23], and the nonlinear simplex by Nelder and Mead [24], referred to as NM. An important issue was to perform a fair comparison between the selected methods. For this reason, the initial population of DE, which contained 1260 points, was generated using the same distribution as used to initialize populations for CMA-ES. DE and CMA-ES were run 25 times and the statistics of runs were analyzed. Local methods are deterministic; therefore each of them will always yield the same result when started from the same starting point. For this reason, they were run once for each starting point generated for DE which resulted in performing 1260 independent runs for both NM and L-BFGS-B. The average values of the runtime and the number of objective function evaluations until achieving stop criteria are presented in Table 2.

Figure 6 presents the curves of the objective function values of the best point found from the beginning of a method's run vs the number of function evaluations, averaged over independent runs. Since the runtime of methods differed by orders of magnitude, two plots are presented: in Figure 6a, the curves for each method are trimmed to the first 50,000 iterations, and in Figure 6b, the curve for CMA-ES is plotted separately.

It appears that on average, the fastest improvement was revealed by CMA-ES, then by the NM. L-BFGS-B got stuck in a poor local minimum and DE yielded results of quality between CMA-ES and L-BFGS-B. For CMA-ES (Figure 6b), after a period of fast improvement of solution quality, the improvement rate gradually decreased, reaching on average a saturation level of about 10^{-11}. The statistics of results obtained in a series of 25 independent runs of DE and CMA-ES and 1260 runs of L-BFGS-B and NM are synthetically presented in Figure 7 in the form of box-and-whisker plots. From Figure 7 it is clear that CMA-ES was the leading method when looking both at the median and the variability of results yielded in independent runs. DE generated solutions of slightly worse quality and with a greater variability. L-BFGS-B performed worst, and NM ranked between DE and BFGS.

Here it is worthwhile coming back to the practitioners' point of view. It should be expected that the performance of an optimization method should not be too sensitive to its implementation. In other words, it should be of small importance which optimization package to choose when looking for implementation of a certain optimization method. A good example is the popular nonlinear simplex method by Nelder and Mead, which comes in three popular implementations under the R environment: *Dfoptim*, which has been introduced in [25], *Neldermead* from [24], and the *Nelder-Mead* method from the Optim package that comes directly with the R environment.

Table 2. Average number of objective function evaluations and average runtime of optimization methods on Xeon(R) CPU E5-2637 3.50GHz processor (single thread)

Method	DE	CMA-ES	NM	L-BFGS-B
Number of objective function evaluations (thousands)	253	1953	33	14
CPU time [min]	21.4	123.4	3.4	1.2

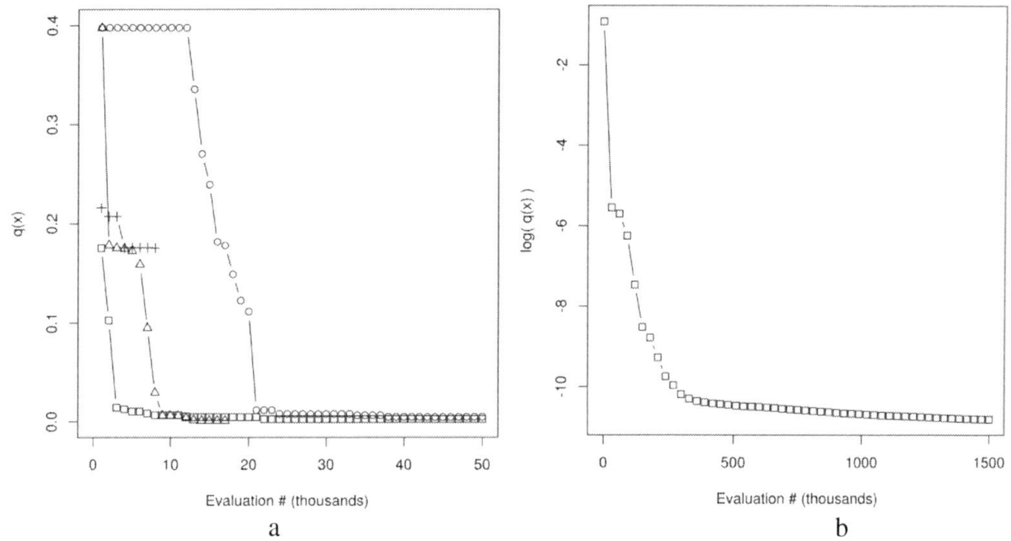

Figure 6. The objective function value of the best solution found so far in function of the number of objective function evaluations. CMA-ES results are marked by squares, DE by circles, L-BFGS-B by plus signs and NM by triangles.

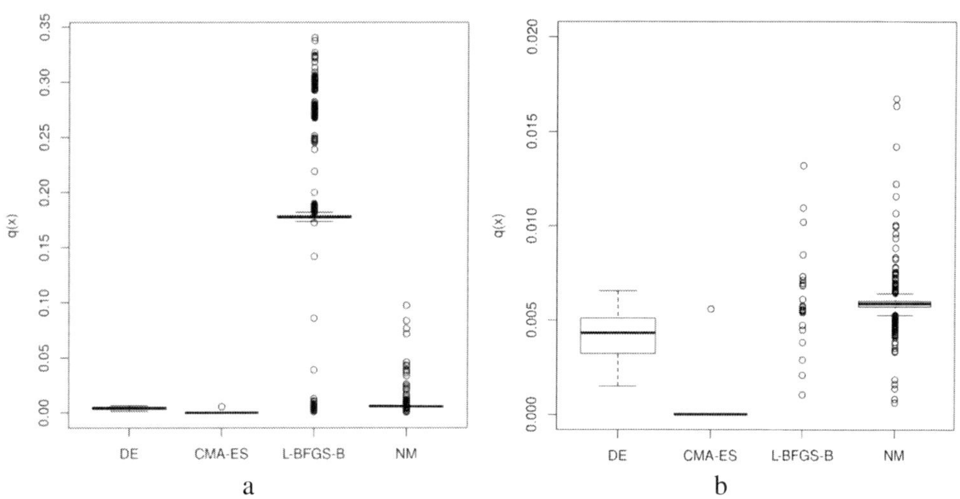

Figure 7. Statistics of results yielded by compared methods: a) full view, b) rescaled y-axis.

In the investigated problem, these three versions gave substantially different results. For example, when looking at the mean value of 1260 independent runs, *Dfoptim* yielded results about 10 times worse than *Nelder-Mead* and about 33 times worse than *Neldermead*. For this reason, results reported in this chapter were produced using the *Neldermead* package.

FROM DESIGN TO IMPLEMENTATION

The best solution generated by CMA-ES, labeled DCM_1, was presented to the technology experts from the Institute of Electron Technology who decided to make small changes in the problem specification. The number of semiconductor pairs was decreased from 60 to 55. The wavelength range was slightly shifted towards longer waves and covered values from λ_l = 1.027 μm to λ_h = 1.047 μm. In the definition of the AR coating it was specified that it should be composed of two layers only: one made of SiO_2 and the other of Si_3N_4. For the first semiconductor layer, it was additionally assumed that its thickness should be no smaller than 30 nm, and the lower limit of thickness for all other semiconductor layers was set to 0.6 nm. The lower limit of thickness for the AR layers was set to 7nm.

The design task was solved in two steps. The first step was aimed at designing the AR coating composed of two layers, while the semiconductor part of the mirror contained 60 pairs of layers. The starting point was defined as follows. The first AR layer thickness and the whole semiconductor part were taken from the DCM_1 design.

The second AR layer was generated randomly with uniform distribution in the admissible range. Then the CMA-ES method with σ= 0.0003 was run 10 times. The best solution found is labeled DCM_2.

In the second step, the mirror structure was further simplified where the number of semiconductor layers was reduced to 55 pairs. The first 112 layers from the DCM_2 structure were taken as a starting point for the optimization process. This involved another 10 independent runs of the CMA-ES method which yielded the final design, labeled DCM_3.

The plot of thickness values of subsequent layers in the DCM_3 design is presented in Figure 8a. In Figure 8b, the plot of the GDD of the DCM_3 solution is depicted.

It can be observed that the GDD curve stays within the acceptable range [-2600, - 2400] [fs^2] in the considered range of wavelength and it is very close to the desired GDD value marked by the dotted line.

The DCM_3 design was accepted for manufacturing. The production process is divided into two steps that use different technology: the semiconductor part is made first and then it is coated with the AR layers. Therefore, to avoid cost and effort, it is advisable to verify the quality of the semiconductor part prior to coating it with the AR layers.

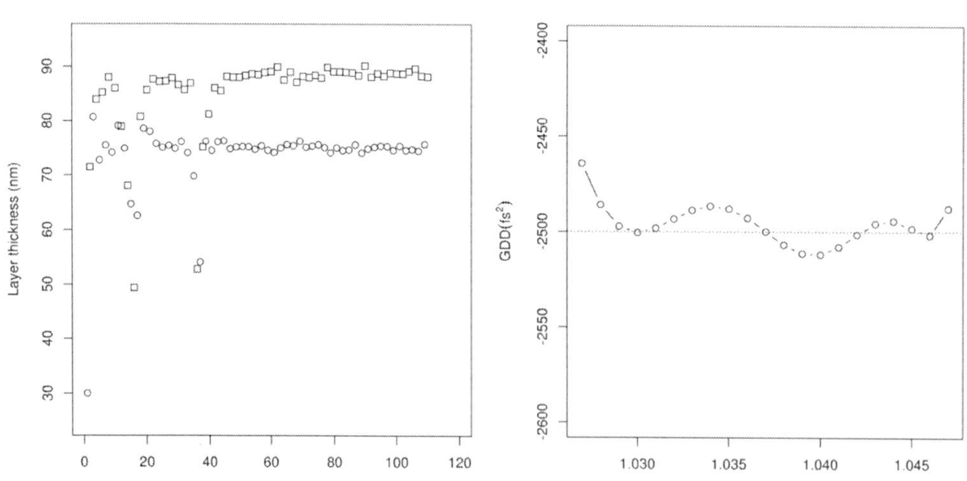

a b

Figure 8. Values of layer thickness for the DCM_3 design (a) and its predicted GDD curve (b).

The semiconductor part was manufactured in the Institute of Electron Technology, and then it was measured in the Institute of Experimental Physics[2]. Special attention was paid to the GDD curve of the semiconductor part. The GDD curve of the mirror is formed by both the semiconductor part and the AR coating, so evaluation of the semiconductor part needs to be performed in relation to the GDD curve obtained for that part using the model.

The predicted and measured characteristics of GDD of the semiconductor part of the DCM_3 design and its implementation are depicted in Figure 9. They stayed in very good agreement; therefore the mirror was passed to the AR coating manufacturer. After completing the AR layer, the mirror will be used as a component of an ultrafast laser which will be built in the Institute of Experimental Physics.

Conclusion

The chapter presented a successful story of a practical application of methods from the evolutionary computation family: CMA-ES and DE. The application field was the computer-aided design of mirrors, produced using semiconductor technology and dedicated for use in ultrafast lasers. The design process was realized in multiple stages, which involved the optimization problem definition, selection and a little tuning of optimization methods, and selection of starting points that incorporated the domain knowledge. In the course of the design process it was also necessary to follow the changes of the design criteria set by the user. Throughout the design process it was necessary to perform optimization in real vectors with, at most, 126 dimensions. The best results were yielded by the CMA-ES method. The mirror defined by the best design was implemented in the semiconductor technology.

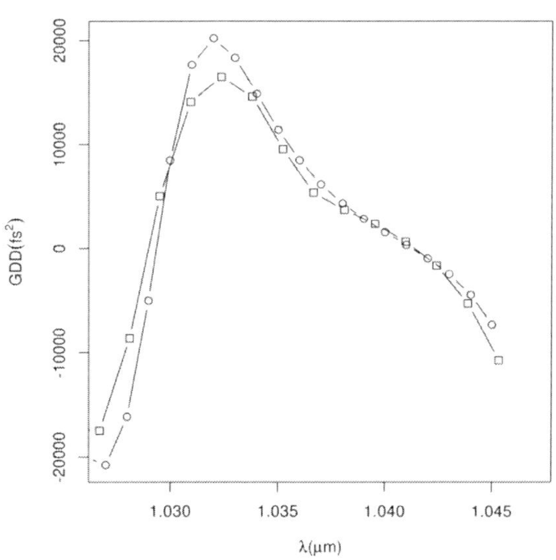

Figure 9. Comparison of GDD curves for the semiconductor part of the DCM_3 mirror: values predicted for the design are marked by circles and values measured for its physical implementation are marked by squares.

[2] Institute of Experimental Physics, University of Warsaw, Poland.

Measurements confirmed that the resulting mirror satisfied the requirements that were set at the beginning of the design process.

ACKNOWLEDGMENTS

The authors kindly acknowledge cooperation with Agata Jasik, Institute of Electron Technology, and Paweł Wnuk, Piotr Wasylczyk, Institute of Experimental Physics.

REFERENCES

[1] Wolpert, D. H., Macready, W. G.: No free lunch theorems for optimization. *IEEE Transactions on Evolutionary Computation*, 1(1):67-82, 1997.
[2] Liang, J., et al.: Problem definitions and evaluation criteria for the CEC 2013 special session on real-parameter optimization. *Technical report*, Comp. Intell. Lab., Zhengzhou University and Nanyang Technological University. 2013.
[3] INRIA: Black-box optimization benchmarking (BBOB). 2013. http://coco.gforge.inria.fr/doku.php?id=bbob-2013.
[4] R Core Team: R: a language and environment for statistical computing. R Foundation for Statistical Computing, Vienna, Austria. 2013.
[5] Matuschek, N.: Theory and design of double-chirped mirrors. *PhD thesis,* ETH Zurich. 1999.
[6] Weiler, S.: Ultrafast lasers: high-power pico-and femtosecond lasers enable new applications. *Laser Focus World*, 47(10): 55, 2011.
[7] Braun, M., Gilch, P., Zinth, W.: *Ultrashort laser pulses in biology and medicine.* Springer, 2008.
[8] Keller, U.: Recent developments in compact ultrafast lasers. *Nature*, 424 (6950): 831–838, 2003.
[9] Chilwell, J., Hodgkinson, I.: Thin-films field-transfer matrix theory of planar multilayer waveguides and reflection from prism-loaded waveguides. *JOSA A,* 1(7):742–753, 1984.
[10] Wolf, E., Born, M.: *Principles of optics*. Pergamon press. 1965.
[11] Bialynicki-Birula, I., Cieplak, M., Kaminski, J.: *Theory of quanta.* Oxford University Press New York. 1992.
[12] Yakovlev, V., Tempea, G.: Optimization of chirped mirrors. *Applied optics*, 41(30): 6514–6520, 2002.
[13] Yan-Zhi, W., et al.: Design and fabrication of chirped mirror. *Chinese Physics Letters*, 26(9), 2009.
[14] Tikhonravov, A. V.: Needle optimization technique: the history and the future. In: *SPIE 3133, Optical Thin Films V: New Developments*, 2. 1997.
[15] Pervak, V., et al.: High-dispersive mirrors for femtosecond lasers. *Optics express*, 16 (14): 10220–10233, 2008.

[16] Jasik, A., Wasylczyk, P., Wnuk, P., Dems, M., Wójcik-Jedlińska, A., Regiński, K., Zinkiewicz, Ł., Hejduk, K.: Tunable semiconductor double-chirped mirror with high negative dispersion. *IEEE Photonics Technology Letters*, 26(1), 2014.

[17] Paschotta, R., Spühler, G. J., Sutter, D. H., Matuschek, N., Keller, U., et al.: Double-chirped semiconductor mirror for dispersion compensation in femtosecond lasers. *Appl. Phys. Lett.*, 75(15):2166, 1999.

[18] Biedrzycki, R., Arabas, J., Jasik, A., Szymański, M., Wnuk, P., Wasylczyk, P., Wójcik-Jedlińska, A.: Application of evolutionary methods to semiconductor double-chirped mirrors design. In: *Parallel Problem Solving from Nature – PPSN XIII*, 8672: 761-770, 2014.

[19] Storn, R.: Differential evolution research trends and open questions. In: Chakraborty, U., ed.: *Advances in Differential Evolution*, vol. 143 of Studies in Computational Intelligence. Springer, pp. 1–31, 2008.

[20] Hansen, N., Ostermeier, A.: Completely derandomized self-adaptation in evolution strategies. *Evol. Comput.*, 9(2):159–195, 2001.

[21] Ardia, D., et al.: DEoptim: Differential Evolution In: *R. Package ver.* 2.2-2. 2013.

[22] Trautmann, H., Mersmann, O., Arnu, D.: cmaes: Covariance Matrix Adapting Evolutionary Strategy. *R package version* 1.0-11. 2011.

[23] Zhu, C., et al.: Algorithm 778: L-BFGS-B: Fortran subroutines for large-scale bound-constrained optimization. *ACM Trans. Math. Softw.*, 23(4): 550–560, 1997.

[24] Bihorel, S., Baudin, M.: neldermead: R port of the Scilab nelder mead module. *R package version* 1.0-8. 2014.

[25] Varadhan, R., Borchers, H. W.: dfoptim: derivative-free optimization. *R package version* 2011.8-1. 2011.

EDITOR'S CONTACT INFORMATION

Assistant Professor Gregor Papa
Jožef Stefan Institute
Computer Systems department
Jamova cesta 39, SI-1000 Ljubljana, Slovenia
Fax: +386 1 477-3882
Email: gregor.papa@ijs.si

INDEX

A

B

C

K

L

M

N

O

P